W. SCOTT POOLE

IN THE
MOUNTAINS
of MADNESS

The LIFE and
EXTRAORDINARY
AFTERLIFE
of
H.P. LOVECRAFT

SOFT SKULL PRESS

AN IMPRINT OF COUNTERPOINT

Library of Congress Cataloging-in-Publication Data is available
ISBN 978-1-59376-647-4

Cover design by Charles Brock, Faceout Studio
Interior design by Tabitha Lahr

SOFT SKULL PRESS
An imprint of Counterpoint
2560 Ninth Street, Suite 318
Berkeley, CA 94710
www.softskull.com

Printed in the United States of America
Distributed by Publishers Group West

10 9 8 7 6 5 4 3 2 1

For Em

One need not be a Chamber—to be Haunted—
One need not be a House—
The Brain has Corridors—surpassing
Material Place—

Far safer, of a Midnight Meeting
External Ghost
Than its interior Confronting—
That Cooler Host.

Far safer, through an Abbey gallop,
The Stones a'chase—
Than Unarmed, one's a'self encounter—
In lonesome Place—

—EMILY DICKINSON

". . . the motor chewed up a whole roll of film as the flash angrily
slashes out at the prevailing darkness, ultimately capturing this dark
form, vanishing behind a closing door . . ."

—MARK Z. DANIELEWSKI, *HOUSE OF LEAVES*

CONTENTS

PART I.

THE NIGHT GAUNTS

"I think I went mad then."

Howard Phillips Lovecraft wrote these words at his window desk in the quickly fading heat of the summer of 1917.

The smooth roll of fountain pen on paper mingled with provoking street noise entering the window at 598 Angell Street in Providence, Rhode Island. The slender twenty-six-year-old found these human sounds excessively bothersome. A decline in family fortune forever separated him from the quiet Victorian dignity that money could buy. He sometimes fantasized about becoming deaf and retreating forever into his interior worlds, realms of darkly intoxicating beauty and horror.

He owned a 1906 Remington typewriter but seldom used it. Nightfall signaled the beginning of his writing workday. He convinced himself that the sound of a typewriter would disturb his neighbors as much as it disturbed him. He came to so dislike its industrial clatter that he sometimes declined to publish his tales rather than prepare a typescript of them.

Many Lovecraft stories would never have appeared in any form if some of his acolytes not taken the trouble to pound them out for him on their own typewriters. This came to constitute a major theme in the

Lovecraft phenomenon. Adoring admirers taking an obsessional interest in his work kept him from disappearing into pulp oblivion forever, a prospect he seemed in some bizarre fashion to desire.

I do not think his current fame would have pleased him. He would have hated the flood of books about him and their speculations or assertions about his personal life. He would have hated the book you hold in your hands and what it tells about the inner worlds of a gentleman from Providence who consistently lied to the world about who and what he had been, performing more radical revisions on his life story than he ever bothered to make in the fiction that has made him famous.

But in 1917, he lived in almost complete obscurity, an obscurity he couldn't escape even when he tried. America had entered the First World War in April of that year and, to the surprise of everyone that knew him, Lovecraft, who turned twenty-seven that summer, volunteered for service. The army almost immediately rejected him, largely because his mother, Sarah Susan Lovecraft, made use of family connections to have him declared medically unfit.

Lovecraft described himself, at various times in his life, as having a weak heart, neuralgic, a sufferer of night terrors, a para-insomniac, and, more generally, the victim of a nervous disposition. None of his alleged ailments kept him from what likely would have amounted to limited stateside military service. In a letter to his fellow amateur journalist Reinhardt Kleiner, Lovecraft described his mother as "prostrated with the news" that he had hoped to join the war effort. He sheepishly admitted that she had "threatened to go to any lengths, legal or otherwise, if I do not reveal all the ills which unfit me for the army."[1]

Howard Lovecraft, who walked with an old man's stoop but could also be seen vigorously cycling the decaying graveyards and dark forest paths of New England, accepted his failed attempt to join the army with his usual fatalism about human existence, a bitterness against life tinged with a peculiar sense of humor. Only those few who knew him best ever fully experienced his unlikely combination of pomposity and capacity for self-parody. Lovecraft, perhaps more than any important writer of the twentieth century, knew that the joke was on him.

In the first twenty-seven years of his life, H.P. Lovecraft had seen his father confined to a mental institution and subsequently die at an early age. At fourteen, while on one of his long bicycle rides, the young Howard contemplated drowning himself in the Barrington River. He dropped out of high school because of a mysterious and unexplained nervous condition that turned him into a virtual recluse between 1908 and 1913.

The boom in amateur journalism of the 1910s brought him out of what he called "a vegetative state" and gave him limited but meaningful human contact through a vast circle of correspondence that replicated certain aspects of contemporary social media. In the years to come, he would marry the unlikeliest woman in the world, move to New York City, get divorced (sort of), ghostwrite for Harry Houdini, watch Tod Browning's *Dracula* and not especially enjoy it (or the city where he saw it) one tropical Miami night, and write stories for the American pulps that transformed the landscape of American popular culture in ways he could not begin to imagine.

Over a twenty-year period, in fits and starts, Lovecraft created a collection of stories that made possible the work of Stephen King, Ramsey Campbell, Guillermo del Toro, and John Carpenter. He dreamed of monsters and fantastic worlds that created cultural behemoths like San Diego Comic-Con. His outré and gruesome imagery influenced heavy metal music and informed the world building of both tabletop role-playing games like Dungeons & Dragons and even direct adaptations of his own imaginative universe. His work has appeared in enormously popular modern video games like *Witchfinder*, *The Elder Scrolls*, and the *Dragon Age* series.

A quick search online locates hundreds of Lovecraftian T-shirts, coffee mugs, fan art, and even versions of his tales produced as early-twentieth-century radio shows. Hipsters tattoo themselves with his monsters. A trendy Manhattan cocktail bar called Lovecraft's uses his stories for their menu while in Boone's Bar in Charleston, South Carolina there hangs an image of the tentacles of Cthulhu, grasping menacingly at you as you scan their long list of upscale bourbons and scotches. The lifelong teetotaler would be astonished by this and by a New England–based brewing company that sells a line of craft beers using both his image and elements of his fiction.

He was dead by age forty-seven. On his last day, suffering horribly from intestinal cancer that had gone undiagnosed and untreated for years despite numerous early warning symptoms, he had no reason to think anyone would ever remember his name.

But then, in the summer of 1917, the street noise began to die away with the late afternoon and the slick, oily skitter of pen on paper grew louder with an almost insistent and defiant scratch. Strange, sickly, geeky, gawky, weird, impossible Howard was about to become H.P. Lovecraft. He could see twilight spreading across College Hill. Night chased close behind. He began to raise his monsters from black depths.

We hear the story from a narrator who begins his tale by informing us he's demented and suffering from an addiction to morphine. Drug-addled and insane, the unnamed storyteller avers that some pre-Cambrian seaborne horror has made its way from a Pacific island to the busy streets of San Francisco to do him in.

The short story "Dagon" oozed from Lovecraft's pen late in that New England summer of 1917. The story's absurdly unlucky protagonist escapes from the German U-boat that sank his merchant ship only to find himself a castaway on an island that's no island at all. A dark maelstrom "of hellish black mire" swamps his tiny boat and he finds himself on land that "by some unprecedented volcanic upheaval . . . must have been thrown to the surface, exposing regions that for innumerable millions of years had lain hidden. . . ."

Smelling of loathsome decay, the muddy landscape features an ancient monolith etched with occult markings and figures that appear a collision of the human and the amphibian. The ancient stone wrenches him with fear. Falling into a troubled sleep, he wakes to a terrible sound, another upheaval from the shadowy sea that brings forth a slippery, slurping, sucking monstrosity that slithers its way to land and crawls over the monolith, almost seeming to sloppily absorb it in a cacophony of rubbery menace. This sight opens up in the narrator the depths of madness and he runs away on a "delirious journey" during which, insane with horror, he laughs, sings, and falls into unconsciousness.

He's not "really scared." What he's seen doesn't make him feel the fear we might experience at strange sounds in the night. Nor does he feel the more complex sense of doom-ridden psychological chaos Edgar Allan Poe evoked. The unlucky narrator simply loses reality, watching it slip beneath the waves from which the living horror first extruded.

Lovecraft's castaway awakens from his terror in a San Francisco hospital, learning from his caretakers of the strange and terrible things he muttered in delirium. Unsurprisingly, no one believes his account. As he tries to recover from the experience, nighttime becomes a theatre of terrors, the darkness reminding him of the Thing and, worse, of what the existence of the Thing implies. Morphine salves his tortured mind but ultimately leaves him alone in the dark with horrors that are older than any human conception of time.

He hears something at the window.

One of the more curious elements of reading the story is that we trust the narrator's description of the monster rising out of the sea, and the monolith that hints at unbearably old civilizations in the vast aquatic dark that predates and will outlast humans and their limited, rather stupid experiences. But we don't trust the narrator's drug-addled account of some Thing from out of the sea showing up on his window casement in California. We find Lovecraft manifesting his ability to make us doubt human experience while giving us a dread certainty of vast, inhuman worlds beyond the ken of our knowledge. In one of his first stories, he begins to convince us that human beings and their illusions are futile.

Containing many of the elements that horrified readers in his later tales, "Dagon" offers the curious an almost perfect ingress into his work.

The beginnings of his malign universe are there, not only because of the nature of the story's monster but also because of the quality of fear it evokes. You not only see the origins of his particular style. You watch the shape of his obsessions emerging much like the story's amphibian horror slides out of the war-tossed sea.

Lovecraft created horror tales without precedent and monsters without antecedent. It's become common in books on Lovecraft to describe the influence of Poe or to talk about his reading of writers in the tradition of "weird" fiction, all little known names like Dunsany, Crawford, and Machen. Although these writers contributed much to Lovecraft's malignant vision, none of them constitute anything like a direct influence on the monsters he imagined. Chasing influences can become a never-ending game that would draw us away from this singular man's nightmares. These Things came to him in his dreams just as now—after we've read him—they come to us in ours.

Not only did he not simply borrow directly from any of these past masters, he also seemed little moved by the long history of human monster obsessions. Readers will search in vain for the creatures that crawl about the castle ruins in the manner of Stoker or Shelley in Lovecraft tales. The one that does appear comes radically, and remarkably, altered.

The monsters of European fiction that made their way first into Hollywood film are creatures of folklore. In creating *Dracula*, the 1897 novel that in effect became the first edition of the rules of vampire behavior, Bram Stoker traded on eastern European folklore about the *Strigoi*. These creatures in the Balkans, the subject of several moral panics in the early modern era when no fewer than three empires sought control over the region, had long been part of folklore and myth. Dying wrong, they came forth from the grave craving blood and, perhaps even more unsettling, yearning to feast on those they loved the most.

Strigoi are monsters of our yearnings and our profound anxiety about those yearnings. After all, it is our tendency to feast on those we love, a possible clue to why the "vampire romance" novel has become outrageously popular early this century, a genre so omnipresent now that a very clever bookstore I once visited placed such tales in what they labeled as "the Kissy Vampire" section.

Werewolves also had a longer history. In the Middle Ages, songs and saga about unfortunate souls cursed with lycanthropy occupied an important place in traditions of medieval romance. By the sixteenth century and the onset of the European witch trials, they had become servants of Satan, diabolical humans who made pacts with demons. In return for their souls, claimed legends especially common in southern France, Satan provided them with a recipe for an ointment allowing them to transform into creatures of magical power and primal pleasure. That the recipe for the mystical salve included baby fat gives some indication of how vile early modern people came to regard the lycanthrope.

Neither of these monsters of legend and twentieth-century popular appeal intrigued Lovecraft. His interest in dark gods and ancestral horrors, ideas nursed by a youthful reading of the darkest of Greek myths and the romances of the Arabian Nights, took him to stranger shores. In "The Shunned House" (1924), he wrote something of a vampire tale, but a vampire with little real connection to Stoker's Count. Werewolves, or at least something like them, make a cameo appearance in "The Shunned House" and at least once in his mostly forgettable poetry. When he did settle in to examine the blurred lines between the human and inhuman world, he created a much more savage vision than had ever appeared in the folklore or popular entertainment of shape-shifting.

The witch, especially the early modern concept of witches as part of a large satanic conspiracy against the order and stability of civilization, does appear in Lovecraft, though in radically altered form. He loved Salem and often visited there to stare at Gallows Hill. Perhaps it's not a surprise that the enduring archetype of the witch haunted him, a man more obsessed with New England than any other American writer, not excluding Hawthorne.

In the early 1920s, Lovecraft read Margaret Murray's *The Witch-Cult in Western Europe* and largely accepted its tendentious claims. Murray's belief in an actual witch-cult that had endured in secret since pre-Christian times fascinated him. Murray did not believe in witches of the spell-casting and hex-making variety. She imagined them as a persecuted religious cult centered on fertility rites that managed to endure into at least the early modern era. Lovecraft found himself fascinated by the idea. Never having read any of the emerging historiography of the European witch trials, he accepted Murray's claims while adding to them a rather vicious racism that played a role in both his worldview and in some of the most questionable decisions he made as an author.

By the time Lovecraft began work on his first tales, two other creatures had become part of the western world's monstrous pantheon. Mary Shelley's 1818 novel *Frankenstein* had become well known in the United States, mostly through numerous stage adaptations. The iconic 1931 James Whale film starring Boris Karloff, a film Lovecraft considered a near-defamation of Shelley even if he liked it on its own terms, made the monster and his maker a household name.

In nineteenth- and early–twentieth-century America, the idea of the mad scientist and the reanimated dead became so readily recognizable that it appeared in political cartoons as often as popular entertainment culture. Early in his writing career, Lovecraft tried his hand at his own peculiar vision of the Frankenstein story, in the process creating a story that became one of his best-known works, despite his personal distaste for it. He eventually found much more peculiar uses for the mad scientist metaphor, blending it with his conceptions of the occult and the power to open portals to other dark worlds. Modern steampunk fantasies that blend technology and magic have some of their roots in this new departure.

In Lovecraft's time, the ghost story probably became the most popular weird form in the U.S. and Britain, so much so that even highfalutin figures like Henry James attempted to tease out the genre's potential for psychological complexity. Ambrose Bierce perfected the form in the United States with tales like "An Occurrence at Owl Creek Bridge," which borrowed its atmosphere directly from the historical horrors of the American Civil War.

M.R. James, F. Marion Crawford, and Algernon Blackwood became the littérateurs most associated with ghostly and fantastic tales. These writers sometimes used traditional gothic trappings like ancestral castles and ancient ruins but often experimented with contemporary Victorian settings that emphasized the "beloved dead," the return of the near and dear or the ancestral and the honored, revenants much-loved but now shambling, grave dirt–encrusted horrors.

Lovecraft never wrote a traditional ghost story though he loved the atmosphere of horror created by writers who did. When he experimented with the form, his improvisations overwhelmed the compositions from which he borrowed. Some of his most interesting stories, such as "The Shadow Over Innsmouth" and *The Case of Charles Dexter Ward* (and to a lesser degree "The Moon-Bog") invoke dreaded ancestors. But the revenants that haunt these stories had a palpability that made them something much more terrifying than a ghost. They did not go bump in the night but instead broke all bounds of space and time. The past took the leash off the present, overwhelming, possessing, obsessing it . . and in fact, threatening its destruction.

"Dagon" offered only one version of the horrors Lovecraft imagined that summer. He wrote another story in 1917 called "The Tomb." The tale takes us to a New England graveyard haunted by some of the terrors of time and ancestry that haunted Lovecraft himself. It reveals that he'd read plenty of ghost stories, though when he rewrote them, the victims manage to haunt themselves.

Jervas Dudley, protagonist of "The Tomb," admits he's confined to "a refuge for the demented" and that he's been "a dreamer and a visionary" from his earliest boyhood. As in "Dagon," our narrator walks the shadowlands of madness, telling us his tale from inside an asylum while assuring us that we'll believe him once he's finished the telling. Nevertheless, he insists we join him in his delusion and discover that it's no delusion at all.

We're fooled by this insidious invitation, a trick Lovecraft plays on us over and over again. "I only seem insane, I have a thing to tell you, just listen a while . . ." and we are suddenly implicated in the labyrinthine insanity of the storyteller and fearful we're participating in it. Some of his best stories pull us in this way, both well-known tales like "The Haunter of the Dark" and undeservedly less famous stories like "Hypnos."

Poe pulled off a similar set of literary shenanigans though he takes us into a rat's trap of human guilt and pain rather than, as did Lovecraft, threatening our sanity with the nihilism of the weird, what Lovecraft calls "unformed realms of infinity beyond all nature as we know it . . . realms whose mere existence stuns the brain and numbs us with the black extra-cosmic gulfs. . . ."[2]

Dudley lived apart from the world in a way that mirrors Lovecraft's own well-documented social alienation. Also like the author, Dudley spent his youth in "ancient and little-known books and in roaming the fields and groves" of his native region. And, again like Lovecraft, his ambles in the past confronted him with the terrors of time, a desire and a horror that formed the substance of both Lovecraft's fiction and his consciousness of the world. History held wonder, awe that turned to terror and back to wonder again. If only he could live in the past, if only he could escape it.

Is "The Tomb" really a bit of Poe plagiarism? It's become de rigueur in most quarters to associate Lovecraft firmly with Edgar Allan Poe and to point to stories like this one as examples. The link between the two writers has too often been assumed rather than explored.

Lovecraft had been reading Poe since he was eight years old. In "The Tomb," his early apprenticeship under his style shows. In the mid-1920s, Lovecraft wrote a study of weird fiction called "Supernatural Horror in Literature" that described the "typical protagonist" of a Poe terror tale as "dark, handsome, melancholy, intellectual, highly sensitive, capricious, introspective, isolated, and sometimes slightly mad gentleman of ancient family and opulent circumstances." Jervas Dudley seems to be most of these things and, notably, Lovecraft himself was at least a few of these things.

Just as a Poe character (or a young Lovecraft) might, the young Dudley becomes obsessed with a "vault . . . of ancient granite, weathered and discolored by the mists and dampness of generations." The ossuary belongs to a family called Hyde, infamous in the region during the eighteenth century because of "mumbled tales of the weird rites and godless revels" that went on in their mansion, a mansion burned to the ground by a bolt of lightning that struck like the wrath of God. These tales lead the increasingly obsessed and unreliable narrator to genealogical research, where he finds a thin strand of familial connection to the Hydes. Young Dudley cannot explain his desire to break into the tomb, simply describing his odd infatuation as the response to "a voice, which must have come from the hideous soul of the forest."

"The Tomb" ends with the possession of Dudley by Hyde, a story of "possession by ancestor" that Lovecraft returned to in later tales. In these stories, all of Lovecraft's historical fascinations ran amok, or perhaps just reached their natural conclusion. The past did not help explain the present; the present doesn't explain the past. The past seeks to possess the present, to invade and penetrate it. Lovecraft suggests that his ancestral enthusiasms didn't need a genealogical society; they needed an exorcism.

We see here Lovecraft's own uncertainty about his devout antiquarianism, his sense that the present could, in fact, become the victim of the past.

Setting "The Tomb" in New England shows Lovecraft's ability to give horror a place, a very American place. He located some of the nation's obsessions, including its belief in its own exceptionalism, in a vault of horror.

In this interest in a history of horror and the horror of history, Lovecraft shows more similarity to his fellow New Englander Nathaniel Hawthorne and to Herman Melville than to Poe. Poe tended to place his haunted ruins in a never-never land, ahistorical moments of psychological terror made more eerie, if also more distant, by being situated in the world of a dark Italianate fairy tale. Lovecraft had already begun giving his stories a history. Although "The Tomb" does not contain the kind of geographical minutiae that became so central to his most important stories, Lovecraft locates Dudley's ordeal firmly in New England, a haunted New England where graves gibber with "uncouth syllables of the first Puritan colonies" that compete with the "precise rhetoric" of the eighteenth century that Lovecraft believed represented a rationalistic high-water mark.

Very early, he started to create Lovecraft country; a geography of terror that came to include "witch-haunted Arkham" and "shadowed Innsmouth," places he describes in such minute detail that ingénues in Lovecraft lore, for almost a century now, have often assumed these places could be located on maps of Massachusetts and set out in search of them.

Lovecraft wrote a new American history and a new geography to match it. And it was not the sort of place anyone would much want to live. And yet, we all do.

———

I'm writing this unorthodox biography of Lovecraft as a historian. I've discovered certain things about my subject you probably don't know, whether you are a Lovecraft aficionado or simply someone who picked up or downloaded this book and wants to see what all the fuss is about, why tentacles are everywhere.

I've learned some odd things concerning how Lovecraft has been written about, defended, remembered, commodified, and obsessed over that are as much, if not more, a part of his story than the anecdotes told by his first circle of admirers and repeated ever since.

Library shelves sag with critical studies of the American master of horror. Most of them are written by a rather small group of people, some of whom have lived and breathed Lovecraft from their teen years in the early seventies.

These Lovecraftians, and it's hard to know what else to call them, feel a sense of territoriality about him, how he's regarded, what he's remembered for, and they're very serious about it. At least one Lovecraft scholar stunned me by rather abruptly breaking off our correspondence when he began to fear that he'd said too much to an author whose book might, to use his word, "denigrate" Lovecraft. We soon resumed our online conversations with my assurance that, while I would tell a critical story about Lovecraft, I also hoped to add to what we know about a figure we both love and admire, if in distinct and complex ways.

So, let's get this straight. I'm a fan of H.P. Lovecraft with all that fandom implies. I was a fan going into this project and I became even more of one as it proceeded.

But it will not always seem that way. As a historian, I will highlight some aspects of his life that reflect and help us to understand the temper of the times—his, ours, and all that came between. This often means writing about issues that cause Lovecraft fans and detractors to work themselves into a lather. I don't expect either group to find their views fully reflected here. As tentative as I am about swimming out to the Devil's Reef at Innsmouth, Things wait for us there that must be evoked, not only if we want to understand Lovecraft and his fiction but if we want to understand the world he lived in and how it provided the raw materials for the cultural world we inhabit.

So, I have some things to say about his sexuality that are both grounded in the sources and, at the same time, openly speculative about things we can't know but can thoughtfully and respectfully surmise. I also highlight the role of women in his life in a way that has not been done before by looking at previous biographers' evidence through a historical lens. I also make some claims about Lovecraft and his relationship to film, video games, comic books, and television that will, I think, show that he's become more than simply an important influence. He's the root of our current fascination with the fantastic in all its forms while remaining, even to Lovecraft "fans," an unknown and perhaps unknowable equation.

Primarily, I wrote this book for people who know about Lovecraft and his tales but only through hints, anecdotes, and fragmentary stories told word of mouth. You've heard of him. You've read "The Call of Cthulhu." You want more. You want to understand why *Gawker* can use the adjective "Lovecraftian" to describe an obsidian-colored cheeseburger marketed in Japan in the fall of 2014. Or why that person at work has a Cthulhu bumper sticker. Or what's so funny about the Cthulhu for President campaign.[3]

You also want to know which stories to read, where to begin. I will spend some time on the ones in which new Lovecraft fans are most likely to discover his genius. Some of these are the well-known stories; some of these you've never heard of before. I see no reason to give a story synopsis for many of these, first because there are plenty of books that already do that and second because I don't want to spoil them for you. As with "Dagon" and "The Tomb," I spend more time on those tales that are the least famous.

You won't find lengthy discussions of the tales considered the center of the Lovecraft canon by most scholars and enthusiasts—those works, mostly written after 1926, that French novelist and Lovecraft admirer Michel Houellebecq called "the great texts." Maybe you've already read them and, if you haven't, dark hints are enough. Let Lovecraft tell you these stories.

Finally, this book will not ignore the issue of race, especially when considering Lovecraft as part of a historical era, or rather, an important figure across several historical eras. As the African American freedom struggle progressed during the mid-twentieth century, his defenders and promoters sought to downplay, even expunge, his peculiar brand of racism from the record. More recent writing, some of it in the midst of controversy, has tried to hold two ideas together in unrelieved tension; the notion that, yes, he held racist attitudes but that, at the same time, they don't really matter that much since in displaying such sentiments he was simply "a product of his time."

The latter point is a risible one for the historian in me. Historical thinking never imagines the period a person happens to inhabit as a sealed corridor of experience where only certain thoughts, feelings, and ideas can conceivably appear. In that phlegmatic view of understanding history, even minds as searching and curious as Lovecraft's must inevitably fall into the prejudices of their times, unfortunate intellectual victims of their era and upbringing.

Sadly, his racism represented a decided choice on his part and a willful rejection of examples of African American achievement, including the kind of literary achievement Lovecraft admired. He remained hidebound in the racial theories of the nineteenth century, a period he in other ways so deeply despised. Worse, he flirted with the rising tide of fascism in the last two decades of his life, sometimes mocking Hitler and the Nazis but also frequently defending them and what he thought to be their aims. All this while maintaining friendships with people who, in that same era, held decidedly different views and often attempted to pull him out of the slough of prejudice that harmed his intellectual acumen and marred his best work.[4]

Ignoring, or even writing an apologia, for Lovecraft in these matters does him no good. A controversy erupted over this issue in 2014 that deserves our attention, a controversy that will have enormous bearing on Lovecraft's influence and reputation over the next several decades as science fiction and fantasy writing emerge from around the globe with Africa producing some of the most compelling material of the last few years.

Sex, gender, race, and emotionally invested scholars war to preserve the real Lovecraft. It really does seem like a morass. But if we want to meet H.P. Lovecraft, we have to walk into this sunken and tangled wood, lit only by moonlight that makes peculiar shadows on the ground.

———

Lovecraft could be a terrible historian but he remained until the end of his days a confirmed, obsessive, and undoubtedly annoying antiquarian, a member of that tribe that selects items from the past as a means of transcending the present or, really, sublimating the present. When, after his mother's death, he began to travel, he unfailingly went to places he could find "antiquities." He started his rambles in Boston, Marblehead, and Salem, walking for hours to stare pop-eyed at Georgian architecture. When the journeys took him further afield, he invariably found himself in places where the atmosphere shimmered with the colonial past: Charleston, New Orleans, St. Augustine. In what became an increasingly illegible longhand, he rendered judgments on the state of preservation of eighteenth-century dwellings, graveyards, and merchant houses to a wide circle of correspondents. He pronounced his displeasure with cities, like Miami, that had no "antiquities."

One form that this obsession with the past took was a firm, enduring and utterly absurd fixation on the eighteenth century, primarily an imagined eighteenth century of English Enlightenment thinkers, Augustan poets, and Georgian architecture. This interest carried over into a weird monarchical romanticism that he held to most of his life (though increasingly as a self-conscious pose in his later years). He saw himself as a citizen of the British Empire, and not the one inaugurated by the Edwardian age. The House of Hanover held his loyalty. In a story we can only hope is apocryphal, Lovecraft once told a correspondent that, when he first saw the monument to the "Minute Men" of 1776 in Lexington, Massachusetts, he caused something of a stir by shouting "God Save the King!"

His Tory pose manifested itself in precocious literary tastes as well. He later described his profound lack of interest in reading "the standard Victorian junk" and instead, as a tween, excavated the eighteenth century with the aid of "crumbling and long-f'd tomes of every size & nature—*Spectator, Tatler, Guardian, Idler, Rambler,* Dryden, Pope. . . ." In other words, the style and poetry of the eighteenth century enveloped him along with an interest in science, "Arabian romanticism," his reading of Poe, and the dreams of sun-haunted ancient ruins and nightmares of dark and forbidden universes granted to him from his Grandfather Whipple. It's the admixture of such disparate elements, some of which had to be held in profound tension, that concocts an H.P. Lovecraft.

His obsession with an artificial eighteenth century constructed in his head never seemed satiated. His "antiquities" always seemed to fail him and his letters are full of laments at finding himself trapped in the twentieth century. Weird fiction helped Lovecraft build a more complex relationship with history and "The Tomb" provides some of the earliest evidence of the intensity of this internal struggle. Like his Poe-esque narrator, Lovecraft yearned to slip into the past even if the trip took him down a charnel house stair lit with a guttering candle. Like the narrator of "The Tomb" he listened to the whispering of ancestors from the vaults of the past. But he also understood that, like Jervas Dudley, he toyed with madness and risked awakening something better left to itself.

More than the psychological terror of Poe slithered from Lovecraft's imagination. Dudley feels the pull of the hidden vault from "the hideous voice of the forest." This evocative phrase speaks to the primal, elemental forces that became the key to the Lovecraft mythos. Poe would have been much more likely to provide a macabre psychological reading of Dudley, his own psychic ghosts leading him to his doom. Lovecraft here hints at power beyond human ken that means us no good, something deeper than the complexities of guilt and inner terror. Something thoroughly unhuman.

He began writing "Dagon" a little over a month after finishing "The Tomb." This means that after completing a story of the New England past clawing its way to the present, he created a tale set far from his much-loved Providence and in places he would never go. The horror of "Dagon" occurs amid world wars and U-boats, real terrors ripped from the headlines. He had begun his troubled negotiation with the past, both his own and with history with a capital "H." He had begun admitting to himself, and the tiny circle of readers he expected to lure, that the antiquarian dream worlds he created might hide deeper terrors and that the present could muster no defense against the terrors of time, monsters both infinitely ancient and remote who came knocking at your window as the moon waned on a San Francisco night.

"Dagon" also introduced the idea that comes to most when they hear the word "Lovecraftian." The morphine addict whose abject terror animates the story "cannot think of the deep sea without shuddering at the nameless things that at this very moment might be crawling and floundering in its slimy bed, worshipping their ancient stone idols and carving their own detestable likenesses on submarine obelisks of water-soaked granite." Horrid Things from the depths, the depths of the sea or space or time, waiting to invade the human moment. Things so ancient that their existence dwarfs any human conceptualization of time. Things that, as Lovecraft writes in "Dagon," "may rise above the billows to drag down in their reeking talons the remnants of puny, war-like mankind."

The past, Lovecraft sometimes asserted, offered a refuge from this future. History, for Lovecraft, was the only stable thing, the only possible refuge from the terror of infinite time. He claimed that his desire to escape from his own century explained his lack of interest in modernism, the new literary, artistic, and architectural mood seen in the work of T.S. Eliot, Ezra Pound, and Frank Lloyd Wright.

Except the past could also become a Thing on the doorstep. He shared with many of his modernist contemporaries the idea of the past as a desert of broken images, the wasteland that woke T.S. Eliot in the cold center of night and eventually sent him fleeing into the arms of the Church as a place of refuge from all time's horrors.

Lovecraft, almost alone among the major writers of his era, refused the solace of religion or Communism or fascism or even the certainties of scientific rationalism—in which he did believe but could never find comfort. He saw the irrevocable power of the past offering the possibility of terror as well as solace, and some of his deepest personal and philosophical conflicts arose from the impossibility of staying afloat on what his most famous tale called "the black seas of infinity."

However, being profoundly anti-modern aligned perfectly with the modernist literary sensibilities of the 1920s. Modernism grew, in part, from a nauseous revulsion toward the crisis of European civilization occasioned by the brutalities and insanities of the First World War. Modernist writers, especially in the United States, worried over a set of rapidly changing conditions that Lovecraft abhorred for reasons not so different from many of the modernists whose work he damned.

Willa Cather suggested, poetically rather than literally of course, that "the world broke in two about 1922 or thereabouts." Ezra Pound took to calling it "Year One" as the publication of Joyce's *Ulysses* and Eliot's "The Waste Land" appeared within months. Something had definitively changed although, unlike Cather and Pound, most historians, poets, and cultural critics didn't bother putting a date on what had become of a Victorian world that now seemed dried up, mummified, and more or less buried by the 1920s.

For many white Americans, especially those living in northeastern and Midwestern cities, a massive influx of new immigrants constituted perhaps their most compelling social anxiety. White Protestant fears inaugurated a wave of nativism unknown since the large immigration of the Irish in the mid-nineteenth century. The era's revived Ku Klux Klan became something of a respectable, open organization in this era. They continued their campaign of terror against African Americans but increasingly attempted to immiserate eastern European and Italian immigrants in both the north and Midwest.

A massive interior immigration to northern cities also began in this era, often termed "The Great Migration." African American families pulled up stakes and headed to emerging industrial centers like Chicago, Detroit, and New York, fleeing near–economic servitude and often-outright peonage in the agricultural South. Needless to say, these economic competitors, already seen through the lens of vicious racist stereotypes, did not receive a hearty welcome. So-called "race riots" exploded across the country, a term of the period used to describe mob actions by white mobs against African Americans and their neighborhoods, sometimes with the blessing or even cooperation of city police.

Meanwhile, big business and a gospel of prosperity became the American religion. Calvin Coolidge, president during some of Lovecraft's most productive writing years, said that "the man who builds a factory builds a temple." The "red scare" that followed the Russian Revolution of 1917 helped fuel a pro-business climate as Americans proved more attached to the corporate revolution than the possibility of a people's revolution. Indeed, in an extraordinary move still little known or discussed today, the United States actually invaded the new Soviet Union in 1918–1919 in an attempt to crush the new Communist state in its cradle, beginning the sense of profound mistrust eventually leading to half a century of Cold War always threatening to become an apocalyptic blaze.[5]

Three pro-business, and highly mismanaged, Republican administrations dominated the decade after World War I and the presidency of the justly unpopular Democrat Woodrow Wilson. Andrew Mellon, the Donald Trump of his day (though arguably a much more successful businessman), oversaw the Treasury Department.

Mellon, technically responsible for enforcing the Volstead Act (Prohibition) that he actually opposed, mostly devoted his time at Treasury to lowering taxes on corporations to diminutive levels not to be seen again until the 1980s. Mellon reduced estate and gift taxes, safeguarding corporate profits in new and creative ways. Antitrust laws became seeming anachronisms as General Electric, American Telephone and Telegraph, and Ford Motor Company ruled their respective dominions like medieval warlords consolidating fiefdoms. "The government has been fused with business," the *Wall Street Journal* enthusiastically crowed.

Lovecraft's world in Providence, especially sequestered East Providence, seemed far removed from many of these changes. But, as he became increasingly aware, you cannot seek shelter from modernity. He would confront it both in his life, his peculiar politics, and in his horror fiction.

The summer of 1917 ended with the chill of an open tomb, the cold and dark menace of the sea. Lovecraft wrote late into the night as his beloved Providence fell into sleep, so late that he worried the constabulary, as was not uncommon in those old neighborhoods on College Hill, might come and demand he put out the light. The constable never appeared.

———

Readers remember when writers come into their lives. The circumstances of this joining stay with us, just like we remember the shape of the light in the room where we first meet a lover or an idea.

I cannot remember when I truly met H.P. Lovecraft. In my study at home, there sits on the shelf an anthology edited in the 1980s that contains selected stories from the pulp magazine *Weird Tales*. Alongside works of the Lovecraft circle, authors like Clark Ashton Smith and August Derleth whose names meant nothing to me at the time, appears a story Love-craft wrote in 1925 entitled "He."

It's a story compelling in its moodiness and ultimately unsatisfying. The tale emerged from the writer's unhappy time in New York City and, indeed, his unhappy marriage. "My coming to New York had been a mistake," the narrator asserts, he had hoped to find "poignant wonder" in the city but discovered only "horror and oppression which threatened to master, paralyze, and annihilate me."

Lovecraft's "He" made little impression on me as a junior in high school. I still think it's one of his magnificent failures, despite its close rendering of Greenwich Village in 1925 and a few final paragraphs that open vistas of horror.

If the story "He" marked an inauspicious first reading of Lovecraft, I never found it possible or desirable to dismiss or avoid him. How could anyone reading as much horror and fantasy as I had over the years not feel him lurking in the attic of my mind? He just seemed part of the infrastructure of the collective imagination of the fantastic. His strangely pleasing surname always evoked for me forbidden knowledge, dark rites, and old gods newly reborn. Saying the name out loud leaves your mouth with the same raw taste as saying "The Old Testament" or "Abraham Lincoln." The name carries an established solidity, so much so that we don't seem to need to know much more about it to understand its sig-nificance. Oddly, when it comes to Lovecraft, it's striking that we have so much information, indeed reams of information, about someone we don't really know.

"Today the whole world knows Lovecraft. Today the mythology of the Elder gods, of the Great Old Ones, of Cthulhu, have become the Horror Pantheon of the science fiction and fantasy reading cosmos." This "step right up" carnival barking appears on the back of a DAW Books paperback from 1976 called *The Disciples of Cthulhu* that also lives on my shelf, in the neighborhood of the *Weird Tales* collection. It's a used bookshop purchase, a very lucky find on a cold and snowy night in Cam-bridge, Massachusetts, if memory serves.

Its overheated back matter actually obscures rather than illuminates the treasures inside. Heavy hitters in the world of horror and the fantastic like Fritz Leiber, Ramsey Campbell, and Brian Lumley write tales set in a recognizable if significantly reimagined Lovecraftian universe. Robert Bloch—the author of the novel *Psycho*, who admired Lovecraft enough to kill him off in a short story—writes in the introduction that the mythos of Cthulhu, Azathoth, and Lovecraft's other malefic gods has a sacred aspect, a metaphysic of horror passed down among the faithful in secret and now blossoming like a night flower into American popular culture. He writes about it as if it's a new religion, a real-life cult of Cthulhu, instead of a fan phenomenon.

Lovecraft's influence over fantasy and horror literature seemingly had reached its peak in the 1970s. This was not the case. His work soon became the guiding influence for a more general interest in fantasy and horror in popular culture. Films based on Lovecraft tales had appeared in the 1960s though they often simply borrowed character names and story titles. But Ridley Scott's *Alien* (1979) and John Carpenter's *The Thing* (1980) made use of both themes and direct imagery from Lovecraft while reproducing his more subtle horrors of nihilism and a sense of a cosmos indifferent to human concerns.

Director Sam Raimi wrote and directed no fewer than three films in the eighties and early nineties that, while using a degree of humor and grotesque slapstick out of step with most of Lovecraft's work, did make use of his fictional *Necronomicon*. This was a book that in Lovecraft's stories and in Raimi's *Evil Dead, Evil Dead 2: Dead by Dawn,* and *Army of Darkness* opens portals to other planes of existence, allowing various nasty things to enter our own.

During this same period, Lovecraft became central to an emerging geek subculture, a peripheral phenomenon destined to make its way to the center of contemporary entertainment. Enjoying the work of Lovecraft, even of the so-called "Mythos" tales based on his work rather than actually produced by him, represented knowledge in nerd arcana that became a badge of honor in parents' basements and the back rooms of comic book stores around the country. Tabletop role-playing games ("RPGs") based on Lovecraft's fiction began to appear, soon followed by PC and console video games. The graphic novel renaissance of the late 1980s soon seized on Lovecraft's work. Enormously popular figures such as Neil Gaiman, who made reading fantasy a mainstream phenomenon, described Lovecraft as "where the darkness begins."

Thirty years later, we live in the age of Lovecraft. Stephen King's 2014 novel *Revival* has been lauded as a return to form, its author perhaps the most recognizable name in horror and fantasy writing since Poe. The influence of Lovecraft, King's fellow New Englander, appears often in his work, dating back to his first novels in the 1970s. King locates his abominations, human and otherwise, in a recognizable New England that yet comes to us reified as the fictional town of "Castle Rock"—much like Lovecraft gave us his fictionalized New England town of Arkham, which seems to attract every transdimensional horror wandering the infinite cosmic planes. Most importantly King, like Lovecraft, has built a universe in which we share physical existence with all sorts of horrors that threaten not only our lives but also our tenuous hold on reason itself.

The literary establishment has never given King his critical due, largely I think because he sells more books than most authors can begin to imagine. But *Revival* represents the consummate page-turner, brimming with Lovecraftian themes of forbidden knowledge and centered ultimately on an unimaginably tormented soul desiring a knowledge that will drive him and all who come in contact with him into madness.

King takes us finally to the dark heart of Lovecraft's vision: "a vast ruined city . . . a dead city of cyclopean stone blocks." As in Lovecraft, and directly echoing his language, King forces his unfortunate characters to visit "a place full of insane colors, mad geometry, and bottomless chasms where the Great Ones live their endless, alien lives and think their endless, malevolent thoughts." In other words, King has evoked the universe of Lovecraft—where human lives are a matter of indifference, and human assertions about any overarching meaning are a blasphemy and a sarcasm.

Revival does more than draw directly on Lovecraftian themes. King actually dedicated it to Lovecraft, his circle of influence, and his influences. King notes the significance for him of Arthur Machen's deeply unsettling tale *The Great God Pan* and, notably, thanks August Derleth and Donald Wandrei, two men largely responsible for keeping Lovecraft in print long enough for him to become a cultural obsession.

Derleth went much further than simply keeping Lovecraft's tales in circulation and created what he denominated "The Cthulhu Mythos." This is an extremely controversial and much pilloried idea among the literary scholars who dominate the field of Lovecraft studies.

The Cthulhu Mythos, a term the Providence author never used, holds that Lovecraft and a small circle of fellow writers intentionally created a self-contained mythological universe with clearly defined conceptions of the Elder gods and the Great Old Ones. Their shared universe contained forbidden tomes that humans should leave unopened. Moreover, they and a third generation of admirers added to the Lovecraftian mythos, expanding and filling in its gaps while also arguing, sometimes absurdly, over which of Lovecraft's stories count as "Mythos" tales and which do not.

So influential has the idea of the Cthulhu Mythos concept become that many fans simply call Lovecraft's work "the Mythos." So despised has the idea become among one group of Lovecraft scholars that they have waged a three-decade assault that has dismantled the idea in literary studies of Lovecraft if not in popular culture. Derleth, a friend of Lovecraft's and the first to publish a book of his stories in 1939, has become a villainous character in some quarters—the man who tried to steal the Lovecraft legacy and hide from the world the true Lovecraft. But neither the controversy, nor the intricate and ever-growing Cthulhu Mythos, draws in most modern Lovecraft enthusiasts.

Role-playing games; short films such as those that premiere at Portland's CthulhuCon and an enormous pile of novels, short stories, and graphic novels that draw on Lovecraft's universe have drawn fans of all ages into Lovecraft's dread universes. Stephen King provides one of the major ways mass audiences meet Lovecraftian themes. King's mammoth, unputdownable novels and well-crafted short stories have become a primary conduit for Lovecraft's conceptual world making its way into American culture. His novella *The Mist* offers an image of what at first glance appears to be a Lovecraftian creature raised from cosmic depths to destroy us and ends on a bitter, rather misanthropic set of ironies Lovecraft would have appreciated.

Guillermo del Toro's body of work represents another pop culture phenomenon that spreads the Lovecraft anti-gospel. Del Toro's films, ranging from horrific fairy tales about the Spanish Civil War in *The Devil's Backbone* and *Pan's Labyrinth* to the adaptation of the popular (and Lovecraftian) comic *Hellboy*, manifests his lifelong love for the author who, in a dark irony, would have considered the Mexican filmmaker part of the immigrant horde coming unbidden and unwanted into the American experience.

Del Toro loves him anyway. One of his lifelong dreams has been, and remains, to create a film version of *At the Mountains of Madness*, the Lovecraft novella that imagines a secret history of the world's beginnings that make humans seem like a temporary growth of weed in a universe that has better things to do. Del Toro's film only failed to receive a studio green light because of the story's similarities to another Lovecraft-influenced tale, Ridley Scott's 2013 film *Prometheus*, that itself tells essentially the tale of *At the Mountains of Madness* even though it places its story in the far corners of the universe rather than the Antarctic's frozen wastelands.

Del Toro has kept to his Lovecraft-inspired program, however. Although promoted as something of a giant robot slugfest along the lines of Michael Bay's childish *Transformers* series, del Toro's more recent work stands out as a good example of Lovecraft in mass culture. *Pacific Rim* features a world where Lovecraft's monsters from the depths rise from their aeons of sleep and humanity fights back. A bit more optimistic than Lovecraft would ever have allowed, del Toro nevertheless used *Pacific Rim* to ask what happens when Cthulhu and his star spawn rise from the depths and humanity refuses to shuffle off the stage.

Of course, if it's true that "the whole world knows Lovecraft," it does not need another biography of H.P. Lovecraft. Unlike most cult figures that become cultural icons, all of Lovecraft's original acolytes and the next generation of the faithful preserved and pored over every piece of printed material he produced. As much as possible, they looked at every piece of paper that even in some tangential way relates to obscure elements of his life, work, and personality.

The proliferation of such materials actually calls out for biography, at least an unorthodox one that shuttles between contemporary manifestation of his fictions, the history that helped create them, and the contemporary history of his role in creating the multibillion-dollar culture of geekery triumphant. Despite the loving attention of Lovecraft devotees, or maybe because of it, Lovecraft sometimes feels like a closely guarded secret. The keepers of the flame also appointed themselves guardians of that flame almost from the moment of his death.

Lovecraft himself did have someone he wanted as guardian to his legacy. Although never creating the requisite legal document, Lovecraft clearly named his young, gay, troubled intellectual friend and companion R.H. Barlow as his literary executor. Personal difficulty prevented Barlow from fighting back when August Derleth wrestled Lovecraft's legacy away from him in the late 1930s.

Derleth, a briefly successful mainstream novelist in the 1940s who also wrote a forest's worth of weird fiction for the pulps, appointed himself Lovecraft's literary heir. He joined with another Lovecraft friend and admirer, Donald Wandrei, in creating a publishing venture called Arkham House. The press primarily sought, at least at first, to prevent Lovecraft's work from descending into oblivion. Until the end of his days, Derleth claimed to hold the copyright to H.P. Lovecraft's work.

He pursued his efforts to disseminate and control the meaning of Lovecraft's work with a zeal often bordering on the maniacal. Along with major compendiums of Lovecraft's stories and piles of imitative

Lovecraft pieces scribbled by Derleth himself, Arkham House published material that sought to shape a public image of Lovecraft. Between 1965 and 1971, Wandrei and Derleth collected and published five volumes of the *Selected Letters*, a mammoth project that only allows us to dip our toes into the ocean of paper Lovecraft mailed to friends, admirers, confreres, and more or less anyone who ever bothered to write to him.

After Derleth's death in 1971, the tidal wave of interest in Lovecraft began in earnest. Ballantine Books began releasing popular paperback editions of his stories. These editions did not include some of his best work and actually contained more of Derleth's "posthumous collaborations" with Lovecraft than the work of Lovecraft himself. These often tepid tales are not collaborations of any sort but rather story ideas, sometimes just images, found in Lovecraft's private "Commonplace Book" and correspondence that Derleth then turned into stories. Nevertheless, these collections sold close to a million copies.

Much like the enormous popularity of the paperback editions of Tolkien's *Lord of the Rings*, these cheap editions became part of the fascination with fantasy and science fiction in the American counterculture. The pages containing terror tales by the conservative gentleman from Providence became crinkled, bent, torn, and deep-baked with the smell of patchouli after their time in a thousand college dorm rooms, becoming foxed and worn from being shoved into hundreds of backpacks. In the late seventies, Jove Books brought out equally cheap paperbacks that now included more of his own stories and reached an even wider audience. Mimeographed fanzines began to circulate in the same era, a phenomenon that would have delighted Lovecraft given his own devotion to amateur journalism.

Meanwhile, something of a scholarly war ignited over his meaning and importance. In 1975, a popular though at times abrasive biography by fantasy and sci-fi author L. Sprague de Camp triggered a contentious academic search for "the real Lovecraft." Efforts to secure Lovecraft's place in American literature produced more printed material than the author himself ever managed. The notion of "The Cthulhu Mythos," perhaps best defined in fantasy novelist Lin Carter's short, tendentious paperback called *Lovecraft: A Look Behind the Cthulhu Mythos* (1972), came under attack from a growing number of scholars who wanted Lovecraft seen as something more than simply popular and who deeply disdained most of the fiction being produced in his name.

A teenager named Sunand Tryambak Joshi, born in India in 1958 and arriving to the States with his academic parents in 1963, devoured every available word of Lovecraft's. He began reading Lovecraft at age thirteen and began writing what he calls "an appalling number" of weird tales imitative of his hero. At age seventeen, he had already planned out his first book of literary criticism that became *H.P. Lovecraft: Four Decades of Criticism.* Published in 1980, it remains a classic in Lovecraft studies to this day. The precocious young scholar came to the attention of Kent State University Press, who asked him to compile a bibliography of Lovecraft's work.

This young man's singular obsession with Lovecraft oddly mirrored the efforts of Lovecraft's first circle of friends and admirers to preserve their mentor's work. Today, writing as S.T. Joshi, he's the acknowledged world authority on Lovecraft. In this role, he continues to lead the charge in the fight for Lovecraft's literary significance—a fight largely won by his efforts.

Lovecraft fans arguably owe Joshi much more than they do Derleth for the rescue of the author's reputation. In fact, it's unlikely we would even be able to read Lovecraft as he wished to be read without Joshi's intervention. Voluminous research into his letters and the original autographs of his manuscripts allowed him to create meticulously corrected editions of Lovecraft's work for Penguin Classics, essentially allowing us for the first time to read Lovecraft as the author wished to be read.

The intriguing, friendly, sometimes frustrating but finally always accommodating Joshi allowed me to engage in an email correspondence with him during the writing of this book. He agreed to talk with me because he was "always interested in new work on H.P. Lovecraft."

Joshi's interest, I would learn, comes from deep affection for Lovecraft and a heartfelt desire to see work on him flourish. It also grows from an absolute insistence on guarding Lovecraft's reputation on some particular points. He will brook no opposition to his views on such matters, even if his rather sharp edges are softened by a genuinely affable personality and a really charming love for the man he's spent more than four decades investigating and explaining to the world.

Joshi can, in fact, seem like some kind of mage right out of a Lovecraft tale who, by his own dedication and intricate, laborious scholarship, has opened a portal from our world into that of H.P. Lovecraft and his monsters. Perhaps not surprisingly, he seems as much a disciple of Lovecraft as a Lovecraft scholar. Protective, combative, and very much aware of his essential role in making Lovecraft both accessible and respectable, he's always up for a tussle. He has little good to say about August Derleth: "[S]ad to say, it seemed to require Derleth's death to bring on the next stage of Lovecraft scholarship."[6]

Joshi also criticizes de Camp, calling his 450-page biography "fragmented and random" and claiming that "it seriously errs in its very conception." Particularly offensive to Joshi is what he calls de Camp's "half-baked, posthumous psychoanalysis" of Lovecraft and his lack of interest in Lovecraft's philosophical worldview. He's also admitted his own tendency to assault efforts by contemporary authors to create stories based on the Cthulhu Mythos idea. Moreover, one can count on Joshi to appear—like a knight at the lists—every time a public controversy about Lovecraft erupts, usually around the author's well-documented racist views.[7]

Lovecraft's world, the one he made for himself and the one he made for us, seems outsized in comparison to these controversies. Joshi and his allies convinced a dubious literary establishment that Lovecraft deserves his literary reputation, that he has every right to belong—as he has since 2005, in the Library of America alongside Hawthorne, Twain, James, Melville, and Poe. Michael Dirda, writing in *The Times Literary Supplement* in early 2015, argues that he's regarded today as "second only to Edgar Allan Poe in the annals of American Supernatural literature." He's no longer a "cult writer," says Dirda, but rather a "cultural icon."

Leslie Klinger, responsible for the beautifully designed and constructed *The New Annotated H.P. Lovecraft* (2015), told *The Wall Street Journal* in an article entitled "Here's Why H.P. Lovecraft Matters More Than Ever" that the teaching of his work in the classroom will be the next natural and logical step for the author of pulp fictions he himself never thought would amount to much.

But the name itself has come to mean something more than the surname of a very good horror writer once despised and ignored by the same literary establishment that sometimes celebrates, and at least grudgingly accepts, him.

More than a literary icon, he's a cultural omnibus who shaped a style of horror that spoke to the terrors of modernism and looked ahead to what's come to be called the postmodern. He's the faux English gentleman who became a bit bohemian, the traditionalist who helped create a revolution in comic books and B movies. A self-declared provincial who never went west of the Mississippi river, he has helped shape a part of Hollywood Babylon that owes more than it sometimes seems to know to this terminally uncool man who at one point in his life believed it unseemly to leave his house without a hat.

He also held to much stranger conceptions about the world than this pose suggests. Some of his best work came from his dreams; intense psychological quests that made him question the boundaries of reality and unreality. These are often trippy experiences, psychedelic in their kaleidoscope of strangeness. He found in his personal dreamlands a place he considered no less real than the physical world, dimensions of the imagination that Poe never uncovered despite the help of morphine, opium, and booze.

———

Whipple Phillips, Howard P. Lovecraft's maternal grandfather, sat in the cold New England sunlight of 1893 chalking an image of the ruins of Pompeii. He made the sketch for his grandson. The three-year-old, already inflamed by the darker visions of classical mythology, saw satyrs dancing in twilight and Pan at play in a nocturnal wood. He had received from Sarah Susan Lovecraft's father a set of dreams and nightmares that opened up vistas of lost cities, time twisted into terrible shapes, and a parade of goblins and ghouls that shambled and swooped amid these ruins.

Lovecraft's emerging genius for horror began to manifest at a very, very early age. His obsessions as a young child took on form as nightmare and poetry, much the same shape in which they would appear in his adult life. By 1896, the alien-seeming six-year-old suffered from terrifying nightmares while in the daylight hours he produced abstracts of Homer and Petrarch in iambic heptameter.

Whipple Phillips helped give young Howard both his fascination with lost cities of legend and his worst night terrors. Phillips had travelled for business to England in 1889 and spent a year touring Europe, spending a significant amount of that time in Italy. His fascination with the ancient Mediterranean past meant that his grandson spent his early years surrounded by Greco-Roman statuary, copies of classical figures that fired the young boy's imagination.

As was true throughout his childhood, Howard could never have a passing interest in a subject. He had to, in some sense, become the thing that allured him. In an essay he wrote on religion in 1922, an essay that dwelt on his reasons for rejecting its claims, Lovecraft recalled that he and his grandfather's reading of classical myth caused him to spend parts of his forest wanderings building "altars to Pan, Apollo, Diana, and Athena." Although he mocks these dramatic bits of play by saying it came from a "half sincere" belief, Lovecraft thought that most religious believers adopted the claims of their dogma with similarly divided minds, and perhaps with less sincerity, than he brought to his childhood play.

A much older Lovecraft told this tale of his personal worship of the Greek pantheon in the context of a polemic against religion in general. This does not, however, subtract from a younger Howard's seriousness about the often chthonic and shadowy world of Greek religion. His mother or grandfather, and perhaps both, took him in 1897 to see a recently opened exhibit of Greek antiquities at the Rhode Island School of Design. The outing seemed to him, he later recalled, a "visit to a magick grotto." He soon would be taken to other regional museums such as the Museum of Fine Arts (MFA) in Boston that contained, and still contain, numerous masterworks of the ancient world. When he moved to New York City in the 1920s, days disappeared wandering the Metropolitan, even though he claimed that its wonders never recreated for him the profundity of his encounter with Hellenic glory at the School of Design.

There are those today who claim that Lovecraft had a secret interest in the magical arcana, indeed a few make the absurd claim that he actually practiced a type of necromancy that gave him experiences reflected in his tales. Those who want to make Lovecraft into an occult figure certainly might latch on to his youthful altar-building as proof of their claims. But we only know about this incident in connection with a polemic against the supernatural.

Lovecraft contended throughout his life that lack of empirical data represents the central fallacy of every set of religious beliefs. Religion's power over hearts and minds, Lovecraft believed, grew out of the poisonous cultural influence of Christianity and the tendency of individuals to present personal experience as evidence. "Once," he remembered of his days of raising altars to the gods, "I firmly thought I beheld some of these sylvan creatures [dryads] dancing under autumnal oaks." He seems to mean it; he really did encounter the gods in a moment of ecstasy that may have been recognizable to worshippers in 400 BCE. But then, here's the polemical kick in the pants: "If a Christian tells me he has felt the reality of his Jesus or Jahveh (Yahweh), I can reply that I have seen the hoofed Pan and the sisters of the Hesperian Phaethüsa."

While he worshipped at the altar of Pan, his mother allowed him an escape from the more traditional religious establishment of Providence, what Lovecraft later called "the venerable First Baptist Church," venerable to him only because its building represented an interesting colonial antiquity dating to 1775. The Phillipses had been Baptist for generations, hearkening back to their earliest days in Rhode Island—a colony founded by the renegade Puritan Roger Williams, generally seen as the originator of the Baptist tradition in America.

By the 1890s, the Phillips family's Baptist identity had become *pro forma* at best. Whipple Phillips seems to have had no interest whatsoever in such matters, and Sarah Susan Lovecraft held to a basic religious skepticism. An aversion to alcoholic beverages constituted the last dying embers of Roger Williams's fiery personal faith in the Phillips household. Still, as a matter of good taste and like most of the East Providence raj, the Phillipses enrolled the child of the family in Sunday school.

No record remains of the woman who taught the young children's Sunday school at First Baptist Church Providence in 1895. Whoever she was, she may have told stories about the odd young Howard Lovecraft till the end of her days. Lovecraft apparently peppered the woman he sympathetically described as "a kind-hearted and motherly preceptress" with a number of questions, including whether or not she used the term "God" in much the same way that parents used Santa Claus. The comparison must have horrified her, and it's easy to imagine that it caused tears and lamentations among the other five-year-olds who learned, as Howard had already surmised, that no rosy-cheeked elf brought toys down the chimney on Christmas Eve. Howard took an extra step that makes it seem like the preschooler had already read in Feuerbach and Freud that adults had also made up a caring and providential God.

It's unclear how long he attended the First Baptist Sunday School but his later memories suggest a series of disasters, as well as enormous discomfort for the teacher and fellow pupils. His love of the classics, for example, had made the Roman world a deep and abiding fascination for him and he took umbrage at the Sunday school representation of them as villainous persecutors of the early Church. "I felt that a good Roman pagan," he later recalled, "was worth six dozen of the cringing scum riff-raff who took up with a fanatical foreign belief and was frankly sorry that the Syrian superstition was not stamped out." He apparently informed his long-suffering Sunday school teacher that "when it came to the repressive measures of Marcus Aurelius and Diocletianus [two emperors who attempted to squelch the growing faith], I was in complete sympathy with the government and had not a shred of use for the Christian herd."

So, his Sunday school experience ended rather quickly. Either he was asked not to return or Sarah Susan Lovecraft removed him from the program or, most likely, a bit of both. Lovecraft describes this memory of the Sunday school debacle long after reading Nietzsche and so almost certainly has a faulty memory regarding the degree to which he mounted a sophisticated critique of the Christian tradition at age five. Still, the evidence suggests that he caused more than a little clamor if First Baptist Providence urged a prominent east side family to keep their heir and his uncomfortable notions at home.

The Sunday school incident deserves some extra attention for two reasons. First, if it did occur at around age five, Lovecraft's early rejection of traditional religion came from his own love for the fantastic, mystical, and magical fancies that lay far beyond the bounds of the staid orthodoxies of Baptist Providence. Sarah Susan had only recently purchased her son an edition of *One Thousand and One Nights* (better known as *The Arabian Nights*) the same year she enrolled him in Sunday school. These stories, filled with enchanted treasure, terrifying Jinn, and dream worlds visited through mystical means, became for Lovecraft one of his many childhood obsessions. He dragged his mother to curio shops around Providence looking for items that he believed looked vaguely "Mohamadean" as people in the late nineteenth century tended to refer to any phenomenon associated with Islamic civilization.

By the time he tormented his Sunday school teacher, he owned a homemade "Arab" costume he probably insisted on wearing in public and, I've wondered, maybe even to Sunday school. His mother oversaw this new interest and essentially made it possible. This deserves special notice, since the 1880s had been scandalized by Richard Burton's multi-volume translation of the tales of Scheherazade, which revealed that *One Thousand and One Nights* contained plenty of sex interwoven with stories of treasures in caves and Sinbad's adventures on the high seas.

So Lovecraft's first rejection of religious faith seems to have come from a yearning for magic lands beyond the narrow path of Christianity's mythic geography rather than from the "scientific materialism" that later became his rallying cry. An older Lovecraft admitted as much in his "Confession of Unfaith" where he describes not just the "absurdity of the myths I was called on to accept" in his Sunday school days but also "the somber greyness of the whole faith as compared with the Eastern magnificence. . . ." Clearly, young Howard had been carried away on a magic carpet and no drab Baptist Sunday school lesson could ever drag him off.

Sarah Susan Lovecraft's role in this story has mostly been ignored. Local medical authorities had placed her new husband in a mental hospital just two years before the Sunday school incident. The talk around town and in her social circle must have been pestilential. And yet, she did not mind taking her son out of Sunday school at one of Providence's most prestigious institutions, even at the risk of more talk about those very odd Phillipses. Surely part of the story concerns the insistence of a doting mother that her son not do much of anything he didn't want to do. But her courage and lack of concern for what other people thought propriety meant also stands out. She did this in an era in which the notion of respectability meant everything when it came to class identity; in fact it created and substantiated class identity. Young Howard picked up some of his distaste for "Victorianism" as a way of seeing the world from his young, pretty, and strange mother.

While Sarah Susan Lovecraft helped her boy explore his fascination with ancient gods, Grandfather Phillips introduced him to the world of monsters. There's evidence that he read *Grimm's Fairy Tales* as early as four, possibly at old Whipple's instigation. Most readers today are probably well aware that the Grimm brothers' collection of central European folktales, though watered down in many a children's reader, actually appeared in 1812 as terrifying stories that involve supernatural creatures eager to cannibalize the young, weak, and generally unfortunate. An older Lovecraft further recalled that his grandfather introduced him to the very idea of horror tales and apparently gave him oral versions of some of the eighteenth-century gothic novels that formed the basis for Whipple's own literary appetites.

The influence of such stories became a more palpable part of his mental geography after his first encounter with death. In 1896, Grandmother Robie died, Sarah Susan's mother and old Whipple's wife of forty years. This introduction to mortality, coming as his father descended more deeply into pain and madness and as Howard's reading took him to fantastical and mystical worlds, had an effect even more profound than the first encounter with death often has on children. Victorian mourning traditions, though in some respects no more bizarre than the practices urged on us by the contemporary American funeral industry, certainly emphasized the tragic and irrevocable nature of death. Writing much later about the experience, Lovecraft recalled that Grandmother Robie's end "plunged the household into gloom" and that the mourning garb of his mother and his aunts, their "black attire," terrified him.

Howard sought an escape from the gloom, as he often would, into worlds more fantastically dire than what he found in real life. He came across an edition of *Paradise Lost* containing the illustrations of Gustave Doré. These drawings are best known for their portrayal of the fall of Satan and his angels, sketched by Doré as titanic figures of immense proportions who appear like the muscled Titans of Greek legend so familiar to Howard from his mythological interests. They also contain dark and brooding images of the rebellious Lucifer, sullen and embittered, gathering about him hosts of flying devils to continue his unwinnable war against God.

Lovecraft, at least in some of his correspondence, claimed that the combination of Doré and the dark cloud of his grandmother's death started his nighttime struggles with what he called "the night gaunts." These creatures infested his dreams at age six, and in some ways for the rest of his life, coming upon him with black leathery wings, giant insect-like horrors whose rubbery skin had aspects of the amphibious and aquatic world already beginning to appall this seaport boy who claimed to despise the taste and even the smell of fish.

He later remembered that in these night terrors "they were wont to whirl me through space at a sickening rate of speed, all the while fretting and impelling me with their tridents." So powerful did these dreams remain that even in his twenties, he claimed that while drifting off to sleep he felt a sudden "thrill of fear" and the need to try and stay awake in order to keep these winged terrors at bay.

He had another version of the origins of the night gaunts he told as an adult. The house at 454 Angell stood on the very edges of residential Providence in the 1890s, giving young Howard unlimited access to the Rhode Island countryside. This allowed him the opportunity to build his altars to the deities of ancient Greece and, according to an autobiographical note in 1933, to expand his conception of the fantastic by brooding right along with what he described as "the brooding, primitive landscape" along the Seekonk River. He claimed that these wanderings took "on an aura of strangeness not unmixed with vague horror" that "figured in my dreams—especially those nightmares containing the black, winged, rubbery entities which I called night gaunts."

There's no particular reason to try and collate these accounts. They aren't exactly contradictory and in fact point to a larger truth about strange little Howard. He lived in a swirl of images that brought together death and the fantastic, a youthful Surrealist a good twenty-five years before the art that combined the beautiful and grotesque by digging into the Freudian subconscious became current. In Lovecraft's imagination, night gaunts flew with fallen angels across windswept darkness while dryads and desert Jinn appeared in the twilight. The thrilling horrors of the smell of death filled the household but the perfumes of a mythical orient wafted from a Baghdad of dreams.

All this at age six. And he had not even read Poe yet.

Grandfather Phillips helped him find his monsters. Meanwhile, his dying father and complicated, fascinating mother provided him with dark materials that shaped his inner life, that urged on his obsession with a past full of promise and wonder and terror. In his father's absence, his mother allowed him the time and the space to ponder this darkness when, especially as he grew older, she had every reason to expect he might help provide for her or, at the very least, for himself.

His family wrapped him in darkness but, luckily for weird little Howard Lovecraft, he used it as a chrysalis and not a shroud.

⌣

Whipple Phillips apparently opposed the marriage of Sarah Susan to Winfield Scott Lovecraft, a silver utensil salesman from New York, from the start.

Old Whipple, the wealthy patriarch of an established family in the East Providence Yankee aristocracy, looked askance at Lovecraft. Although born in Rochester in 1853, Winfield Lovecraft affected the English accent of his parents and apparently cut a poor figure before his future father-in-law. The shady young man had just a dash of the British dandy about him, an attitude that did not comport well with his occupation as a "commercial traveller" (in other words a travelling salesman) for Gorham and Company silversmiths. In fact, he does seem a shadowy figure as the details of his life before his marriage to Sarah Susan Phillips have remained obscure even to some incredibly detailed genealogical investigations undertaken by Lovecraft enthusiasts. None of this could have served to give Whipple much confidence in the match.

Whatever rich, old Whipple thought, Sarah Susan Phillips seems to have finally been swept off her feet, or at least she was up for something new, something not tied to her father and the family home. In her early thirties when she married, Sarah Susan had long been considered something of a delicate beauty in her little corner of New England brahminhood. One longtime neighbor described her as "very pretty and attractive with a beautiful and unusually white complexion." The neighbor, a childhood acquaintance of Howard's named Clara Hess who reported her memories about the Lovecrafts in the 1940s, noted that most thought that Sarah Susan kept her porcelain skin "by eating arsenic." Victorian folk wisdom held that the poison, taken in small doses, promoted both beauty and sound nerves.

Most everyone who has ever written a word about H.P. Lovecraft has portrayed Sarah Susan as a malefic influence. She vamped him from his very infancy, the story goes, and while as a child he may have had dread dreams of what he called "night gaunts," it was really the Dark Mother of his daylight hours that should have worried him. Young Howard's failure to launch in his early years has been laid squarely at his mother's feet.

There's really no way, and no need, of getting around her oddities. She found herself subject to a history and a culture not of her own making that brought its assumptions to bear on her behavior. Current attitudes about her depend on an interpretation generated by the Victorian world that entrapped her. She deserves better as we look back at that era from the distance of more than a century.

At the time of H.P. Lovecraft's birth, the middle class represented a somewhat new phenomenon in world history. The term itself only appeared in the mid-eighteenth century, used to describe a social reality born from the industrial revolution. This world-historical transformation of the relationship of work to wages and labor into the supervision of labor created Americas's first industrial working class. Above them rose a new class of supervisors, managers, bankers, retail salesmen, insurance companies, and all manner of people making money off the infrastructure of this new, vibrant form of capitalism.

The middle class emphasized a new set of values in order to fully secure its legitimacy. Aristocracy depends on the power of name and the lands and privileges that go along with it. Aristocrats, or at least their ancestors, forged their status with swords. The new middle class in Britain and America had no storied names and no battles their ancient ancestors had won. They needed something other than money to establish a right to their business ventures and managerial positions and the social position that went along with them.

Out of this search for legitimacy emerged the notion of "respectability," a set of interrelated concepts that became the badge of identification for what counted as "middle class." A respectable member of the middle class exhibited the virtues of frugality, self-discipline, and sexual purity. The first two are the virtues that make for a disciplined work-force and it's really no wonder that, through organized efforts such as the Temperance movement, the bourgeoisie sought to inculcate these values into the working class. Before the arrival of the factory, American artisans and their apprentices had stopped their work in tanning, candle-making, and cobbling shops for a midday tipple of whisky or rum. The new factory system, as it transformed into what became the twentieth-century assembly line, could not allow its workers such luxuries.

The emphasis the middle class placed on sexual purity confronted middle-class women with a conflicted set of expectations. On the one hand, motherhood represented the apex of their achievement. Thus, their worth to the middle-class household depended on both their sexual performance and a successful procreative outcome. At the same time, middle-class ideology assumed that the mother took on the role of "the angel of the household," a guiding light for the young and a beneficent comfort for the male patriarch. This set of expectations came with all the assumptions of asexuality implied by angelism.

In other words, middle-class values grounded women's very identity in sex and reproduction while insisting they have no knowledge, experi-ence, or interest in the first and only concern themselves with the latter after they had borne another young, angelic presence for the household. This set of contradictory expectations offered enough psychic confusion to drive a whole generation to laudanum addiction.

Sarah Susan Lovecraft lived amid all of these strictures. The limita-tions of her world are plain in her family, where a dominant father ruled with sentiment and concern but—let it not be doubted—ruled nonethe-less. Sarah Susan had two sisters, Annie and Lillian, and all three mar-ried quite late, living in their childhood home into their thirties. While Whipple Phillips travelled widely and for extended periods, his family stayed at home.

Biographers have emphasized the role of Grandfather Phillips in shaping young Howard's imagination and intellect. More attention should be given to his grandmother and aunts, who played a decisive role in his interest in science, and to his much maligned mother, who encouraged his interest in literature, including some of its forbidding, dark corners. Living entangled in a complex skein of Victorian expectations, the Phillips women seemingly carved out a world for themselves and, at least intellectually, allowed young Howard to do the same.

In 1889, Susan's marriage to the man with the interesting accent may have been a bid for independence as much as infatuation. Marrying Lovecraft entailed a move to Boston where the silver salesman headquartered. In 1892, the family went to live briefly as boarders in Auburndale, a suburb of Boston. The Lovecrafts rented from Louise Imogen Guiney, a minor poet who took a limited interest in the couple's two-year-old. Lovecraft clearly remembered her reciting poetry with him, though her friendly Saint Bernard apparently made the biggest impression on the man who would become such a vehement cat person that he wrote an essay defending the cat's alleged aristocratic superiority over the proletarian canine.[8]

During this period, W.S. Lovecraft's work prospered enough to allow the purchase of a building plot in Auburndale. Two-year-old Howard was about to become a Bostonian.

Whipple Phillips may have been right that his son-in-law had a bit of the ne'er-do-well about him. Winfield Scott Lovecraft confirmed these fears just as he seemed on the verge of establishing his young family's respectability. Lovecraft set off for Chicago in April of 1893 on a sales trip, a trip that changed Howard and his mother's life forever.

"The chambermaid has insulted me! Brutal men are raping my wife upstairs! I can hear her cries, oh God!" W.S. Lovecraft came running out of his hotel room screaming these words, or some approximation of them, on the night of April 21. Hotel management called in a local doctor who sedated him, though Lovecraft's medical records note that he remained "noisy and violent" for two days. Doctors administered enough drugs, possibly morphine, to render Lovecraft unconscious. This enabled Whipple Phillips to take him to Providence and place him in Butler Hospital. He died there five horrific years later.

Like an unhappy satire of the stereotypical travelling salesman, Winfield Scott Lovecraft, somewhere and from someone, contracted syphilis. The disease began to manifest on his Chicago trip. Dementia and extreme paranoia are symptoms of a particularly malignant form of tertiary syphilis. Although some Lovecraft enthusiasts who have considered his case note that a brain tumor might have similar results, it's highly unlikely that Winfield Scott Lovecraft would have lived another five years after the Chicago incident had a tumor been responsible. A complete mental break, such as the one he suffered in 1893, would suggest a lesion of a very advanced stage.

Grandfather Whipple paid for Winfield Scott Lovecraft's extended time at Butler Hospital in Providence. It's doubtful that Lovecraft's precocious son would have been taken to see him over these five years, when Howard was between the ages of three and eight. Whipple and Sarah Susan would not have wanted him to see his father's state. Medical records of the elder Lovecraft's final years, exhumed by S.T. Joshi, tell a story of a complete descent into madness. W.S. Lovecraft's doctors describe him as at times so physically uncontrollable that only morphine quieted him. Although occasionally allowed into the hospital courtyard, the descriptions of efforts to get him fresh air end with more vague talk of him being "noisy."[9]

Winfield Scott Lovecraft died in the chaos of physical and mental agony. Ulcerations appeared on his genitalia, likely a sign of compulsive masturbation rather than symptomatic of syphilis, since ulcers tend to appear at earlier stages in the disease. In May of 1898, he suffered convulsions and gastrointestinal agonies made more horrible by being treated with an enema every few days. Doctors pronounced him dead on July 18, 1898.

There's no meaningful reason to believe that Winfield Scott's son did not know the details of his father's illness or death. I agree with previous writers on Lovecraft who claim that the family undoubtedly attempted to veil the story in silence. But Providence was a small place, especially upper crust East Providence, and it seems more than likely that the true story made the rounds. Sarah Susan Lovecraft sank into a deep depression around the time of Winfield Scott's hospitalization, driven further into her personal darkness by the disreputable nature of his disease as much as by his impending death. How could he have been protected from these neighborhood stories and the occasional odd comments his mother undoubtedly let slip?

Meanwhile, the three-year-old already reciting reams of poetry and well on his way to a full-blown obsession with the eighteenth century probably listened and learned from whispered conversations taking place between his grandparents, mother, and aunts at 454 Angell Street. He and Sarah Susan Lovecraft had, probably with little discussion of the matter, gone to reside in the family mansion very soon after his father's incapacitation.

Although family catastrophe triggered the move, this house became the epicenter of Lovecraft's adult yearnings for a home. He never discussed how the collapse of his father led to his living there beyond the stark fact of the move. His correspondence in the 1910s shows little or no awareness of the reasons for his father's death, but there's good reason to be suspicious of this—that we are reading a feigned ignorance.

Lovecraft claimed in 1916 that "In April of 1893 my father was stricken with a complete paralysis resulting from a brain overtaxed with study and business cares." It's of course possible, and even likely, that his mother, in collusion with the rest of the family, told the young child that his father had gone away simply because he needed a rest.[10]

The story that exhaustion from business and intellectual activity became paralysis that then led to his father's early death may have held some purchase in Howard's eight-year-old brain. Most of us inherit from childhood the basic lineaments of magical thinking, fairy tale logic about the relationship between seemingly unrelated events that adults foist upon us in an effort to protect us from various harsh realities. We absorb many of our adult mythologies, both mundane and transcendent, from such benevolent lies: the grandfather dying in a hospital bed "is just resting" or a young friend suddenly taken from our lives for uncertain reasons and being planted before our eyes into the ground has "gone to be with the angels." In our early years, we generally buy into these well-intentioned scams without too much thought.

But then we aren't H.P. Lovecraft—who by the time of his father's death spent his dreams with the night gaunts, had absorbed whatever knowledge he could find of the classical world and the eighteenth century, and soon embarked on a massive project of autodidacticism in chemistry and the discipline that became most significant for him in his early years, astronomy. Of course, none of these intellectual enthusiasms suggest an early worldliness; and it's been the habit of most writers considering Lovecraft to portray these geektrests as simple escapism—a nerdy retreat into literature, science, and fantasy that provide evidence for a deep lack of awareness of the world.

While I do not contest that he found an escape in his precocious intellectual pursuits, it's unclear to me how they mark more of an escape than Lovecraft's contemporaries' fascination with baseball or the growing national obsession, college football. Besides, maybe eight-year-old boys with dying fathers shouldn't be asked to spend their hours staring into the abyss. Why shouldn't he be allowed such an escape?

Moreover, if colonial antiquities, Greek gods, his grandfather's monster tales, Dryden's Augustan poetry, and the Arabian Nights provided Lovecraft with a distraction from his institutionalized father, they also opened to him a wider world of narrative. These stories hinted at impulses, motivations, and tragic consequences that taught something about the world that it would have been much easier for the boys on the sandlot to miss but that Lovecraft absorbed from Bulfinch and *One Thousand and One Nights*. In sum, there are elements of Howard Lovecraft that suggest he knew the score despite his family's best efforts to protect him.

There's at least some evidence that Lovecraft guessed at the meaning of his father's demise. Howard proved precocious about matters more earthy than the Augustans and the classics. He did, despite the frequent assertions by some biographers about his allegedly preternatural asexuality, develop an interest in what exactly the grown-ups hid about the possibilities of what could happen between men and women. Perhaps he'd come across some of the naughty bits in *Arabian Nights* at about the time his father's death from an illness that, from all the talk around him, seemed to have a mysterious and guilty origin. Everything we know of him suggests that he would have tried to divine the mystery of his father's disappearance. It's not a giant leap that he figured out that sex had some role to play in his father's rather abrupt disappearance from his life. Whatever the exact trigger, at age eight he sought out knowledge of sexuality with the same alacrity he brought to making sense of eighteenth-century prose and poetry.

It goes without saying that asking questions of his distraught and anxious mother would have been culturally impossible at the end of the nineteenth century. Grandfather Whipple would have greeted his questions with a startled glare, despite his willingness to initiate his grandson into the world of weird fiction. So, the young Lovecraft did what he'd spend most of his life doing . . . finding books, with little guidance and direction from others that might tell him what he wanted to know, and trying his best to puzzle the matter out for himself.

The family library contained at least two volumes that would give him the facts of life, or at least what passed for those facts in 1898. These included the illustrated *Quain's Anatomy* and *Dunglison's Physiology*, guides to the human body and its possibilities that have about as much erotic appeal as a plumbing manual.

Lovecraft gave an interesting explanation for his interest in the subject, given the context of his father's death. He later said his reading on the subject rose "because of curiosity & perplexity concerning the strange reticence & embarrassments of adult speech" on the subject. Again, the dark whispers behind closed doors at 454 Angell. More whispering from neighbors as the family passed on the street. Forbidden knowledge that young Howard had to bring to light, a deadly fault in nearly all the protagonists of his later horror fiction.

Much later, Lovecraft claimed that his reading, "instead of giving me an abnormal & precocious interest in sex . . . it virtually killed my interest in the subject. The whole matter was reduced to prosaic mechanism—a mechanism which I rather despised or at least thought non-glamorous because of its purely animal nature. . . ." Although this assertion of a lack of interest, even abhorrence, of all things libidinal has often been taken at face value, there are plenty of reasons not to do so. We are not hearing a male eight-year-old report his feelings at learning about the possibilities of sex and orgasm, ideas that he later suggested became an unwanted fascination for him during an adolescence almost perfectly suited to frustrate any effort to fulfill these urges. We are instead listening to an account of the man trying to make himself fully into stuffy old Providence gentleman H.P. Lovecraft, the character he played for the small group of friends that counted as his audience during his lifetime.

No definitive evidence proves that H.P. Lovecraft learned the reason for his father's death. In fact, we have letters that seemingly make it clear that he did not. These denials do seem like exercises in profound naiveté but, despite how he's often pictured, naiveté cannot be listed as one of his failings. So it's more likely that he lied to correspondents about his father's death, lies he was of course perfectly within his rights to tell people who had no need and certainly no right to know about his father's syphilitic madness and death if Lovecraft did not wish them to know it.

Why does his possible knowledge of his father's fate matter? For the cultural historian, if Lovecraft did know of the causes of his father's death, it certainly explains some puzzling aspects of his life and fiction, shedding light into some of the darkest corners of Lovecraft's interior world.

"Sex, though, it's just all dark hints, unnamable couplings, just stuff like that." A detective investigating a murderous sex and drug cult in the 2011 graphic novel *Neonomicon* authored by the legendary Alan Moore describes Lovecraft's work in this way. The comic series, built around the idea that Lovecraft describes actual cosmic monsters contacted by devotees, dwells much on the idea that the very repressions and silences about sex in Lovecraft's oeuvre actually underscore the sometimes blatant erotic language he used for his nameless horrors. Another detective in the series tells his captain that "I've read his books . . . perhaps it's me but it seemed like it was *all* sex. You know? The monsters and all that? They're like a lot of cocks and pussies crawling around."

Well, many of Lovecraft's monsters don't even begin to resemble genitalia. A full examination of his work, even by someone intent on the most radical and thoroughgoing Freudian reading, would conclude that sometimes a sea monster is just a sea monster. Still, Moore's onto something here and it's likely traceable to Lovecraft's earliest confrontation with sex and learning its meaning even as he watched his father go mad and die in agony from a sexually transmitted disease. It's not armchair psychiatry to assume such a thing had a profound effect on hypersensitive Howard and the stories he told us, particularly given the nature of the historical context in which he wrote.

Lovecraft returned to the relationship of sex, death, and madness in both his fictions and his intellectual interests. His fascination with Freud in the 1910s and 1920s, sometimes verging on careful acceptance of some of his ideas and sometimes complete rejection of all of them, seems out of step with his other intellectual pursuits. But it makes much more sense if stemming from an effort to comprehend his father's life and death. Most Lovecraft biographers have passed over his frequently sympathetic reading of Freud—an odd intellectual inquiry for the conservative young man with an allergy to modernism—rather quickly. This is in part because Lovecraft himself made utterly contradictory statements to different people about the value of Freud's work.

A conservative young man of East Providence writing monster stories. But what if Lovecraft represents something more? What if he unlocked a door in the head of the twentieth century and let all our dark angels out in a manner no different from the famous Vienna psychiatrist—himself a sort of gothic author that imagined the ego in a three-way S&M relationship with the savage and civilized regions of mind and culture?

Lovecraft's deepest literary influences are significantly more diffuse than commonly assumed. There are early doses of Hawthorne that show up in his creation of horrific atmospheres, Rappaccini's garden transformed into dream worlds and dimensions of horror that the original model only suggested. Ambrose Bierce may have appealed to his cynicism more than he later admitted. Poe and Dunsany became his idols but his work shows their fingerprints rather than their guiding hand.

In Lovecraft's own mind, only one predecessor mattered in an ultimate way. Edgar Allan Poe, he insisted, always remained his master.

He claimed to have first read Poe in 1898. Not only does this represent a feat on its own terms for an eight-year-old, it further underscores how his diverse interests gave him an awareness of the wider cultural landscape at a ridiculously early age. Poe had just begun to enter the popular consciousness in a meaningful way when Lovecraft read him. The French poet Baudelaire, a favorite among absinthe drinking goths of the nineteenth century, celebrated Poe's work, as had the littérateur Mallarmé. His reputation grew more slowly in America, although during the 1880s two major biographies of Poe appeared in English.

Among the respectable middle class, this did not matter much. Poe still had the whiff of the disreputable about him, despite and even because of the growing adulation of his work by outré French poets. Poe himself had helped create the atmosphere of brooding self-destruction that surrounded him. In what he himself would have described as a sudden possession by "the imp of the perverse," Poe made perhaps his most bitter enemy, the Reverend Wilmot Griswold, his literary executor. He and Poe had tangled over mutual love interests and literary reputation, and the spite that Griswold held for Poe drips from his announcement (under a pseudonym) of Poe's death in the *New-York Tribune* on October 9, 1849; "Edgar Allan Poe is dead. He died in the streets of Baltimore the day before yesterday. This announcement will startle many *but few will be grieved by it.* [emphasis in original]."

Taking over Poe's literary interests made Griswold a pile of cash and also allowed him the pleasure of spreading tales of Poe's prodigious drinking, alleged opium and morphine addiction, and general dissolution. It didn't help Poe in the eyes of Victorians that some of these stories had the advantage of being true. Moreover, he had plenty of detractors based solely on his authorial skills. The powerful voice of Henry James damned Poe and his readers in 1878 by writing that "to take him [Poe] with a certain degree of seriousness is to lack seriousness in one's self. An enthusiasm for Poe is the mark of a decidedly primitive stage of reflection."

Poe simply had not yet become the iconic American writer he'd become in the twentieth century, and he certainly had nothing like the level of fame he attained in recent years. We don't know how Howard found him. Grandfather Phillips may have introduced the young Lovecraft to Poe—even if old Whipple's tastes in weird fiction ran more toward the Walpole–Radcliffe–Reeves gothic novels of the eighteenth century.

However the child came across Poe's work, the adult version of H.P. Lovecraft perceived and represented it as the watershed moment of his youthful fascinations. Lovecraft later insisted that Poe's more macabre works had even caused a break with his interest in classical history and mythology. Poe's tales had joined the night gaunts in haunting his dreams. "It was my downfall," he laughingly noted about his discovery of Poe, "and at the age of eight I saw the blue firmament of Argos and Sicily darkened by the miasmal exhalations of the tomb!"

The mention of "the exhalations of the tomb" and the very title of Lovecraft's first mature effort at horror fiction in 1917 suggest that Poe's dark incantations are what drew him into the world of the macabre. But perhaps a better grasp of Poe helps us understand what Lovecraft received from him and what he did not.

Although thoroughly associated with the beginnings of horror, Poe wrote in a variety of forms, including comedy and adventure. He created modern detective fiction with his *Murders in the Rue Morgue*, a story that may have been a partial influence on what would become Lovecraft's childhood interest in literary detectives. Poe's C. Auguste Dupin may also have been the inspiration for, as we will see, Howard's creation of what amounted to a detective agency role-playing game.

Poe's influence may have been most important as an early impetus for Lovecraft's desire to write fiction. After his introduction to Poe, he earnestly began to try his hand at his own weird fiction. It's unclear, however, whether Poe definitively prompted him to evoke literary nightmares. His first effort, entitled "The Noble Eavesdropper," actually came to him before his reading of Poe. No copy of Lovecraft's first tale of terror exists, though we do have his description of the plot that involved "a boy who overheard some horrible conclave of subterranean beings in a cave." Although probably failing in its execution, it's certainly not a bad concept.[11]

Over the next few years, more juvenile tales followed, bearing such titles as "The Mysterious Ship," "The Secret Cave," and "The Mystery of the Graveyard, or a Dead Man's Revenge" (which contained yet another subtitle, "A Detective Story.")

The tendency of Lovecraft enthusiasts to associate him so thoroughly with Poe largely came from a desire for their idol's reputation to grow right along with Poe's in the literary community. This has trickled down to Lovecraft fandom, where mentioning Poe and Lovecraft in the same breath has become de rigueur if you want to portray yourself as a sophisticated reader of horror fiction.

Some of the best popular writing on Lovecraft has, unfortunately, strengthened what's mostly a false connection. Jess Nevins, maybe the most important writer on the meaning and history of comic books working today, wrote two essays published as appendices to *Fatale*, a graphic novel edition of a brilliant 2013 comic series by Ed Brubaker and Sean Phillips. *Fatale* manages to fuse the work of Lovecraft with midcentury noir films while mounting a critique of misogyny in popular culture. Nevins's appended essays in *Fatale Vol. I* explain the work of Poe and of Lovecraft, intertwining them to the themes of *Fatale* and to each other.

The only problem is that Poe's nowhere to be found in the Brubaker and Phillips series. It's breathtakingly original, taking Lovecraft's notion of secret cults and elder gods and mingling them with a midcentury Los Angeles of dirty cops and organized crime in the golden age of Hollywood. Brubaker and Phillips make it seem as if Lovecraft himself could have written these stories and the inks bring some of Lovecraft's darkest imaginings to life. The cover art for the original comic series alone makes it worth picking up for Lovecraft aficionados. You'll look far and wide in popular culture for such a creative use of tentacles and tommy guns.

But, contrary to what Nevins's essays suggest, Poe's influence appears exactly nowhere in this work. This makes the effort to link them in Nevins's otherwise excellent writing simply a function of the connection made between Lovecraft and Poe that has become nearly inevitable in the popular imagination.

So inescapable does the coupling seem that the earliest effort to bring Lovecraft to film linked him with Poe. B-movie impresario Roger Corman directed a version of Lovecraft's short novel *The Case of Charles Dexter Ward* in 1963. Billed as *The Haunted Palace*, studio execs insisted that Corman give it the full title *Edgar Allan Poe's The Haunted Palace* even though the script makes reference to the *Necronomicon*, Cthulhu, and other Lovecraftian inventions. Moreover, the film takes Lovecraft's fictional New England town of Arkham as its setting and, while not following the plot of *The Case of Charles Dexter Ward* especially closely, it's certainly a recognizable interpretation even as it includes bits and pieces of "The Shadow Over Innsmouth" and "The Dunwich Horror."

The reasons why a Lovecraft adaptation became a Poe adaptation are complex, related in part to the Poe renaissance of the sixties and the popularity of other Corman films like *House of Usher* and *The Pit and the Pendulum* that borrowed Poe's titles and tropes. Studio executives simply decided that Poe sold well. Whatever the pecuniary motivations, even on the verge of Lovecraft's own renaissance he and Poe are welded together as twin, indeed interchangeable, masters of American horror.

And, really, who can blame the fangirls and -boys, or the scholars and the artists, and the entertainment industry itself? Lovecraft nourished the alleged connection in his essays and with his correspondents. Poe became essential not only in his representation of himself, but to his own personal conception. By the time Lovecraft sought to convince others of the influence of Poe, his life's work had become writing for almost no pay in a highly disreputable genre that literary critics lampooned for decades after his death. Poe offered him the chance to place his work within a literary legacy that by the 1920s had come into its own. Poe's growing influence offered him a way to appear as something other than a not very successful pulp writer.

Lovecraft himself sometimes left Poe out of the narrative of his influences. Asked in 1933 to write a short autobiography set to appear in *Unusual Stories* (it never did), Lovecraft does not mention his first reading of Poe as the trigger for his interest in weird fiction and horror. The night gaunts are there, as is the *One Thousand and One Nights*, *The Rime of the Ancient Mariner*, Gustave Doré's nineteenth-century illustrations of Milton, and even his rabid fascination with the eighteenth century. He is silent about his discovery of Poe. Late in the essay, Lovecraft does mention Poe as one of his two "chief models" for his writings, but only after 1920. The Anglo-Irish writer Lord Dunsany is mentioned as the other . . . and for a period when his stories seem unlike anything either of his "chief models" ever wrote.

The work of a lesser-known American literary light suggests another element of Lovecraft's early influences that biographers have perhaps downplayed. In a 1921 essay Lovecraft wrote for his amateur journalism friends in defense of his interest in the "weird tale," he called Ambrose Bierce "the greatest story writer except Poe that America ever produced." If you've never heard of Bierce before, don't feel left out of the conversation. Lovecraft said in the same piece that "nine out of ten persons have never *heard* of Ambrose Bierce" [emphasis in original], a claim just as true today.

S.T. Joshi's investigation into Bierce's influence on Lovecraft suggests that the latter did not read Bierce until 1919. However, Bierce began publishing weird fiction in the 1870s and had a collection of stories, *Can Such Things Be?*, that appeared in 1893 and might have been especially pleasing to Whipple Phillips. It's very possible that Lovecraft may have heard abbreviated oral versions of some of Bierce's tales from his storytelling grandfather. If this is not the case, it's notable that Joshi located incontrovertible evidence that Lovecraft did read Bierce for himself in 1919, right on the verge of one of the first productive periods of writing as an adult.

Bierce's misanthropy, indeed his bitterness against the universe itself, would have seeped into a young Lovecraft's consciousness if he only heard oral versions of some of the former Civil War officer's tales. Bierce played the supernatural as a trick pack of cards the universe dealt humanity, dark ironies piled on one another. In his most famous short story, "An Occurrence at Owl Creek Bridge," a hanging becomes an occasion for someone to be haunted by their own ghost as well as a parable about what Bierce saw as the miserable fate of all life.

Bierce's hilariously embittered *Devil's Dictionary* defined "Worm's-meat" as "the finished product of which we are all the raw material." Dark clouds gathered over Howard's worldview even as an eight-year-old although an older Lovecraft, writing to August Derleth, actually distanced himself a bit from Bierce's brand of cynicism. Why be cynical when you can be indifferent? Lovecraft strived to attain this old Roman sense of passivity toward the horror of life but, whether he achieved it or not, it's a worldview that depended on the assumption of the triumph of meaningless suffering in human experience.

This growing sense of unease eventually fostered some of the most interesting, if also disturbing, elements of Lovecraft's fiction. And like so many things in his psyche, it sat uneasily with other, seemingly apposite elements. His love of the fantastic blossomed while the weeds of nihilism shot up everywhere. Some of these tensions found release in what became his next obsession. In 1898, Howard Lovecraft discovered science and, he thought, his future career.

Lovecraft claimed in a 1918 letter that his interest in science began with *Webster's Unabridged Dictionary*. Dictionaries have become significantly less impressive in intervening years, due to cheap abridged versions and Wikipedia making them appear unnecessary. Perhaps bibliophiles prone to purchase the complete *Oxford English Dictionary* in its multivolume physical manifestation have some sense of what a dictionary or encyclopedia meant in Lovecraft's boyhood.

In the late nineteenth century a dictionary, often rich with detailed illustrations, opened worlds of wonder to someone with young Howard's predilections. After making his way through various kinds of zoological knowledge, and probably feeling a bit ill if he came across anything amphibious or amphibian, he lighted upon an article entitled "Philosophical and Scientific Instruments." Chemical apparatus of all kinds thrilled him and he desperately wanted to plumb the mysteries they proffered.

His Aunt Lillian shared his interest and gave him a text entitled *The Young Chemist* written by a family friend, a professor at Brown named John Howard Appleton. Sarah Susan Lovecraft and Lillian Phillips also made sure that, at great danger to him and to themselves, eight-year-old Howard soon had his own chemical apparatus and full permission to transform the basement of 454 Angell into a young mad scientist's laboratory.

Old Whipple's classical statuary decorating the parlor rattled and rocked at least once when a loud explosion resulted from one of young Howard's experiments with potassium. He also worked with gunpowder and carbon cell batteries. He once attempted an experiment in an open field behind Angell Street that resulted in a brief brushfire. More or less unsupervised and given access to any compound or instrument the well-to-do family could procure, Lovecraft pursued chemistry with the same fascination that caused him to lose himself in classical mythology, mystical orientalism, or the dark vision of the macabre in his grandfather's stories. As with so many of his hobbies, he couldn't simply have an interest in chemistry. He had to become a chemist. Only good fortune prevented him from blowing his own face off in the process or burning his beloved childhood home to the ground.

Howard's interest in chemistry expanded into a more general interest in science and most especially in astronomy, a field he and his family came to assume would become his profession. By 1902, he discovered, as he put it in an essay written twenty years later for an amateur journal, "the myriad suns and worlds of infinite space"—an encounter whose significance he placed alongside his six-year-old discovery of the mysteries of ancient Greece. Chemical interests quickly faded, in part because he had begun his lifelong struggle with understanding mathematics. But, as with so many things, stumbling across a set of books set him on a new trajectory, if one where math also waited for him like a night gaunt.

He had his deceased grandmother to thank for what became a lifelong obsession with the infinite dark. Robie Phillips, whose death painted Lovecraft's world black in 1896, undoubtedly influenced him more than even he seemed willing to credit in his later correspondence on the topic. She certainly played the Victorian matron to Whipple Phillips's entrepreneurial go-getterism, staying at home while he made his extended travels for business and much pleasure to London and Italy. She raised three daughters and took special delight in her very young grandson.

We also know that she had a special interest in astronomy, one of a number of facts that suggests that the women in Lovecraft's life have not been given their due. Howard's first astronomical texts came from a collection of such materials that had belonged to his grandmother. Along with Lillian's continuing interest in the smattering of chemistry she gained in her boarding school education, the picture that emerges reveals what Victorian notions of womanhood would have considered an unconventional interest in the male-dominated sciences among the women of the Phillips family.[12]

Robie's books on astronomy sated him until 1903, when his mother and aunt began to provide him with a wealth of new astronomical texts. During the same period, the family began purchasing him beginner's telescopes, leading finally to the procurement of a more expensive and professional model in 1906. At age thirteen, he would give a lecture and slide presentation at his home, possibly only for immediate members of his family and a few of their friends, on very basic astronomical phenomena. The slides he used included "Sun Spots," "A Total Solar Eclipse," and "Comet of 1811."

Science became for Lovecraft the very foundation of his philosophical worldview. Biographers have often noted that an older Lovecraft linked his interest in the wonders, and the terrors, of "infinite space" to his earlier acquaintance with astronomy.

The fantastic, however, never receded into the shadows and we have to remember how ably he filled those "infinite spaces" with monsters. He discovered chemistry the same year he discovered Poe. He explored chemistry and then astronomy while reading pulp adventures and continued his imaginative immersion in the worlds of Hawthorne and *One Thousand and One Nights*. His interest during this period in the scientific explorations of the Antarctic may have drawn slightly on Poe's *The Narrative of Arthur Gordon Pym of Nantucket* and, much later, formed the basis of one of Lovecraft's most ambitious tales of the weird.

A seemingly contradictory love for the world of the imagination and the rational empiricism of the sciences coexisted in Howard Lovecraft's mind from an early age. There's no evidence that what looks to us like an incompatible set of impulses troubled him in the least. In fact, he melded them so successfully that they became crucial to his understanding of horror. He happily let the night gaunts fly through the infinite spaces. Long before Hollywood's vision of mad scientists gave us the imagery, monsters roamed his secret laboratory.

He may later have spoken of 1898 as the year he discovered Poe and science simultaneously. It's marked most significantly, however, as the year his father died.

He knew his father had disappeared as irrevocably as Grandmother Robie. He also fully experienced his mother's grief, a cold and obdurate shadow that stalked her for the next two decades. He later described 1898 as the first of the "near nervous breakdowns" of his youth, a term he frequently employed to describe various moments of crisis throughout life.

Soon after he became initiated into the dark and guilty mystery of Winfield Scott Lovecraft's death, he found himself in what must have been an excruciating experience for a boy mostly allowed to live in his own inner worlds. In the fall of that year, he began his spotty attendance at the Slater Avenue School. He only lasted until the spring of 1899. He would return again, briefly, in 1902–1903. He later wrote that he found his stints in what we might regard as middle school as "quite useless," adding, "I tried attendance at school, but was unable to endure the routine."

So, of course, Sarah Susan Lovecraft removed him from a situation he disliked. There's every reason to believe that part of his struggles with school came not only from the "quite useless" instruction he received. He was, as everything you've read so far suggests, a decidedly and unrepentantly weird kid. Memories of the young Lovecraft provided by children from his neighborhood all recall his intense oddity.

His peers may or may not have bullied him during his brief time at Slater Avenue, though it's reasonable to assume that some had heard stories about the cause of his father's death from the echo chamber of gossip about the matter that surely existed in East Providence. Lovecraft must have seemed like some bizarre and exotic thing materializing in their classroom, as if a giraffe who understood chemistry and eighteenth-century literature suddenly appeared to take lessons in basic spelling and grammar. "He gave a queer, eccentric impression," de Camp said, or, as one classmate simply put it, he seemed "crazy as a bedbug."[13]

Grandfather Whipple has often appeared in biographical accounts as a heroic father figure for young Howard. He did, after all, act as psychopomp for the future H.P. Lovecraft into the world of the night gaunts and probably led him to Poe, and maybe to Hawthorne and Bierce as well. There may have been another side to this relationship, especially as troubled business affairs and the increasing influence of all the Phillips women became the shaping force for Howard's life. Old Whipple worried that his grandson had not become manly enough.

Manliness became a cultural obsession in turn-of-the-century America. Public schools, beginning in the Midwest, established the first physical education programs between 1892 and 1899. This development coincided with the rise of college football as a new national obsession, though it lagged far behind the intense fervor attached to baseball. Theodore Roosevelt, president of the United States, gave a well-known speech in 1899 called "The Strenuous Life," celebrating manly achievement in sport, hunting, and exercise. Just before World War I, Philadelphia public schools forced male students to wear first-, second-, and third-place buttons that categorized them according to their physical development.

"These were catastrophic developments for nerds," writes Benjamin Nugent, the author of the book *American Nerd* that details the genealogy of nerddom from its humble beginnings to its current cultural triumph. These developments certainly had an ill effect on boys like Howard Lovecraft, who had a lifelong distaste for sports. He couldn't be called sedentary since by age ten he seemed to bicycle the entire state of Rhode Island and would walk for miles a day, exhausting anyone who joined him. But neither of these activities fit into the turn-of-the-century fascination with dumbbells and hitting or throwing cowhide. He bicycled because it helped him think. He walked to look at colonial architecture.

Whipple Phillips's concern that his grandson manifest more masculine traits began early. He complained in 1894, for example, that Sarah Susan Lovecraft should have had the boy wearing trousers much sooner. Whipple insisted that he receive a bicycle in 1900 so that he might have a modicum of physical activity and less time to set off explosions in the basement. Likely at his grandfather's insistence, Howard made the completely unimaginable and doomed effort to take part in the activities of the Providence Athletic Association during a brief period in 1899–1900. No information exists concerning the family discussions about this ill-considered plan. Lovecraft, perhaps on his first visit, had what he later described as a "fainting fit" and never had to return. Sarah Susan almost certainly refused to allow it and, without a doubt, young Howard happily agreed with her.

Soccer moms, and equally enthusiastic soccer dads, will only shake their heads in pity for Howard and disdain for Sarah Susan's parenting skills. Perhaps most of my fellow geeks reading these words, however, join me in envying Lovecraft his childhood. No matter how useless and commercially unviable his interests became, Sarah Susan made his pursuit of them possible.

This does not make her a Victorian-era helicopter parent, so familiar in contemporary American suburbia. Typically, the parenting philosophy of Generation X encourages the same kind of narcissism that Sarah Susan Lovecraft did, without exhibiting her singular saving grace; she insisted that her son invest himself in whatever weird and ultimately useless hobby captured his fancy. Howard's mother never did a single thing to ensure that her only son would became anything but a creative and interesting layabout.

Worse charges can be laid against her, and have been. She didn't teach him to love, she may not have taught him to think of himself as worthy of love, though it's really an open question whether such things can be taught and how well anyone ever learns them. A few times she kept him from experiences that arguably could have made him a better writer. She had been dosed with enough Victorian prudery to suffer a mental shock from her husband's death that does seem to have crippled her emotionally. In other words, the world that shaped her punished her and it punished Howard Lovecraft as well.

But so what? Sarah Susan Lovecraft did something that modern parents of privileged millennials don't even imagine achieving. She gave him unlimited freedom to pursue more or less anything he wanted to pursue and, in the process, to utterly fail in every attempt he ever made at making money. She opened to him magical worlds of fantasy and made possible his introduction to science. She derailed the family patriarch's efforts to turn him into an "All-American boy" and allowed him time to become one of the most influential authors of the twentieth century.

Thinking about peculiar young Howard in this earliest period of his life yields no final answer as to how he became H.P. Lovecraft. Too much quibbling over his "influences" can actually cause us to miss some essential secrets about what becoming H.P. Lovecraft meant, the effort it required from this young child and how others—especially his mother, his grandfather, and indeed his syphilitic and insane father—helped shape the most important horror author of the twentieth century.

Perhaps a much older Lovecraft's description of his first story idea, "a boy who overheard some horrible conclave of subterranean beings in a cave" best describes young Howard himself. As he sat in his room at

454 Angell reading Poe at the dawn of the twentieth century, he would overhear whispers in the gathering shadows of a century that no one in 1899 guessed could take such a sudden plunge into utter darkness.

———

"It seemed like a damn futile business to keep on living."

This is Howard at fourteen. Or, rather, a much older H.P. Lovecraft remembering the direction his thoughts travelled during his first real bout with the black and all-embracing morass of depression. In 1899, he had had his "near nervous breakdown" that had let him take a break from school. In 1904, he began to ponder the possibility of taking a break from life.

A set of spectacularly terrible circumstances, almost perfectly suited to wrecking the psyche of a young boy of Howard's disposition, help explain this mental state. The death of his father had created in his mother a vast, unmappable glacier of pain, a sense of loss compounded with embarrassment, anger, and a host of unanswerable questions she probably didn't want answered.

Old Whipple, meanwhile, made a lousy investment in a Colorado irrigation company, so bad that it sapped the Phillips family capital for years. A major flood in early 1904 caused the concern's complete collapse. Although in his seventies by this point, the nervous strain of the failure likely contributed to his stroke and sudden death in March of the same year. Old Whipple, whose presence must have seemed to Howard as solid and certain as a stone monument, disappeared from his life forever.

Passing through the third major family mourning ritual of his life at age thirteen, Howard also found himself uprooted from the family home he so idealized. His aunts Lillian and Annie had both recently married and moved out, leaving Sarah Susan and Howard alone in a house that desperate financial straits did not allow them to keep up. Soon after Whipple's death the family sold 454 Angell, and Howard and Sarah Susan moved to 598 Angell, sharing the western side of a duplex.

Lovecraft, writing in his forties about the move, describes it in terms that make empathy difficult. He says that "for the first time" he came to know the horrors of "a congested, servantless home." Such ideas are understandable in a thirteen-year-old of the upper bourgeoisie, but let's hope the forty-four-year-old man had some sense of irony about them. A generous reading suggests that in this letter he's remembering a more generalized sense of loss that came with the move into a house he described contemptuously as "five rooms and an attic."

The move did represent much more to him than a change of residence. His mother's "permanent grief" had found yet another focus with the death of her father. Young Lovecraft had been uprooted from a home that, with its basement laboratory and windowless attic, represented a kind of material extension of his vast, imaginative interior life. On top of this tonnage of existential grief suddenly landing squarely on the young boy, even his beloved cat had run off.

Let's ponder Lovecraft and his boyhood animal companion. As unimportant as the relationship might seem, it highlights a burden that any honest fan confronting Lovecraft bears. Lovecraft at times seems intensely likable, indeed loveable. So much of what we know about him comes from his brilliant correspondence in which he appears, like many of our contemporaries on social media, as the hero of his own story. Reading through what amounts to an autobiography told in hundreds of letters, it's easy to fall in love with his modesty, and his ability to move effortlessly between the erudition he attained with his own unrelenting effort and a kind of early–twentieth-century street speech that he both parodied and used to parody his usual formal tone.

Most enticing, his letters to what became a huge circle of correspondents shows the capacity to make fun of himself, a virtue that we all know covers a multitude of sins. Certainly his ungainly awkwardness appears charming in the age of *The Big Bang Theory*, an era in which we seem to have experienced not only the revenge of the nerds but their complete and utter hegemony.

Then, suddenly, our affection turns to repulsion. He becomes something beyond unlikable, indeed he appears as reptilian as some of his cosmic horrors. One of the first moments we feel this while exploring his young life comes when we learn that he named his cat, his longtime boyhood companion, "Nigger-Man."

S.T. Joshi comments that the name, especially for a cat, "was not regarded as offensive at the time." I regard it as instructive that Joshi uses the passive voice here. Who didn't find it offensive? Upper–middle-class whites like the Phillipses of Providence did not. Plenty of working-class whites in the urban North used it regularly. White Southerners made a fetish out of the word and it regularly appeared at the public torture, lynching, and burning of African American men that became common across the United States between the 1880s and 1940s. Five thousand such horrific spectacles occurred by 1948, a number that does not take into account a monstrous record of secret murders, rapes, and acts of random violence. The number also does not include innumerable "legal lynchings," a term that refers to the near-impossibility of black men and women receiving anything like a fair trial in an era when many states barred them from juries.

In other words, domestic pets did not receive the name "Nigger Man" in a social vacuum where casual bourgeois racism prevailed. Such words are intertwined into an American experience where it had become open season on black men, men often described by politicians, the press, and even white physicians and religious leaders as "black beasts" hard-wired for rape and murder.

Some find reason to excuse him even given this horrific historical record. But, as the story of how racism shaped Lovecraft's life, thought, fiction, and relationships shows, he's not simply—in that truly meaning-less and redundant phrase—a "product of his times."

Lovecraft did not simply reflect the atmosphere of the early twentieth century, despite the incessant claims of most of his acolytes. Even L. Sprague de Camp, often criticized for writing character assassination rather than biography, cuts Lovecraft whole bolts of slack when it comes to his racial attitudes. "In those days," he writes, "ethnic prejudice was so rife that it seemed the natural order of things."[14]

This is not a total falsehood. But it ignores a massive movement emerging in the United States that soon resulted in the beginnings of an African American freedom struggle. By the time that Lovecraft mourned the loss of Nigger-Man the cat, a generation of New England Brahmins had cut their teeth on a radical, anti-racist version of abolitionism that continued to influence their politics in the years after the American Civil War. Frederick Douglass had become one of the country's most recognizable public intellectuals, continuing the struggle for black civil rights and linking it to women's struggle for the franchise. A vast network of political and social organizations, many of them connected to the founding of black colleges like Fisk, Atlanta University, Howard, and Spelman, began to coalesce for a century of struggle.

W.E.B. Du Bois, the first African American to receive a PhD from Harvard University, had begun his lifelong war with white racism and structural oppression of all kinds. While young Howard pined for his lost cat in 1904, Du Bois had just published *The Souls of Black Folk*, one of the classics of American literature and an uncompromising, full-throated broadside against white racism in tones that prefigure the unbending rhetoric of Malcolm X almost sixty years later.

In short, it's a willful denial of the larger context of Lovecraft's life to use the "back then, that's just how people thought" argument, a favorite canard for those who wish to provide a retroactive forgiveness for a historical figure's attitudes and actions about race, racism, and its practical effects on the lives of actual human beings in the past. Paul Roland, Lovecraft's most recent biographer, makes this point plain when he notes that "While it may be true that racial prejudice was endemic in the 19th century, many were immune to such reprehensible beliefs . . . a number were considerably less well-educated than Lovecraft."

This may seem a lot of weight to place on the name of a cat. And, frankly, I agree that a pet's name might not mean so much if race did not seem to become something of a personal obsession for Lovecraft in later years, appearing in essays, fiction, and some of his most embarrassing correspondence. In fact, he composed an absurdly ignorant poem, even

for a fifteen-year-old in 1905, that attacked the Emancipation Proclama-
tion, compared African Americans to apes, and suggested that the end
of slavery would inevitably lead to the death of the formerly enslaved,
presumably because they could not adequately care for themselves.[15]

Young Howard did love his offensively named cat. He had been
convinced that they shared a secret language. He wrote about the sleek
black cat with continued and enduring affection over the years and his
"Cats of Ulthar" and parts of his short novel *The Dream-Quest of Unknown
Kadath* are really tributes to his animal companion. He befriended and
obsessed over various felines for the rest of his life, regularly adopting
outdoor cats and developing what his friends saw as an odd, seemingly
mutual, sympathy with his own pets.

But, as with many of the human beings in his life, Howard loved
best at a distance. He sometimes did this quite well, giving not a little joy
and pleasure to his circle of family and friends and living, fairly content-
edly, with the immense caverns of loneliness such a life carved within his
own heart.

What do we make of racism when it's part of a general attitude
toward the world and its inhabitants rather than the systemic oppression
of most societies in human history since the early modern era? What does
it mean when it's a feeling and not a lever of social and economic power?

———

He'd been riding his bicycle fervently since his mother and grandfather
purchased it for him in 1900, when he was ten. He used it to quench
his thirst for the historical sites of Providence, especially the Georgian-
era architecture that fostered the beginnings of a lifelong obsession. He
cycled through the "brooding hollows" he'd explored for years on foot,
rattling down rough paths that likely necessitated frequent repairs in this
time before the appearance of the mountain bike. Although there are
twice-told tales of Sarah Susan's unrelenting and overbearing concern
for her son's physical safety, she allowed these lonely ramblings though,
probably, not without understandable concern.

During one of these rides in 1904, having fallen into an abyss of depression, he contemplated suicide. His cycle frequently bumped along the Seekonk River and he first considered drowning himself here.

He had other methods available to him. We know for example that his family allowed him to play about with a .22 pistol at an absurdly early age, another aspect of his boyhood that argues against the idea of Sarah Susan as the overbearing mother. In a decision that to me suggests that he was quite serious about the matter, he decided against the firearm because he didn't want his mother to find his remains in such a state.

He further concluded that if he drowned himself, he would do so in the Barrington River just southeast of Providence, in order to lessen the chances that the family endure what he saw as the added grief of finding the corpse. As is so often the case with Lovecraft, a cold logic coupled in the same brain with a willingness to sympathize with the rather small number of human beings he came to know intimately.

Also typical, and deeply revealing, his decision not to end his life had no relationship to his attachment to other people or even a sentiment as simple as the effect this would have on his mother. She, most would feel, might be far more damaged by the sheer fact of his death rather than the manner in which the body was discovered.

Instead, Lovecraft reasoned himself out of his own suicide. He concluded that the cessation of his consciousness meant the end of intellectual inquiry. He would leave what he considered an overwhelmingly bitter existence without having learned as much about it as he wanted, and needed, to know.

"Much of the universe baffled me," he remembered, "but I knew I could pry the answer out of books if I lived and studied long enough." This was not a depressed teenager's search for the meaning of life, since Lovecraft had already come to the conclusion that it had no inherent meaning. In response to the well-meaning bromides offered today about suicide being "a permanent solution to a temporary problem," Lovecraft would likely have insisted that it provided a permanent solution to an obviously permanent problem: the burden of consciousness that offers such intense suffering.

So, he didn't decide against self-destruction in hopes that life might present him with a deeper meaning or any meaning at all. He did not call the suicide hotlines that did not exist in 1904. He didn't learn to look on the sunny side. But he did say that he had not, after all, had the chance to study geology yet. He asserted that extinguishing the candle of his brain assured that he'd never learn more about the secrets of Antarctica as new scientific expeditions continued to explore these frozen wastes that fascinated him. Moreover, what he called "tantalizing gaps" existed in his knowledge of history, including the history of Asia and Africa. How could he leave behind consciousness when, along with heaps of suffering, it presented him with the possibility of knowledge?

The need to know things lashed him to the mast of human experience. Even as he contemplated self-extinction, he never gave up his love of prying out the secrets, and being overwhelmed by the unknowable mysteries, of "infinite space." Since the late 1890s, the young Lovecraft had "published" a series of essays and "volumes" (really pamphlets) that paraphrased what he learned from his chemistry books and recorded the outcomes of his basement lab experiments.

He produced these, ordinarily for family members and perhaps a small circle of interested adults, using a process known as the hectograph. Hectography involved hardening gelatin in a pan with glycerin and making a master copy with either special ink or a typewriter ribbon specially prepared for imprinting on the heated slab. The printer pressed the master copy onto the gelatin and then up to fifty copies of the imprint could be made on blank paper.

A flood of publications using this technique emerged from Angell Street after his discovery of astronomy. A "nine-volume series" of pamphlets appeared in 1903–04 bearing titles such as "Optics," "On Saturn and His Rings," and "The Moon" and "The Moon Part II."

Beginning in January 1903, the thirteen-year-old began producing what he rather ambitiously titled the *Rhode Island Journal of Astronomy*. We know he printed at least sixty-nine of these weekly newsletters. They came to a halt during the period of his darkest depression in 1904 but, as his reasoning for extending his young life suggested they would, they resumed in January 1905.

The specifics of astronomical study only played a role in his fiction a few times. But the larger conception it gave him of the universe played a decisive role in both his worldview and his sui generis conception of monstrosity and the meaning of horror. Writing in 1922, he claimed that by age thirteen his study of astronomy had made him "thoroughly unimpressed with man's impermanence and insignificance," and that by this time he had "formed in all essential particulars my present pessimistic cosmic views." Although Poe, he claims, shaped his fantasy life, he understood that the fantastic offered a set of illusions about reality, even if they represented a set of aesthetically pleasing illusions.

Lovecraft decided against his own death, and quickly decided to continue his experiment with consciousness. In his young mind, science and history, knowledge of the world as it is, and a philosophical materialism brought empiricism together with a way of thinking about the meaning—or rather the essential and unavoidable meaninglessness—of the universe. In the very same mind, without much tension and conflict, lived the world of the fantastic, adventures into the irrational that captivated the depressed young man. In an apparent conflict between the pure enchantment of the fantastic and the hard rationalism of the sciences that thoroughly disenchanted the world, we have the hammer and anvil that forged an H.P. Lovecraft.

In 1904, recovering from his despondency, the fourteen-year-old announced the founding of the Providence Astronomical Society with, of course, H.P. Lovecraft as president. He was not, as the reader might expect, the only member. Contrary to everyone's expectations, including his own, Lovecraft had entered high school and formed the first of his many strong male friendships.

Taken out of the Slater Avenue School in 1898 by Sarah Susan after his "near nervous breakdown," he had only returned briefly for at least part of the 1901–02 school year. Otherwise, Lovecraft continued his life-long project of self-education. We do know that his mother enlisted a private tutor at some point, a theological student whom the now teenaged Howard viewed with a mixture of sympathy and contempt. The tutor's tenure must have been brief, as Lovecraft later crowed that his youthful paganism drove the young man away.

High school loomed in the fall of 1904, and Lovecraft later recalled that the few people who knew him literally "predicted disaster" for him and, indeed, for his teachers. To everyone's surprise, including his own, Hope Street English and Classical High School did not become a living torment for everyone involved. His teachers seemed fascinated with his encyclopedic knowledge that extended to the utterly obscure. He maintained a friendship formed earlier with two brothers, Harold and Chester Munroe, his earliest and only youthful friendships. The brothers seem to have been a bit enthralled with Lovecraft's odd hobbies and shared at least a modicum of his interest in science. They, for example, acted as his research assistants and formed the rest of the membership of the Providence Astronomical Society.

However, it's absurd to assume that Lovecraft had anything like a normal experience with teachers, peers, and the institution itself. Fellow students generally found him unapproachable. A few claimed later that they actively sought to make friends with him and found their efforts rebuffed. At least one English teacher accused him of plagiarism, a charge he answered by showing that he had indeed copied the assignment—in essence plagiarizing himself from an article he had written about astronomy for a local paper. This episode probably did nothing to endear him to the faculty.

Lovecraft's high school transcripts show that he mostly proved a mediocre student, especially in math. While making uneven marks he managed to become a skillful smart aleck, the unloved kid smarter than his teachers and simultaneously uninterested in putting forth the effort to make good grades.

In 1938, a year after H.P. Lovecraft's death, Almina and Ernest Gygax brought Gary Gygax into the world. Obsessed with chess and adventure tales, Gygax and his friends created games set in worlds of fantasy and science fiction that they read about in the pulps. They ran about in abandoned sewers and drainage tunnels, settling their epic battles with aliens and monsters by designating one of their friends as a referee.

By the 1960s, Gygax became heavily involved in the world of military war gaming and created play-by-mail games that worked via a "choose your own adventure" mechanism. Gygax also experimented with the use of the die in gaming, coming up with the innovation of employing dice with more than six sides in order to create more random numbers.

Gygax and his partner Dave Arneson created the tabletop RPG Dungeons & Dragons in 1973. For more than forty years it has remained the world's best-selling fantasy role-playing game; with its semi-medieval world peopled by humans, elves, orcs, dwarves, various deities, and, of course, dragons and the dungeons where they can be found.

The rules of D&D have evolved and expanded many times, but the game's central theme has remained the same. Gaming can afford you the opportunity of entering fully into a world of antique fantasy and becoming a character utterly different from the one you must play in daily life. D&D allows you to transform from a cubicle worker into a monster-slayer. You become a hero of legend and plunderer of treasure rather than someone servicing a drive-thru window or delivering pizza or attending bothersome academic gatherings.

Had Lovecraft and Gygax been compatriots, they no doubt would have built an even more enthralling system of role-play than even Gygax managed with his singular creation. Lovecraft obviously had a gift for fantasy and, long before tabletop role-playing became the pastime of generations of nerdy kids, he had, sometimes with the help of the Munroe brothers, made some forays into the kind of LARPing (a contemporary acronym for Live Action Role Playing) that became the rage in the geek world of the late 1990s.

　Young Howard at least made it to the gates of what later became tabletop role-playing games. Up to the age of thirteen, and perhaps beyond, Lovecraft built complex dioramas used to enact scenes from ancient history, fantasy, and horror using small lead soldiers of the 70mm variety. In some of his 1933 correspondence, he recalled the creation of games involving "widely extensive scenes" in which he would "devote an entire table-top to a scene" that he then used earth, clay, and rock to transform into a tableau of "villages with small wooden or cardboard houses." He used "people . . . mainly of the lead-soldier variety" although Sarah Susan seems to have gotten into the act by helping him "modify many in costume with the aid of knife and paint brush."

　Although model railroading first became a passion of many children in the decade of his birth, Lovecraft created a different set of worlds (but railroads held a deep fascination for him as well). Many of the dioramas that he built featured scenarios from his beloved eighteenth century. But he also promiscuously mixed historical eras. The Roman world collided with the Victorian era that he in turn collapsed into Dryden's and Pope's England. "Horror plots were frequent," he tells us, though he notes that he never built "extraterrestrial" scenes.

　It's pleasing to imagine H.P. Lovecraft playing out some version of the role-playing games that, eighty years later, grounded themselves in the mythology created from the tales he wrote. If only we could know that Howard and Sarah Susan took a toy truck and shaped it into some kind of proto-Cthulhu, an eldritch horror emerging amid the tiny 70mm soldiers transformed into hapless victims of the Great Old Ones by craft knife and paint by young Howard and his mother.

　"I kept this up till I was eleven or twelve," Lovecraft wrote, "despite the parallel growth of literary and scientific pursuits." His seeming reticence, or perhaps simple surprise, at admitting this appears self-mocking. He had long combined Poe and *One Thousand and One Nights* with chemistry and astronomy. In any case, his adventures in role-playing may not have ground to a halt quite so suddenly.

The Providence Detective Agency certainly suggests that Howard's inclination toward rendering his fantasies into life continued well after he claimed he had moved on to his "literary and scientific pursuits." In 1903, he enlisted the Munroe brothers, and apparently several other younger kids in East Providence, in what amounted to live action role-playing. They took on the roles of detectives modeled on both Arthur Conan Doyle's Holmes tales and adventure stories that had come to form a regular part of the young Lovecraft's literary diet.

The boys of the Providence Detective Agency outfitted themselves with magnifying glasses, handcuffs made of twine, a police whistle, tin badges, and, at least in Howard's case, the .22 revolver that he briefly considered using on himself. They shadowed any citizens of Providence who bore a passing resemblance to criminals appearing in a sensation-alist national tabloid called *The Detective*. Meanwhile, Lovecraft, like a "Dungeon Master" from the golden age of role-playing in the 1970s and '80s, created scenarios for his friends to solve, at one point recreating artificial bloodstains on the floor of a deserted house as the basis for one of their games.

During 1904, his year of nearly fatal despondency, role-playing disappeared from the life of Lovecraft, like so much else. But, as with many of his other interests, it revived in 1905 with the announcement (in the renewed *Rhode Island Journal of Astronomy*) that the agency had gone back into business. In 1906, when Howard turned sixteen, he and Chester Munroe had begun calling themselves "Carter and Brady," an imitation of the fictional turn-of-the-century detectives Nick Carter and King Brady, crime-solving heroes of the dime novels.

Young Howard's fascination with detective fiction grew out of his reading of the Sherlock Holmes tales, a figure he later said he became "infatuated with." His love of Holmesian mystery perhaps prompted him in his reading of other kinds of adventure tales, including material that critics in Lovecraft's time and since have tended to classify as trash lit.

Frank Munsey began publishing the ancestor of the pulp magazine, called *Golden Argosy*, in 1882. Munsey built *Golden Argosy* around stories for children. The effort failed, perhaps because middle-class parents proved too suspicious of the new form. A new pair of magazines in the 1890s, called simply *Argosy* and *Munsey's*, found a more compelling and successful formulae. Printed cheaply on pulp, a by-product of the manufacture of more finely textured and expensive papers, the magazines catered to adults as well as teens and precocious younger children. They carried a variety of stories ranging from detective tales to westerns. Humor and romance made frequent appearances in the magazines as well. By 1905, the Munsey publishing concern produced *All-Story*, a pulp that Lovecraft, in 1914, claimed to have read "every number" since the first issue.

Lovecraft also apparently read dime novels dealing with detective and frontier adventures from a very early date, perhaps four or five years of age. He began his obsessions with the Munsey magazines around 1903. Ten years later Lovecraft had read hundreds of thousands of words from the early pulps, obviously displaying a special taste for the weird and the outré such as the "Mars" tales being produced by Edgar Rice Burroughs. It's worth noting that Lovecraft would have been twenty-three at the time he wrote the "fan letters" to *Argosy* magazine that praised these stories, showing that the influences that led him to his fantasy games with his friends did, as we well know, endure into adulthood.

The creation of fantasy worlds by the teenage Lovecraft, despite his later claim that he had only "kept this up" till he became "eleven or twelve," continued in other forms that proved just as elaborate. He and the Munroe brothers created an intricate set of gardens and forts on a vacant lot that involved drainage pools, graveled paths, and even a "Georgian Lawn" complete with a sundial. This lasted, by Lovecraft's own admission, until his seventeenth year.

Although it's absurd to claim that Lovecraft and his small circle of boyhood friends invented live action or tabletop role-playing, their activities are at the root of this cultural phenomenon, particularly since Lovecraft's fiction became secondary only to the work of J.R.R. Tolkien in developing today's world of fantasy role-play.

Intriguingly, an author who became—though did not remain—a favorite author of Lovecraft's published what's regarded as the first effort to create a basic set of rules for tabletop gaming. In 1913, H.G. Wells published a book called *Little Wars: A game for boys from twelve years of age to one hundred and fifty and for that more intelligent sort of girl who likes boys' games and books*. Wells designed the basic rules for movement and protocols of shot and shell for use with the small lead figures produced by Britain's, the leading manufacturer of toy soldiers in the era. Not unlike Lovecraft, they created dioramas and built fortifications. A referee regulated time and troop movements with a stopwatch. Wells was a well-known pacifist, and this text contains asides on the silliness of war that do nothing to dilute the glee with which he describes the playing of the game.

Lovecraft and his nerdy pals would have delighted in *Little Wars*, and it's easy to see young Howard extrapolating from Wells's rules a much more complicated set of games involving all manner of historical and fantastical scenarios. But the world had to wait another seventy years for twenty-sided dice, critical hits, and saving throws. Even so, Lovecraft's horrors rustled in the shadows around the card tables, beer cans, and empty pizza boxes when Baby Boomers and Gen X'ers searched their dungeons for dragons.

Lovecraft's involvement in the world of pulp fiction and his excursions into a certain mode of role-playing locate him at the very roots of geek fandom. By the 1960s, Stan Lee's Marvel comics and Forrest J. Ackerman's *Famous Monsters of Filmland* built on the foundations of pulp enthusiasts like Lovecraft, marginalized people who found little or no comradeship in their small towns and smaller social circles.

The world of the fan had its beginnings in the letter columns of the original issue of comics like *Spider-Man* and the *Fantastic Four*. The letter sections of early *Famous Monsters of Filmland* magazines became a way for kids rediscovering the classic monster movies of the thirties to connect with like-minded youngsters and adults, functioning as what might be considered in the Internet age as a much slower version of a fan forum or Reddit thread.

Isolated nerds, maybe unable to locate more than one or two friends who shared their interests in their hometowns, suddenly found themselves taken up into something expansive, something that linked them with other kids all over the country. Forrest Ackerman became "Uncle Forry," producing the notion of classic monster fandom as something of an extended family with himself as affectionate patron and patriarch. Stan Lee wrote notes from "the Marvel Bullpen" in each new issue. This practice gave the (largely falsified) impression that his new, edgy comics came out of the daily interaction of a kind of family of artists and writers that fans could personally make connection with through the letters page.

The early pulps provided the model for what Marvel and *Famous Monsters of Filmland* so successfully achieved in postwar America. Lovecraft would, by 1914, become a regular letter writer to *All-Story*, critiquing tales and getting into sometimes fairly major brouhahas with his fellow readers about the value of certain authors. In this, he and his fellow correspondents presaged today's message boards and fan forums on sites like *I09* and *Fangoria*, in which the comments sections under movie reviews and top ten lists are set aflame by a fandom utterly dedicated to this or that science fiction or horror franchise—often devoted to it over another. They argue for the superiority of authors, directors, and screen adaptations of their favorite works while damning, in language often reserved for political and ideological disputes, products of geek-dominated popular culture they consider inauthentic or inferior.

It's a world Lovecraft would have readily recognized.

⌒

After his first year at the Hope Street School, Lovecraft dropped out and never returned to any kind of formal academic program. Seemingly recovered from suicidal depression by his thirst for knowledge and his consummate abilities as an enthusiastic hobbyist, he became overwhelmed with some variety of what our current therapeutic culture would call social anxiety. He later recalled in a letter that he "suffered a nervous collapse" because, although he claimed to enjoy high school, "the strain was too keen for [his] health." The same letter lies about the time of this "nervous collapse," suggesting that he had, in fact, completed his secondary education and that his health difficulties kept him from being able to attend Brown University.[16]

This misrepresentation, the desire not to be thought a high school dropout, became a theme in much of Lovecraft's correspondence on the subject. It's thoroughly understandable. He liked to play the scholar he made himself into, a need that coalesced with his tendency to patronize his friends and loved ones—a trait of scholars the world over.

The abrupt departure from school had several causes. At its heart, his nervous collapse represented the coming together of his desire to retreat into his inner world and Sarah Susan's desire to allow him to do so. S.T. Joshi notes that Howard continued to do poorly in mathematics, suggesting that he would not have gotten into Brown anyway and, if he had, he had little hope of becoming a chemist or astronomer. Maybe he realized this and gave up on education altogether. Or maybe not, since we find him trying to learn chemistry again and playing the astronomer, in the years ahead.

A second-, in some ways third-, hand account from the year of Lovecraft's departure from school described him as having "terrible tics" that certainly must have been startling in class. According to this account by a fellow student "he'd be sitting in his seat and he'd suddenly up and jump—I think they referred to them as seizures."

This story, combined with Lovecraft's own account of his numerous facial tics, has caused some writers to suggest that he suffered from chorea minor, often today called Sydenham's chorea. A childhood neurological disorder, Sydenham's chorea causes involuntary spasms and movements. Maybe he did suffer from this affliction. But he probably would have stayed in school nonetheless had he wanted to do so. Sarah Susan granted him an almost absolute freedom, and school was not for him.

So, according to some biographers, began his long seclusion from the world. He himself never really knew how to explain the more than six years that he spent mostly at home and interacting with no other human being other than his mother. This period has become something of a biographical black hole because H.P. Lovecraft decided that it had to become an autobiographical black hole. Those of us who want to give an account of him have followed his lead; let his embarrassment and perhaps his incomprehension of these years guide our own ruminations about what exactly happened to him.

The dearth of hard evidence for what became of Howard as he turned from a teenager into a twenty-three-year-old has led to wild speculation. Biographers have been allowed to range freely over their favorite theme: the all-consuming Vampire Mother, Sarah Susan Lovecraft. Paul Roland says of these years, without basis in any evidence, that Sarah Susan Lovecraft "could not restrain herself from indulging in periodic outbursts of self-pity" and that young Howard witnessed and "was profoundly affected by her suffering."

Kenneth W. Faig, Jr. has investigated the biographies of Lovecraft's parents more thoughtfully than anyone and has some positive things to say about Sarah Susan, emphasizing her willingness to introduce Howard to literature and make possible some of his other intellectual endeavors. But even Faig concludes, rather brutally, that Lovecraft's mother's hospitalization and death "saved the very sanity of her son." He suggests, based on nothing but pure speculation, that she "transferred the fear and loathing caused by the illness of her husband onto her innocent young son." S.T. Joshi, in his overall evaluation of Sarah Susan Lovecraft, calls her "clearly neurotic" and asserts that she "psychologically damaged" her son. August Derleth described her as doting on young Howard with "aberrant affection."[17]

L. Sprague de Camp uses all his skills as a novelist in conjuring the relationship of Howard to his mother. He entitled the chapter dealing with Howard's early manhood "Haunted House" and does in fact turn 598 Angell into something along the lines of the Bates Motel. Sarah Susan

Lovecraft becomes the incapable hysteric who held Howard back and even the reason that he gave up chemistry. Their home had a "haunted house atmosphere" and she created the kind of "shunned house" that her son later wrote about in his 1924 story of the same name.[18]

De Camp's account blames her further for Lovecraft's unwillingness to seek out an occupation. She made him into a hypochondriac. He's the "unfortunate youth" destroyed by "a neurotic mother." In a remembrance of Lovecraft (actually based on the remembrance of someone who only knew the author from his occasional attendance at an amateur journalism club in Providence), de Camp refers to Sarah Susan as Lovecraft's "dotty mother." In one especially purple passage in his Lovecraft biography, de Camp calls her "a monster mother."[19]

Responsible for most of the lurid imagery of monstrous motherhood written about Sarah Susan and Lovecraft, de Camp became a successful weird fiction writer before he embarked on his Lovecraft biography. He became best known for writing a new Conan the Barbarian cycle of tales, based on the original writings of perhaps Lovecraft's most famous correspondent, Robert E. Howard. His Conan stories helped lead to an increased fascination with the character and to the creation of a *Conan the Barbarian* comics series in the seventies.

In evaluating de Camp's estimation of Sarah Susan Lovecraft, it's worth noting that in his own writing de Camp tends to describe women not as characters but as objects for his ferocious Conan to seduce and/or rape (he seldom draws a bright line between these activities). Women are, in most of his Conan tales, little more than "tantalizing perfume" wafting off of "soft, sweet, firm flesh." It's hardly to be expected that de Camp would have given a woman of Sarah Susan Lovecraft's disposition and demeanor much notice, respect, or meaningful analysis.[20]

He's not the first, or greatest, offender in this respect. Perhaps no one has written more cruelly of Sarah Susan Lovecraft than Winfield Townley Scott, a very minor poet based in Providence and the literary editor of *The Providence Journal.* In the mid-1940s, during the first strong revival of interest in Lovecraft's work, Scott took it upon himself to construct a biographical sketch of Providence's increasingly famous native son. Although praised by Lovecraft scholars like Peter Cannon, Scott's short work damns Lovecraft with faint praise and damns Sarah Susan Lovecraft outright.

Scott managed to get his hands on Sarah Susan's files from Providence's Butler Hospital, a document that became central to the case made against her by Lovecraft admirers. He also spoke with the family lawyer and took his word when the lawyer referred to Sarah Susan Lovecraft as "a weak sister." He makes much of a story that Howard did not visit his ailing mother at the hospital in her last days because he was "a fearful and selfish young man." Scott concludes, with off-handed viciousness, that ". . . it was not his fault. His mother had herself to thank."[21]

Various strands of cultural DNA have spliced over the last forty years or so to make being odd into a way of being hip, or at least intriguing, in current white American culture. But even now, men are allowed more leeway with this than women. Most everyone, outside of certain realms of suburbia in the most carmine of red states, gets at least some applause if they fly their freak flag. Indeed, the eccentricity option has become an important element in contemporary white privilege, especially white male privilege.

Sarah Susan Lovecraft raised her odd boy at a time when this was simply not the case. The cultural capital of the Phillips name in Providence probably stood between her and institutionalization after Whipple's death, although she endured even this fate at the end of her life. She lived at a cultural moment—a moment that continued well into the American fifties—in which women found themselves shut up, literally, in asylums.

The reasons given for women's institutionalization could range from their drinking too much, losing their temper in public, involving themselves in politics, having sex with whomever they wanted to have sex with, and a variety of other behaviors that fathers, husbands, and male doctors defined as presenting a danger to themselves and to the social order. Once buried inside these horrific places, they lived with the truly psychotic and schizophrenic while enduring hydrotherapy—a treatment that resembles nothing so much as waterboarding. Sarah Susan Lovecraft's odd behavior could have placed her in one of these institutions, known colloquially as "snake pits," given different circumstances and a different genealogy.

Lovecraft's biographers have metaphorically institutionalized her in descriptions they've created or accepted. Most of those who write about Lovecraft tell his life story as a narrative of escape from his mother's spiderweb of hypochondria and neurosis. Writing about her mostly replicates the Victorian notions that the sources themselves use to describe the relationship between Sarah Susan and her exceptional and exceptionally weird son, making enormous allowances for Howard's sometimes bizarre behavior while making her responsible for it. She deserves better.

Two documents have been given enormous weight by everyone who has written about H.P. Lovecraft's mother and the childhood she gave him. Both are, in different ways, highly problematic as historical sources.

The first comes from a 1948 account by a woman named Clara Hess, a neighbor of the Lovecrafts in the nineteen-aughts. She did not record her childhood memories of Howard and Susan until 1948, at about age sixty. Kenneth W. Faig calls it "the most remarkable portrait of Susan Lovecraft that we possess," by which he means almost the only portrait of Susan Lovecraft we possess.

Hess claimed she knew Sarah Susan better than Howard who, she notes, "was strange and rather a recluse." Hess also remembered that, in the period after the death of Whipple Phillips, Sarah Susan "was considered to be getting rather odd" by the wagging tongues of College Hill. She alleged a visit to the Lovecraft home that, she recalled almost five decades later, "had a strange and shutup air and the atmosphere seemed weird." She laments that such a home "was an environment suited for the writing of horror stories but an unfortunate one for a growing youth who in a more wholesome environment might have grown to be a more normal citizen."

Hess's account reeks with the demands of the Victorian era warmed over by the revival of domesticity that took place in the years after World War II. When Hess gave her account, the word "normal" had only recently become a much-used term in the American English of the late forties. The concept suited an era of red scares and a middle-class retreat into the domestic seclusion of the suburbs where they built increasingly palatial homes understood as nurseries for "normal citizens."

Hess's early memories of Howard and Sarah Susan are weighted with all this cultural baggage. She's basically telling us that East Providence at the turn of the century thought the Lovecrafts rather odd, a fact we could have guessed on our own. They were odd, and odd in ways that American geek culture and anyone who cares about good books have reason to be glad.

The oft-told tale that Sarah Susan saw "weird and fantastic creatures" rushing about in the twilight also comes to us only from Hess. In fact, it's not in her original account given to Scott at all, but in an even later interview given to August Derleth. There's every possibility that what Hess described here simply records the family tradition, going back to old Whipple, of telling tales of monsters in the dark. There's good reason to think that mother and son continued this tradition after Whipple's death. The night gaunts didn't disappear, as Lovecraft's fiction reveals on every page.

Hess's dated remembrance becomes even more suspicious since we also know that gossipy neighbors who lived near 598 Angell often confused other elements of Howard and Sarah Susan's relationship. Marian F. Bonner, a former neighbor, explained that the stories of alleged "quarrels" between mother and son actually came from the Lovecrafts' pastime of reading aloud from the work of Shakespeare. In fact, the whimsical nature of their relationship, and the fact that they may have taken special delight in annoying their nosy neighbors, led them to read the scenes of bloodletting and murder with special gusto. "The more cruel the part, the better he liked it," Bonner remembered, "and would shout it out to be heard by the neighbors. I have had neighbors tell me of his 'quarrels' but I know that it was only Shakespeare being read."[22]

The second source heavily relied on by those with less than kind things to say about Sarah Susan comes from a seemingly more authoritative, but in some ways even less credible source, than Clara Hess. It's the file that we do not have, of Dr. F.J. Farnell, psychiatrist at Butler Hospital. He noted in Sarah Susan's file that she was "a woman of narrow interests who received, with traumatic psychosis, an awareness of approaching bankruptcy."

Winfield T. Scott himself constitutes the only source we have for this file. He's also the only one who saw the file and we have nothing but his word, and his interpretation, for what it contains. As a historian, I can only look on in wonder at the immense weight biographers place on this nonexistent piece of evidence. Still, it's likely that Sarah Susan's file contains a number of uncomplimentary statements about her mental state. But even this tells us more about the Victorian concepts of the troubled female mind rather than the mother of H.P. Lovecraft.

The medical care Sarah Susan Lovecraft received in her last years would have been heavily influenced by the work of Dr. George Man Burrows who believed that nonspecific disorders in the uterus led to mental disorders. This idea assumed that women had a special affinity for depression and nervous anxiety. The Victorian-era medical community tended to agree that women had a weak nervous system, either because they allegedly had thinner blood than men or, again, due to the very existence of the uterus.[23]

By the 1870s, Sarah Susan's own lifetime, the idea that the speed and noise associated with the second industrial revolution had created a number of new "nervous disorders" became prominent in the emerging profession of so-called "mind-doctoring." Women, physicians argued, proved especially susceptible to the "nervous weakness" caused by the pace and clangor of the era. Increasingly, mind-doctors gave the diagnosis of "neurasthenia," a term coined by an American physician in 1869 for a range of illnesses that also came to be defined as "nervous collapse" and "nervous exhaustion" and that doctors most frequently applied to women.

In other words, the diagnosis of Sarah Susan Lovecraft, including how deeply dismissive and aggressive it appears, falls within the parameters of the medical profession's treatment of depressed women in this era. Farnell had likely read an 1881 treatise by Philadelphia physician Silas Weir Mitchell, whose *Lectures on Diseases of the Nervous System: Especially Women* spoke patronizingly of the "couch-loving invalid" who needed "a rest cure" that separated her from relatives and friends so that, presumably, she'd pull herself out of her malaise.

In fact, Farnell probably accepted the profession's general attitude that the doctor had an essentially adversarial relationship with the "hysterical" women in his care. Literature on the topic spoke of treatment of the "nervous problems" of women using metaphors of combat, victory, and defeat. In 1888, Dr. L.C. Grey told a graduating class of medical students that, in dealing with such women, "you must expect to have your temper, your ingenuity, your nerves tested to such a degree that cannot be surpassed even by the greatest surgical operations." These nervous women would actually threaten the citadel of the male nervous system, he seems to suggest, and they must be met with "steady, resolute, iron-willed determination." It's as if Grey thinks that the act of treating such women placed Victorian men in danger of emasculation, of facing their own "nervous collapse."

So, given the general tone of the medical literature on women and "nervous conditions," it's little surprise that Farnell chose to characterize Howard's mother in such demeaning and false tones. Nor can we really take seriously Farnell's comment on her terror of "approaching bankruptcy." The Phillips–Lovecraft family had been in dire financial straits for almost twenty years when Farnell wrote these words. Back in 1911, Sarah Susan's brother Edwin managed to lose even more of the capital of the family legacy in a bad investment. Worries about money didn't suddenly confront Sarah Susan in 1919.

A few writers on Lovecraft have especially seized on the "woman of narrow interests" comment as it seems to dovetail rather well with the picture of a woman who put nothing but restrictions on her son's development, impeding his maturity at every turn. It's a throwaway comment that has been written about as if it should appear on Sarah Susan's tombstone.

It's also completely untrue. "A woman of narrow interests" would not have introduced her five-year-old to classical mythology and the literature of the Islamic world. She would not have encouraged his interest in chemistry, purchasing his first assemblage of lab equipment and later paying $161 (no small sum in 1909) for him to take an essentially useless correspondence course in the subject.

We also have not a peep out of H.P. Lovecraft about any attempt by his mother to restrict his access to his rather outré tastes in fiction. Or even to keep him from his more proletarian love of the pulps. In fact, we have evidence she both encouraged his nightmare visions and read Shakespeare with him, apparently with special regard given to the tales with bloody blades and a high body count.

Sarah Susan had important accomplishments in her own right. She had studied French in boarding school and kept up with it her whole life. Lovecraft later recalled his mother's intense interest in French literature, an avocation he never shared but admired. She would have been delighted that literary acclaim came to her son in France; and indeed his work received laurels there decades before the American literary establishment recognized him.

I spent a pleasant part of an afternoon at Providence's John Hay Library reading Sarah Susan's "Commonplace Book," which suggests that Howard received parts of his love of the eighteenth century, and auto-didacticism, from Sarah Susan. She filled page after page with quotations from writers ranging from Goethe to Dryden to Hawthorne—the latter making it possible that she served as Howard's introduction to one of his earliest and favorite writers of dark fantasies. It also contains extensive outlines of history, compiled seemingly so she could provide herself with a clear picture of world events, her special focus being the Middle Ages through her son's beloved Enlightenment era.

On that same afternoon spent amid piles of Lovecraftiana, I had the chance to read annotations in her own student copy of Jean Gustave Keetels's *Analytical and Practical French Grammar,* published in 1878, that she apparently used in the fall term of the same year. An extensive Latin quotation on "The French Language," written on the flyleaf, argues that France, and its language, represent the survival of the great legacy of Rome. Her ideas and interests certainly seem much wider than a neurotic focus on her son or obsessive grief over the loss of her husband and father.

We also know Sarah Susan Lovecraft to have been an enthusiastic landscape painter and a drawer, though none of her work has survived. It's pleasant to imagine her with easel and paints along the Seekonk River as a warm spring day turns New England chilly in the afternoon. We know she did take such outings. Clara Hess claimed she saw her on the streetcars all the time. She had a life outside of 598 Angell and out-side of her beloved, but undoubtedly sometimes impossible, son.

Perhaps most interesting, she had an investment in politics—espe-cially what was known as "the woman question." Muriel Eddy, whose husband later became a friend of Lovecraft's and a fellow *Weird Tales* writer, first knew of Lovecraft because Sarah Susan and Muriel's mother-in-law attended women's suffrage meetings together.[24]

I diligently searched the Rhode Island Historical Society for a spe-cific mention of her in the records of the Rhode Island Equal Rights Association, the incarnation of the women's suffrage movement at the time Eddy remembered Sarah Susan attending their meetings. Although no specific mention of her appears, this is not surprising since the asso-ciation had a rather large membership in 1916 for a state the size of Rhode Island: five thousand members.[25]

Biographers have made much of the friendship between Eddy and Lovecraft. The friendship has received the attention it has because Love-craft did heavy revision work on Eddy's tales of horror, revisions that may have come so close to rewrites that they are, in essence, Lovecraft tales. However, the two may never have met had it not been for Sarah Susan's very real, if perhaps limited, political engagement.

None of this biographical detail assures us that Sarah Susan did not damage her son, in the current nomenclature of mental health. None of it means that he did not damage her as well. The nature of human relationships manifests in various kinds of suffering on everyone's part. Why we need to create narratives of villainy and victimhood to explain this is obscure, particularly when talking about the secrets of the dead.

The ways we hurt one another are manifold, complex, and difficult to explain. The ways we hurt the people we love the most are even more irreducible and inexplicable. So, we construct narratives about these secret terrors and, if we become famous, biographers also try to shape these mysteries of memory and pain into stories.

Did Sarah Susan Lovecraft harm her son? Did something lie in the dark places of his psyche because of her, dead but dreaming, and certain to wake to bring catastrophe like great Cthulhu? Probably. But we have more historical evidence for the things she gave him, the imagination she nurtured and set free. She failed at creating "a normal citizen" and winning Victorian Providence's mother of the year award. She succeeded in helping to forge an H.P. Lovecraft.

The history of early twentieth-century America tells us much more about what the world did to Sarah Susan Lovecraft than what she did to her son. The rest is whispers and secrets. We won't ever really know.

———

Lovecraft's years of seclusion are no great mystery. His activities between 1908 and 1914 didn't change too much except that he could slough off the burden of human contact and the anxiety-producing experience of school. He remembers this time in his correspondence as a period of overwhelming depression and "nervous exhaustion." But in this he's explaining, and explaining away, what he, and some of those who have written about him since, saw as an appalling lack of productivity in an America where Henry Ford's go-getterism (the Model T went on sale in 1908) and "let's make some things and sell them" and "you better make your way in the world" became the prevailing mood. He did none of this. Mostly, he just went about the business of being Howard Lovecraft.

He studied chemistry even though the mathematics gave him headaches and he finally gave it up. He read Edgar Rice Burroughs's *John Carter of Mars* tales and, though he later damned them, he seems to have loved every word at the time. In fact, he read piles of pulp stories about detectives and adventurers and cowboys and the occasional "weird tale" that *Argosy* and *All-Story* published. He continued his astronomical enthusiasms, keeping a fairly detailed notebook of his observations. In May of 1910, he saw Halley's Comet and, I suspect, it became a day he remembered forever. The "infinite spaces" had passed within sight and Howard Lovecraft caught a glimpse of the cosmic.

In November of 1911, Thanksgiving Day, he wrote a poem to Sarah Susan making light of his nocturnal habits and tendency to sleep during the day. He wished her good times with Aunt Lillian and her husband at their dinner while he dozed till it was time for his "Quaker puffed wheat" or "biscuit." Sarah Susan added an affectionate note at the bottom, explaining when he had written her the piece.

Howard Lovecraft's discovery of the world of amateur journalism has been turned into one of his watershed moments and nothing I say here is meant to detract from its significance. He did change in interesting ways because of amateur journalism and these changes made possible his first tales and even his marriage. But that discovery was not his transformation into H.P. Lovecraft.

In 1913, Lovecraft wrote a letter to the *Argosy* criticizing the work of Fred Jackson, whose tales of adventure and romance appeared regularly in the pulp. His critique drew the anger of the *Argosy* readership and Lovecraft, obviously, wrote a forty-four-line satirical poem about the fan page imbroglio that he describes in a 1916 letter to a friend as being "in the manner of Pope's *Dunciad.*"

Poetic satire mimicking Augustan poetry provoked more confusion than anger among Jackson's defenders in the *Argosy* but Lovecraft had managed to stir a minor tempest. Howard claimed that the next month's issue of the pulp contained nothing but "anti-Lovecraft letters," prompting him to write "another satire, flaying all my tormenters in stinging pentameter." That his tormenters felt properly flayed by an eighteenth-century poetic style that depended on a facility in classical literature and Latin puns for its punch seems unlikely. But, the controversy did bring Howard Lovecraft to the attention of Edward F. Daas of Milwaukee, one of the deeply enthusiastic proponents of the amateur journalism movement that flourished in turn-of-the-century America.

Amateur journalism involved the production of independently published papers, often produced by one or two people gathering materials that varied in size between four and twelve sheets. A few used the old hectograph method into the 1910s but most made use of the small printing presses then commercially available—oily and complicated little cranking mechanisms that often required significant skill in type-setting to make the final product look even a little polished. Reportage, of course, formed a significant element in these materials, though a combination of literary efforts and political editorializing seems to have formed the bulk of what the amateurs produced. Circulation for these publications, by nature, remained tiny.

Amateur journalism proved especially attractive to young people and had its beginnings in the late 1860s. In 1876, the National Amateur Press Association emerged out of early efforts to organize these independent and fairly solitary hobbyists. In 1895, a fourteen-year-old formed the United Amateur Press Association with the stated mission of giving amateur journalism a more intellectual cast. Little wonder that Howard Lovecraft found himself involved in such a movement since his various chemical and astronomy journals mimicked the style.

Rather redundantly, much of the writing about amateur journalism has focused on the amateurish nature of its production. More interesting is the fact that it emerged during a time historians have called "the incorporation of America." During this period, vast swaths of American commerce came under the control of the hierarchs of the second wave of the industrial revolution. In the year of the founding of the UAPA, William Randolph Hearst built on his success with the *San Francisco Examiner* to purchase the *New York Journal*, laying the foundations of a media empire that, today, includes three hundred magazines and twenty-one television channels.

Although they chose the adjective "amateur" to describe their lack of desire for profit, the term "independent journalism" explains much better in today's parlance what they attempted. In some respects, their efforts reflected the work of the artisan printers of the early American republic, amateurs who mixed literary aspiration with political entrepreneurship in a wide-open frontier of publishing possibilities rife with dissent and partisanship. Or, to give an even more germane contemporary example, these turn-of-the-century amateurs embodied elements of twenty-first-century blogging. Amateur journalism contained many of both the positive and negative elements of that movement.

Howard Lovecraft fell in love with this network of independent producers of the printed page, many of who shared his anti-commercial outlook. Although first a member of the UAPA, he also became involved in NAPA. Both organizations went into decline in the 1920s under the increasing pressures of regimented, Fordist journalism and the simple demographic fact that many of the very young members of the movement aged and moved into paying occupations. Lovecraft himself remained very active in the mid-1920s and in fact served as interim president of the UAPA in 1922–23, at a time when membership and activity in the organization had dwindled significantly. He never entirely cut his ties with amateur journalism, engaging in some activities until close to the time of his death.

Amateur journalism proved important for the making of H.P. Lovecraft in two primary ways. His involvement opened his life to a circle of friends and acolytes who encouraged his interest in writing, provided him with early outlets to publish, and, eventually, provided the basis for the survival of his work after his untimely death. Second, through amateur journalism he met Sonia Haft Greene who became, along with his mother, the woman he had the most significant relationship with during his almost forty-seven years.

The friends that Lovecraft made became the first recipients of what would become a voluminous and never fully collated correspondence, thousands of pages and hundreds of thousands of words pouring forth from 598 Angell—and later Brooklyn; 10 Barnes Street, Providence; and finally, his last home, 66 College Street—to friends and admirers in California, Texas, Wisconsin, Florida, and points all across the nation.

Maurice Moe and Reinhardt Kleiner became two of Lovecraft's first regular correspondents, starting with an introductory letter to Moe in 1914 and Kleiner in the same period. His first letter to Moe tells us a great deal about the twenty-four-year-old's state of mind. First, though he's not Clara Hess's "normal citizen," all of his years alone with his mother hadn't turned him into Norman Bates either. Second, he very much wanted to establish human contact, at least of a limited sort.

Moe's criticism in an amateur journal that Lovecraft needed to "get away from the heroic couplet" in the poetry he produced provided the occasion for the letter. Lovecraft's letter to his critic offered, urged, and almost bashfully begged for friendship, but he introduced himself in terms that would not immediately appeal to most. "I ought to be wearing powdered wig and knee britches," he told Moe, confessing that he did not think he could ever escape the rigors of Augustan poetry. However, he wondered, did Moe "care for the science of Astronomy?" Lovecraft goes into some detail about his own enthusiasm for the topic, including how his study of science encouraged his skeptical materialism, a set of ideas that would eventually provoke conflict with his new compatriot.

Moe, a major figure in the small world of amateur journalism, could have been put off by the peculiar letter but the two became fast friends instead, at least fast pen pals. Lovecraft and Kleiner formed an even quicker bond, secured by a mutual interest in astronomy and speculative fiction. In a letter to Kleiner, we hear Lovecraft connecting his interest in the macabre to Poe, whom he calls "the God of Fiction." In a 1916 letter, about a year before he began writing weird fiction regularly, he tells Kleiner that he "used to love the horrible and the grotesque—much more than I do now."

He's being duplicitous, because the rest of the letter expresses his devotion to tales of horror and details some of his own early efforts at writing weird fiction. He admits a mind full of "tales of murderers, spirits, reincarnations, metempsychosis, and every shudder-producing device known to literature!" In an earlier letter to Moe, he leaves out Poe in the story of the development of his literary tastes but pledges allegiance both to Hawthorne's *Wonder-Book* and *Twice-Told Tales.* He worked to redact his biography, even at this early stage of building his vast network of correspondents.

He was learning to become H.P. Lovecraft and this involved deception and misdirection, a style and mode of being in the world that has long been the province of creative sorts. He notes to Moe, for example, "In 1908, I should have entered Brown University, but the broken state of my health rendered the idea absurd." What's absurd is the claim that ill health kept him out of Brown. His health problems, mostly related to what we would call social anxiety, made him quite simply a high-school dropout.

By 1916, Lovecraft's correspondence entered a new phase. He and his new circle of friends began a practice that has intriguing connections with geek culture in the twenty-first century. In a June 1916 letter, Lovecraft outlined to Kleiner a plan for "a rather unique sort of rotating correspondence" in which Moe, Kleiner, Lovecraft, and Ira Cole would participate. One member of the group began a letter on some topic of literary, political, or philosophical interest who would send it to another. After that correspondent added his thoughts, it would be sent to the next member till it had come round full circle and the first member of the group would launch a new topic. The conversation would move on, conceivably to infinity.

Collectively, the group called themselves "The Kleicomoloes," a bit of whimsy composed out of parts of each of their names. Lovecraft insisted to Kleiner that each member must omit their part of the name when they write, so that all Lovecraft's addressed his contributions "Dear Kleicomo" while Kleiner's salutation began "Dear Comolo." Lovecraft concluded his description by exclaiming "What a nomenclature!" but he clearly delighted in what originally seems to have been Maurice Moe's plan. The Kleicomoloes circulated letters for many years to come; the first of several such circles in which Lovecraft participated.

The Kleicomoloes are very much like the first online forums that appeared on the Internet in the early 1990s, many of them emerging out of the fandom of text-based adventure games that are close to the origin of computer gaming culture. Occasionally it's suggested that the fans that corresponded with one another in the 1930s because of their interest in pulp science fiction initiated the first version of nerd networking. Lovecraft and his circle seem much closer to the origins of the culture of exchange between otherwise isolated enthusiasts that today has become a significant part of the Web.

He sometimes had actual human contact during these years. In 1917, W. Paul Cook, a fellow amateur journalist with whom Lovecraft developed a long correspondence and working relationship, dropped in on him at 598 Angell. Although he appeared at the door first thing in the morning, Sarah Susan and Aunt Lillian greeted Cook at the door with the explanation that "Howard had been up all night studying and writing, had just now gone to bed, and must under no circumstances be disturbed." Suddenly, however, Lovecraft himself appeared in an old-fashioned dressing gown and slippers and ushered Cook into his room to give what his guest called a "long lecture" on the significance of amateur journalism.

Now and again, Cook's story of his visit with Howard Lovecraft has been trotted out as more evidence of how his mother and aunts turned him into an invalid and recluse. Truthfully, it's mostly a story about what had become for Howard a nearly nocturnal existence. Another 1917 visitor to 598 Angell, Kleiner, found Sarah Susan Lovecraft "very cordial and even vivacious." Lovecraft, after a long chat in his room, took his friend for a stroll around Providence, primarily to show his guest some examples of his beloved colonial architecture. Kleiner remembered wanting to stop at a local cafeteria for a snack and Lovecraft joined him although he ate nothing himself and, in Kleiner's memory, "watched me dispose of coffee and cake, or possibly pie, with some curiosity." Kleiner recalled thinking that his strange friend had perhaps never eaten in a public place before, and there's no reason to doubt Kleiner's suspicion.

By the time Lovecraft met with Kleiner and Cook, he had written both "The Tomb" and "Dagon"—an outgrowth in his lifelong interest in the fantastic. His reading habits had also begun to change and he had started plumbing the depths of the literature of the macabre and the fantastic. Not all his new friends took to his increased interest in such work immediately, although a few seem to have been delighted that he had taken to writing less imitative poetry modeled on Dryden, Swift, and Pope.

Amateur journalism ensured that his circle of friends and admirers continued to grow. Lovecraft first met Kleiner in 1916 when he went to the Providence docks to meet a group of amateur journalists on their way to a convention in Boston. By 1919, he formed a correspondence with Samuel Loveman who, despite Lovecraft's oft-stated prejudice against Jews, became one of his closest friends. Loveman, nearly thirty years after their first acquaintance, recalled with delight the stream of letters from Providence that covered a wide range of topics, including "Astronomy, Sorcery, Witchcraft, Archaeology, English literature, Cabalism, Dutch New York, Eighteenth century poetry, Alexander Pope, Roman sculpture, Greek vases. Decadence of the Alexandrian period, Baths of Caracalla, T.S. Eliot, Hart Crane—Heaven alone could enumerate their infinite range. . . ."

During the late 1910s, he also formed his lasting friendship with Alfred Galpin, whom Lovecraft affectionately nicknamed "Alfredus." We don't know the details of their first correspondence, although it seems to have begun around 1917 when Galpin was a junior in high school. Galpin, after twenty years of writing to his friend, destroyed all of their letters for reasons that are unclear beyond a vague allusion to "a change in his interests." About ten years Lovecraft's junior, Lovecraft took the pose of being Galpin's "old grandpa" and the two first wrote copiously about amateur journalism, religion, Sherlock Holmes, and eventually weird fiction. They would grow apart for a time in the late 1920s but reconnect before Lovecraft's death, by which time Galpin had become an accomplished composer.

These friendships had a surprising intensity given that they primarily took the form of correspondence. But, this apparently pleased Lovecraft. Congenial and polite to a fault in social gatherings, he had little experience with them and, only during the brief period that he would spend in New York City, did he have a circle with which he socialized with any frequency. Setting aside his mother and aunts, he spent extended periods of time with only two people during his life: Sonia Haft Greene and R.H. Barlow—who brought him a rich companionship at the twilight of his life that he perhaps never knew previously, even with Sonia.

This came to him much later. Lovecraft once wrote to Kleiner that "Like you, I am absolutely devoid of actual friends outside of correspondence." He seemed to say this as a simple acknowledgement that gave him no displeasure, not as some cry of despair. He liked, and maybe needed, the distance.

Although Edward H. Cole, an early friend from amateurdom, once suggested that "his [Lovecraft's] friends were innumerable," he describes this mainly in terms of his voluminous letter-writing. Cole estimates that at one point, Lovecraft may have been trading letters with up to one hundred regular correspondents, often sending twenty- to forty- to seventy-page theses to his closest friends on subjects of every intellectual interest imaginable. These hours at his desk, like our hours on Instagram and Facebook, remained essentially solitary and seldom became for Lovecraft a point of entry into anyone's daily life. In fact, a few correspondents made repeated and failed efforts to meet with him in person, including several who lived in or near Providence.

The correspondence did become a bridge for him to a larger world. He had begun to venture forth, possibly sleeping outside of his own bed for the first time at an amateur journalism convention in Boston in 1920. In 1919, he had joined several amateur friends in Boston to hear a lecture by Lord Dunsany. Still more trips to Boston came in 1921 and he would soon pay a visit to Sam Loveman in Cleveland, a town Lovecraft judged utterly un-Lovecraftian (but which also provided him one of the occasions he met the already famous poet Hart Crane). The near-recluse had begun moving in some very interesting literary circles, at least now and again.

⌒

Sarah Susan Lovecraft entered Providence's Butler Hospital March 13, 1919. She died there on May 21, 1921 from a botched gallbladder operation.

The narrative constructed about Lovecraft has often portrayed this as his moment of freedom, the moment when he broke the bonds from the vampire mother and became H.P. Lovecraft. If you're inclined toward tempting Oedipal interpretations, you won't be shocked to learn that he met the woman he married within six months after Sarah Susan's death.

Lovecraft's actual response to his mother's hospitalization and death are oddly ignored in discussions of what his mother's death "meant" for him. The possibility has been ignored that the travels and literary work that consumed him over the next several years consisted of one long cry of trauma, this time finding expression in at least some outside social interaction rather than his normal habit of seclusion and disappearance into the maze of his own eclectic interests.

The fact that he hoped to find a substitute for the relationship with his mother, and did so quickly and disastrously, needs no psychoanalysis to explain. When we're in pain, as Howard Lovecraft certainly was during his mother's two-year death march, we become desperate for solace. Unlike earlier times in his life—the death of his father, the loss of his grandfather and his boyhood home, whatever exactly happened to him in 1908—this time he embraced more opportunities for exterior solace than he'd ever done before. It's extremely odd that Lovecraft has received heavy-handed psychoanalysis and biographical head-shaking for one of the few times in his life that he behaved like the average person.

Missing evidence makes the circumstance that led to the family

placing Sarah Susan Lovecraft in Butler unascertainable. We've already
seen that a fire destroyed much of the hospital records. We know she
had gone for a rest at her sister's. S.T. Joshi writes that "she was admitted to Butler hospital," a telltale passive voice and perhaps the best that
we can make of it based on the black hole in the record.[26]

These years, the first of two incredibly productive periods in the
creation of his early works, obviously represented a constant trial. Writing to Kleiner on January 1, 1919, while Sarah Susan stayed with Aunt
Lillian, he described himself as unable to eat or stay out of bed. Another
letter to Kleiner, written about seventeen days after his mother entered
Butler, exuded even more despair. "Existence seems of little value," he
wrote "& I wish it might terminate."

He wrote and visited her on the grounds frequently, taking long
walks along the Seekonk River. Winfield T. Scott's 1940s hatchet job
made much of the fact that he "did not venture inside the hospital."
We actually have limited evidence of this, outside of Scott's venomous
assessment of Lovecraft's relationship to his mother. Muriel Eddy, a local
Providence friend, claims that "he visited Sarah Lovecraft quite often."
She acknowledges that he never went inside the hospital but that they
walked the grounds that she calls "huge and beautiful." The idea that
Lovecraft ignored his mother in her final days ranks as one of the major
absurdities circulated about him.

Writing to a correspondent soon after her death, he consoled himself with thoughts of suicide. "During my mother's life-time, I was aware
that voluntary euthanasia on my part would cause her distress," he
wrote, "but it is now possible for me to regulate the term of my existence
with the assurance that my end would cause no one more than a passing annoyance—of course my aunts are infinitely considerate and solicitous, but the death of a nephew is seldom a momentous event." Perhaps
thinking back fifteen years to his first plans for suicide, he suggested that
he might "possibly . . . find enough interesting things to read and study
to warrant my hanging on indefinitely."

He concluded the letter by suggesting to his reader that she give up on reading Kant and describing how much he had been enjoying the work of this very intriguing Viennese thinker, Sigmund Freud.

⁓

In 1920, he wrote to "The Gallamo," a new correspondence circle Lovecraft had started with young Alfred Galpin and Maurice Moe. He reported a dream that incarnated him as a retired army surgeon living in upstate New York, the region from where his long dead father hailed.

He tells his circle about walking to see a colleague who had been causing much alarm for "conducting secret experiments in a laboratory attic of his home, and beyond that locked door he would admit no one but himself. Sickening odours were often detected near that door and odd sounds were at times not absent." Lovecraft the army surgeon sees "a large glass slab . . . damp, gelatinous, and bluish white" and learns to his horror that his insane colleague has begun to fashion the glob into a living thing. In the irrational logic of dreams, he looks at the glass panel of one of the mad doctor's instrument cases and notices, to his chagrin, that his tie needs straightening. And then he woke up.

Every reader of Lovecraft will notice bits and pieces of some of his best tales in this dream: "Herbert West—Reanimator," "The Dunwich Horror," "From Beyond," and, perhaps most especially, *The Case of Charles Dexter Ward*. All feature unnatural things born out of the collusion of science and magic. A closed-off secret laboratory from which issues hints of something ghastly beyond a locked door.

Every dreamer will notice the trick that the psyche plays on us in our sleep, those moments when we seem to be on the verge of a revelatory explanation of the secret, and possibly terrifying, nature of all life and remember that we forgot to pay the wireless bill. Our dream double sets out for a happy reunion with a lost loved one and the dream narrative lurches from sublimity into a search for a lost umbrella.

Some of Lovecraft's letters between 1919 and 1921 make it seem he had lost himself in a world of nightmare as his mother's condition at the sanatorium worsened. In truth, he had used the time to enter into the first of several productive periods of writing horror fiction. "The Tomb" and "Dagon" had come to completion two years before her hospitalization, but "Dagon" finally came into print in 1919—though only at first in an amateur journal published by his friend Paul Cook. "The Tomb" appeared in Cook's journal in 1922. *Weird Tales* reprinted both of these stories later in the twenties.

During this time, Lovecraft read much of Dunsany, whose lecture in Boston had so impressed him. Elements of Dunsany's tales of otherworldly quests and adventures in lands ruled by a pantheon of new gods show up in early stories like "The White Ship" (1919) and "The Quest of Iranon" (1921). Darrell Schweitzer finds all manner of connections between Lovecraft's stories of this period and the work of Dunsany. Lovecraft became enough of a Dunsany fan to write two rather bad poems about him and send him a gift of a letter signed by Abraham Lincoln that belonged to the Phillips family library.

Lovecraft quickly broke Dunsany's spell. He very soon produced a far more sinister vision than the British writer ever conjured. His own dark dreams cast their shadows over Dunsany's Celtic worlds of wonder, dreams, and midnight terrors and suggest that his boyhood night gaunts continued their romps through his sleeping mind. Indeed, even Schweitzer notes that he began writing tales of otherworldly dream quests before he'd read a word of Dunsany.

Lovecraft's own dream quests explain his growing interest in Freud during the 1920s and his description in a letter to Kleiner that he found himself "forever dreaming of strange barren landscapes, cliffs, stretches of ocean and deserted cities with towers and domes." The creatures that lived amid these ruins, the shadowy things old Whipple had helped him meet and the strange creatures he and his mother apparently played at seeing, slowly transmogrified into the recognizable abyss of Lovecraftian horror in the early 1920s. He insisted to Kleiner that he went to these strange places without the aid of opium or cannabis. "Should I take that drug," he wondered, "who can say what worlds of unreality I might explore?"

Maurice Levy, a French admirer of Lovecraft, beautifully and terrifyingly described how H.P. Lovecraft *"dreamed his repugnances"* (emphasis in original). He found us the monster stories we needed from him and raised them out of the abyss in our collective psyches as much as his own. He didn't need opium, or Poe, or the pulps he'd been reading or even the nightmares his family liked to trade with one another. He needed the American experience joined with his own strange, inexplicable life. He needed to tie them together and find the terrible secret that no one in his own time, with few exceptions, wanted to know.

He never successfully came to grips with America, or wanted to. His romanticized, ancient, terrifying, and wondrous New England had a tenuous relationship to the New England where he made his home, tied by the same loose cords with which his consciousness connected his dreams with his waking hours. The parts of North America he visited, and loved, floated in an ether of somnolent time: Salem, Marblehead, Quebec, Charleston, St. Augustine. His love of the world as it existed before 1775 clouded his relationship to the realities of American history and inevitably, to the actual history of his own region.

Lovecraft never wanted to be anything but a New Englander, though he desperately disliked the founders of the region. The Plymouth settlers, separatist Calvinists who showed up in 1630, and the Puritans, who came to kill Indians and burn witches and Quakers in 1636, represented for Lovecraft all that he hated about religious fanaticism. In later letters to Robert E. Howard, he used the Puritans as perfect examples of Freud's concept of extreme repression leading to manifestations of neurosis.

The Puritans are almost the only colonists who came to the New World "for religious reasons" although some conservative American exceptionalists even today claim that theological scruples motivated all the early English, Dutch, and German settlers of the New World. In truth, much of the rest of the original colonies first emerged out of entrepreneurial gambits, the schemes of hopeful capitalists who aspired to own land and slaves and merchant capital. Hard men who wanted to tame a wilderness whose resources they could spin into gold.

The founders of Lovecraft's New England wanted to build the king-dom of God. They imagined themselves on an "errand into the wilder-ness," building a beachhead in a place they called a "howling wilderness" filled with the children of the devil. Black bears and black dogs actually came as manifestations of demon spirits when they wandered into their settlements. The native peoples, Reverend Cotton Mather wrote, repre-sented the very children of the devil living in a dark forest where the light of the gospel had not penetrated.

These ancestral spirits lived in the heart and mind of Lovecraft no matter how much he wanted to claim Roger Williams, rather than John Winthrop, as the father of his Yankee heritage. As strange young Howard grew into H.P. Lovecraft, as he created H.P. Lovecraft, he embarked on his own errand into the wilderness: a tangle of dreams, of nightmares, of national horrors, of a moment in the experience of America and the world in which the stars aligned and the dead but dreaming Cthulhu awakened and wreaked havoc on the earth.

PART II.

FORBIDDEN BOOKS

S tuart Gordon began his career directing an all-nude, psychedelic, politically radical production of *Peter Pan* in 1968. He had marched against the war in Vietnam. Mayor Daley's goon squads gassed him at the protests at the Democratic National Convention in Chicago. His theatre company, called Screw, put on a satire entitled *The Game Show* in which actors threatened, attacked, and sexually assaulted audience members (actually just more actors planted in the audience). The performances ended in riots, exactly as Gordon hoped. He wanted to shock his generation out of apathy, make them stand up and fight when they confronted evil or make them think about why they had sat there and let it happen.

And, he loved H.P. Lovecraft.

Lovecraft and Gordon are an unlikely duo. Nevertheless, Gordon symbolizes the generation of the counterculture who seized on Lovecraft and other fantasy writers because they provided alternative visions of the world and teased out the dark and primitive terrors that lived underneath America's postwar suburban haze. The generation getting high to the Who and fucking in the back of VW vans to the dissonance of the Doors devoured the writing of someone who, at their age, edited an amateur paper called *The Conservative* that whined about saving Anglo-Saxon civilization. They read Lovecraft while taking to the streets or taking over whole campuses to protest segregation, economic inequality, gender discrimination, and an increasingly brutal, savage war against a popular post-colonial revolution in Vietnam.

Gordon's fascination grew as Lovecraft's tales became available during the 1970s. His devotion to the author resulted in the 1985 cult film *Re-Animator*, based loosely—very loosely, purists insist—on Lovecraft's serialized tale of the early twenties entitled "Herbert West—Reanimator."

The film has become a cult classic because of its combination of creative gore effects, straight-faced humor, and willingness to go places audiences didn't think they'd ever be taken. The reanimated dead do more than walk in this film and, in its most infamous sequence, scream queen Barbara Crampton has a romantic encounter with a severed head that cannot be explained, but must instead be viewed. Horror maven John Stanley writes that it's "disgustingly sickening as it panders on one hand and amuses cleverly on the other." More than thirty years later, it remains smart, hilarious, and utterly gross.

Perhaps Lovecraft himself would have cared little for the nudity and the crude nature of the sexuality of Gordon's flick. Or maybe he would have understood why his tale had to be told in such terms. He often professed to feel nothing but disgust for what he usually called "the erotic" or "the erotic instinct." And yet, as he once told his friend Reinhardt Kleiner, "all ethical systems based on erotic repression have been futile and hypocritical." As a young man, he disliked stories that explored sexuality and never wrote one himself that explicitly did so. But he came to despise all forms of censorship and to see eroticism as essential in some stories. He encouraged August Derleth in his reading of Huysmans's *Là-bas*, a book he called "really nauseously disgusting" but "worth reading."[27]

So who knows what kind of impression a naked Barbara Crampton facing some unwanted zombie attention on an operating table would have made on him? I have some suspicion he would have found it a bit funny, exactly the sort of thing human beings' mad dreams could bring about. He, after all, had written the lurid and sensationalist tale upon which Gordon drew inspiration.

"Herbert West—Reanimator" appeared in serial form from February to July 1922 in the amateur journal *Home Brew*, a little magazine of humor and oddities that S.T. Joshi calls "crude and flamboyant." The publication of the stories marks a turning point in Lovecraft's writing life, as it's the first time he actually received payment for his horror stories, a full five dollars for each of the six episodes. He wrote, with delight that seeps out of the page, that he had conceived "a most hideous conception of yarns."

He took obvious pleasure in the stories, at one point writing that he doubted the success of *Home Brew* as a going concern but thought the tales might aid his own reputation for "sinister diabolism." He complains to Kleiner that he's become "a Grub Street hack" while relishing the completion of the first two episodes of his "daimoniack tales." He claims that, as a true artist, he had first refused because of the idea of accepting payment "for fiction written to order." But he then claims that "the jovial editor convinced him," and seemingly did so rather easily.

"Herbert West—Reanimator" clearly stands in the tradition of the mad scientist raising monsters he cannot control. Although the tale makes much of its villain's scientific materialism, West arguably represents the first of Lovecraft's many insane inventors and explorers of the unknown whose work walks a twilight path between scientific and occult experiment—a reflection of Shelley's Dr. Frankenstein, whose studies began with reading the occult works of necromancy and alchemy before exploring the findings of modern medicine.

Herbert West's activities begin at the medical school of Miskatonic University, a fictional institution of higher learning that became central to Lovecraft tales and lore. He based Miskatonic heavily on Brown University, even though it appears in the town of Arkham—his fictionalized Salem—rather than Providence. "Miskatonic U." T-shirts proliferate today online, perhaps the most clever being one that advertises the "Miskatonic University Department of Necromancy," a pretty clear allusion to the Herbert West tales. Of course, the real Lovecraft insiders can show off their biographical knowledge with a "Miskatonic U. Department of Astronomy" tee.

Lovecraft's complaints about hack work aside, the "Reanimator" tale shows he had a taste for blood and gore that Stuart Gordon simply picked up and ran with. A young protégé of West's narrates the serial, journeying with West in search of fresh specimens with "spade and oil dark lamp" into a potter's field graveyard. West was himself kicked out of Miskatonic by the sympathetic and caring physician Dean Alan Halsey, who we think might become the hero of the tale. Instead, West takes Halsey's death as an opportunity to turn him into a postmortem stalking maniac who kills indiscriminately, tearing apart his victims in a frenzy of bloodlust. Night after night, Arkham's fiend rips apart its victims and sometimes, Lovecraft writes, it "had not left behind all it had attacked, for sometimes it had been hungry."

A band of "angry villagers" (long before this image became a staple of the Universal Studio monster movies after 1931) hunts the creature and inters it in the asylum where it "beat its head against the wall for sixteen years." West assumes he could have had more success had the specimen been even fresher.

More lurid half-resurrections follow, including a viciously racist passage in which a black boxer, "The Harlem Smoke," becomes one of West's victims whom Lovecraft describes as "a loathsome, gorilla-like thing . . . and a face that conjured up thoughts of unspeakable Congo secrets and tom-tom poundings under an eerie moon." In a comment reserved only for West's African American victim, Lovecraft writes, "the body must have looked even worse in life."

By the end of the serial, West and his assistant have been to the trenches of World War I—the land of horrors where Lovecraft imagined himself going, and West's experiments have become even more bizarre as he uses reptilian genetic material to awaken the freshly dead. Finally, as befits what later became the mad scientist formulae, his own "human, semi-human, fractionally human, and not human at all" horde of the living dead revolt and tear their maker to pieces.

Dark humor and gore spouting in red flumes off the page made this story the basis for a nearly perfect 1980s horror flick. *H.P. Lovecraft's*

Re-Animator became the film's official title and advertising posters reiterated the connection with a tagline that read "H.P. Lovecraft's classic tale of horror . . . it will scare you to pieces."

Lovecraft deserved such praise. He'd written a tale in 1922 that intertwined elements of the *Frankenstein* films of the '30s, the slasher films of the '70s and '80s, and the endless stream of zombie flicks that lurch toward us in the present. Howard Lovecraft had escaped the anxiety of his influences, his Hawthorne and his Poe and his Dunsany and Bierce, all these dark masters congregating into the shadows that gathered behind his writing desk even as he transubstantiated their imaginations into something new, original, and terrible.

He had also tapped into one of the great terrors of his own era: The war that killed eight million men and left twenty-one million wounded. Bodily mutilation, men who had come back from war seemingly as reanimated dead, had become part of life in the western world in the years following 1918.

Combat medicine advanced significantly during the First World War, allowing men to survive gruesome wounds that previously would have sent them to their graves. The new Maxim guns and the use of shells that exploded into flying shrapnel could do things to the human body that made it nearly unrecognizable even if medicine could keep it alive. Facial mutilation led to some of the first instances of plastic surgery following the Battle of the Somme, while artists and sculptors made veterans tin or plaster masks that sometimes lent them an aspect as horrifying as the wounds themselves.

The war that Lovecraft had hoped to participate in had raised a world of horrors, and both horror films and the weird tale proliferated in the aftermath of World War I. In 1922, Albert Grau and F.W. Murnau created the modern vampire film with *Nosferatu: A Symphony of Horror*. Grau remembered that bits and pieces of the imagery of the film had come to him one dark and shell-ridden night in the trenches when the war had come to seem like "a cosmic vampire, sucking the blood of millions." In 1931, James Whale, a former British officer in the trenches and one of Hollywood's first openly gay directors, relived his wartime trauma when he directed the iconic film version of *Frankenstein*.

Lovecraft's new kind of horror owed much to this willingness to experience what Freud called in a 1919 essay "The Uncanny," which Freud contemplated even as he considered the effects of war trauma. But, while Europe lay in ruins, the American twenties roared both with the speakeasy world of jazz and gin and a new, rambunctious brand of conservatism embodied in a revivified Ku Klux Klan and America's first "red scare." Neither American constituency yet had the frame of mind suited to Lovecraft's grotesqueries even as—like Herbert West—he labored in the small hours to bring them to terrifying half-life. No one, outside of the tiny circulation of *Home Brew*, saw his gore-soaked "Reanimator" tales until after his death.

Literary critics and historians love to argue about periodization. Some claim Lovecraft went through a period of being influenced mainly by the Decadent Symbolists before the mid-twenties. Others see his work as all Poe all the time before 1926. These arguments have helped shape a Lovecraft canon, one regarded by scholars as "the Great Texts" and mostly written after his return to Providence in 1926. "The Call of Cthulhu" itself gets credit as the beginning of a period when he put his creative genius on full exhibit.

When—and I very much expect this to be true—we are still talking about H.P. Lovecraft in thirty years, I think the classic stories "The Call of Cthulhu," "The Shadow Over Innsmouth," "The Haunter of the Dark," and "The Colour Out of Space" will not receive the degree of attention they do today. They will not be the horrific things baristas and bartenders of the next generation (post-millennial, we'll maybe call them, or Generation Water-Shortage) will want to talk about with middle-aged patrons pondering over Lovecraft books (or e-books or holographic readers or whatever technology we'll have in our hands or implanted in our heads in that not-so-distant future).

Right now, simply typing in "Cthulhu" on Etsy garners 4,074 hits. But Cthulhu will get some competition. I expect the tentacle horror of this and other justly famous stories will be showing some wear and tear after having become so recognizable, so much a part of the cultural DNA that laying claim to "The Call of Cthulhu" as your favorite Lovecraft tale will seem rather a truism.

I'm not suggesting that his key canonical stories will lapse into obscurity. Instead, I think more readers will begin to discover the haunting vision quests he wrote between 1918 and 1923. These mostly short pieces are some of the strangest, even gnomic, tales that he ever created. One or two feel more like Zen koans than short fiction. They have names like "Celephaïs," "Polaris," "The Quest of Iranon," and the "The Doom that Came to Sarnath." One of the best is simply called "The Nameless City" and like 1917's "Dagon" presages some of his late masterpieces. Many of his explorations of fantastic worlds have a grotesque beauty about them that reappears in those tales of cosmic dread he began to write in the late twenties.

Lovecraft calls "The Nameless City" (1921) an "archaeological phantasy." It did not find publication in his lifetime outside amateurdom even though it contains one of the most terrifying passages that he ever wrote. His unnamed traveller "wanders the deserts of Araby" and transverses ruins whose very age evoke horror. This desolate place, despised by the locals, calls to him in a way that Lovecraft sees as "unwholesome," a yearning that evokes in his traveller not only horror but desire and "wonder."

The narrator enters deep vaults that tell a story of an inhuman history. The walls are traced with tales of monstrosities that Lovecraft compares to the reptilian while assuring us that what his traveller views is something much worse than he knows how to describe. Exploring further, gusts of air brush his face from out of an abyss that echo with a horrible squall of voices, "the ghastly cursing and snarling of strange-tongued fiends," out of a "grave of un-numbered aeon-dead antiquities." I'll let you discover what he finds there and what becomes of him.

These early stories all allegedly have the spark of Lord Dunsany's *Book of Wonder* in them. Lovecraft alludes directly to that work in "The Nameless City." But most of his fantasies of this era leave their seekers of wonder—and us—in a black abyss of uncertainty, horror, or disillusion; they mistook an endless cycle of meaninglessness for a mystical journey to worlds of indescribable beauty. This aesthetic of hopeless quest continues, and expands, through his work.

These are terrors that no one before Lovecraft had explored, or perhaps even been willing to face. These are not ghosts in a haunted house, horrors avoided if you don't darken the door of the forbidden place. They are the terrors of time and even if you don't journey into ill-rumored caverns, Lovecraft assures you that things older and more terrible than humanity wait to rise and squelch us. He notes in a letter to Frank Belknap Long that he borrowed one phrase from Dunsany as inspiration for "The Nameless City" while he tried to "aim at a cumulative succession of horrors."

"Hypnos" offers another example of an early story that future Lovecraft impresarios are likely to put forward as representative of his early literary power. I wonder, and worry, that "Hypnos" might even become a standard college reading for the hip classroom.

If this occurs, maybe the idea of "Hypnos" being on a college syllabus will acquire the same outré patina as reading *Naked Lunch* in the 1970s, or seem as exciting as Charlotte Perkins Gilman's "The Yellow Wallpaper" in the 1990s. Maybe its reputation will say to future college students what it says to them today when they read a David Foster Wallace essay or check out one of Chuck Klosterman's more incisive and less opaque essays. An adult who "gets you" has given you this VERY RELEVANT work that will change your life and open the gates of perception.

I say I worry as well as wonder about this because canonizing means domesticating and containing the power of such texts and their histories.

It's a tale that deserves something better than such a fate. Hopefully, to quote Stephen King writing about Lovecraft, "the chickenshit academics" won't get their tenured mitts on this one.

"Hypnos" tells the story of a friendship that may have existed or may have been the result of utter madness helped along by morphine, opium, or a mystical relationship with a real entity, a terrible Thing drawn into this world by spells, hallucinogenic dream quests, and ill intention.

The story envelops you like a fever dream or a passage from a Beat novel: a sculptor meets a stranger on a railroad platform, a stranger in the throes of an unexplained "convulsion" from which the "vulgarly curious had backed away." The narrator, however, finds himself drawn to the stranger's face, a visage he calls "actually beautiful," and when the stranger opens his eyes the narrator sees in their bottomless pools the bioluminescence of forbidden knowledge.

In the logic of dreams, the sculptor knows this man must become both his only friend and his master. He "drove the crowd away" and, as his new acquaintance comes out of his apparent seizure, the narrator asks him to come and live with him, "be my teacher and leader." The stranger agrees, again like the impossible happenings of a dream state, "without speaking a word."

This story stands out in the Lovecraft oeuvre for two reasons. First, it's an example of how he very early began to shape his work around themes of monsters from the depths and things that, once encountered, drove the seer into a madness they could not escape.

More importantly, it's a tale that some current critics chalk up to his alleged slavishness to Poe. The superficial relationship to Poe's style, and an homage or two in the tale, actually highlight how much Lovecraft had wrestled free of the master's influence. Poe would have used the plot to work the psychological complexity side of the street, the ambiguity about the narrator's sanity. However, he would never have created visceral descriptions of forbidden voyages into transdimensional spaces filled with creeping terrors. Nor would he have created these other worlds, worlds the narrator describes not as places but as "plungings and soarings" that suggest to the reader that the journey takes on characteristics impossible to describe in terms of recognizable physical space.

Something awful comes at the end of the tale, awful and inexplicable—or rather possible to explain in several different ways, each more terrible than the last. Some readers might read the conclusion as Lovecraft trotting out the old, dusty idea of gothic double or as the supernatural blurring into the horrors of madness.

Lovecraft doesn't really allow us to read the ending as simple hallucination. He makes clear in "Hypnos" that the narrator and his friend's dark explorations into drugs and the occult touched what he called in his astronomical enthusiasm "infinite space." There they locate things that the narrator's friends must never have dealings with again. And even after they try to step away from their otherworldly journeys, he catches his friend looking "furtively at the sky as if hunted by some monstrous thing therein." Here waited "spheres forbidden, unimagined and hideously remote."

If my prediction concerning how a new generation of Lovecraft fans will seize on the tale comes true, it's difficult to envision how it will figure into the ongoing quest to monetize Lovecraft. Will it replace the Cthulhu T-shirts, coffee mugs, and Christmas ornaments? It is pretty straightforward to imagine "Hypnos" tattoos of the future, if tattoos remain as mainstream as they've become. The story ends with a simple word in Greek, Attic lettering perfect for a youthful shoulder blade or forearm or lower back.

In January of 1923, Lovecraft complained that when you give critics a weird tale "they all cry Poe" and in this way are a bit like "trained animals." Although not particularly thinking that "Hypnos" came off very well in this period, he also sees it as different from what he calls his writing of "Dunsanian things." Although certainly enamored of Dunsany, a point many of his critics have complained about, Lovecraft only took bits and pieces of the Irish author's style and narrative interests. In his hands, flights of fancy transform into dangerous journeys through opaque darkness. His characters, always filmy and insubstantial, began to take their amorphous shape in these dreams.

In "Hypnos," he made something new: a tale of psychological terror without ghosts, a tale of madness that did not depend for its effect on the fear of madness but instead on the Things that lived beyond the borders of what counts as human sanity. Call it his cosmicism, his Cthulhu Mythos, or, in Lovecraft's own words, his "Yog-Sothery." But no one had done it before, not Poe, not Bierce, and not Dunsany—whose work contemporary audiences would think of more in terms of light fantasy than horror. "Hypnos," like his other great early tale "Dagon," announced a new terror upon the earth, qualitatively different from any of the other horrific creatures of fiction and folklore before him.

S.T. Joshi, not always complimentary toward Lovecraft's earliest work, believes "Hypnos" has received too much "casual dismissal" from critics, perhaps because Lovecraft later disdained it in his correspondence. Lovecraft expressed his dislike for the tale at a point when he felt generally downcast about his writing career, and the critics have picked up on his distress.

He wrote tales like "Hypnos" in the depths of the New England night after spending most of the daylight hours exploring dream dimensions. It's a little unclear just when this nocturnal lifestyle began, though he certainly spent much of the night awake and at his desk by the time Cook came to visit him that brisk morning in 1917. It certainly became a well-established habit at least by his early twenties.

He seemed to become free at night and it's impossible not to wonder if he began sleeping through the day to escape some of the strangeness of the household. Or perhaps it's a much simpler issue and he liked the quiet, finding it conducive to work. He clearly did a lot of writing at night, though when he moved to New York in the mid-twenties he became a sort of midnight rambler, walking the streets till dawn. So it's probably not about writing or about getting away from his mother and aunts and how their collective oddities must have made the house feel at times.

I think nighttime allowed him to alter his consciousness. The night became a kind of waking nightmare that created the feeling of swimming out into the infinite dark, just as had his fascination with astronomy. Like Jervas Dudley in "The Tomb," he paid more than one visit to an aged cemetery in the morning's small hours. In later years, visiting friends found themselves sitting on seventeenth- and eighteenth-century tombs till 2:00 AM telling ghost stories. The old burying ground of St. John's Episcopal on College Hill, what Lovecraft described in his own lifetime as "a spectral, sloping ossuary completely concealed from every public thoroughfare," offered him and his horror nerd friends the perfect setting for such nighttime jaunts. One August night, Lovecraft told a correspondent they "all sat down on an altar-tomb & rhymed acrostics on the name of Edgar Allan Poe."

Maurice Levy described how some of Lovecraft's most unnerving horrors are things that come from depth. "The abnormal, the disquieting, and the unclean are," Levy writes, "always, on the vertical axis of the imagination, always situated toward the bottom, in the zone of the deepest shade." Lovecraft did, in fact, unleash horrors that came from the depths, the depths of time, the seas and imagined interdimensional spaces from where Things clawed their way into what humans imagine as their world. In the dark, Lovecraft had his monsters to himself in a way he did not have in the bright and busy sunshine.[28]

Clara Hess would have undoubtedly pointed to his mother allowing him to be up at all hours as one of those things that prevented him from becoming a normal citizen. But his nocturnal ramblings, both his literal night walks and his interior journeys, allowed him to trouble the denizens of the diurnal world, to make all those normal citizens see their experience as the abnormal state of things, a shade behind which gibber a thousand terrors.

Lovecraft's nightmares soon found a wider audience than amateur journals like *Home Brew*. In March 1923, the first issue of *Weird Tales* appeared on newsstands and several of Lovecraft's correspondents urged him to submit his fiction. James F. Morton, an unlikely friend to Lovecraft as his politics had inclined toward anarchism in his youth and remained radical throughout his life, played the most significant role in convincing Lovecraft to send his stories to the new magazine. Writing to Morton in May 1923, Lovecraft playfully proposed a bet over whether or not the editor would simply return the five stories he sent them without a letter. He assumed this would be the outcome.

In fact, Edwin Baird, the first editor of *Weird Tales*, had been intrigued with all the samples sent to him, though he requested in a personal note that Lovecraft return them, retyped with double spacing. "Yah! I hate typing," he complained to Morton, but also that he was "so damn hard up I may try one as a gamble . . . 'Dagon' I guess. . . ."

He dutifully retyped the story and Baird both accepted it and wanted more. "Dagon" appeared in the October 1923 issue of *Weird Tales* and generated significant reader interest. Complaining to Morton even more about the horrors of typing, he confessed to wanting "to grind out a deuce of a lot of shocking monstrosities."

The John Hay Library sits atop College Hill, the old section of colonial East Providence that Lovecraft adored. Named for Lincoln's personal assistant who later became Secretary of State in both the McKinley and Roosevelt administrations, it's a neo-Federal building that once served as Brown's primary library for undergraduates. Today it's a refuge for researchers and undergrads seeking a quieter spot for reading than the main library offers. Or for researchers who have decided to voyage to strange places.

The special collections feel like part of Lovecraft's mythic world because of an intriguing series of coincidences and supremely odd connections that have made it into one of the leading repositories of books on magic, arcana, and occult lore in the United States. I spent part of my own time at the Hay looking at bits and pieces of the H. Adrian Smith Collection of Conjuring and Magicana. The Smith collection contains materials as diverse as a complete run of the pulp magazine *Tales of Magic and Mystery* or a set of sixteenth-century materials on necromancy, neo-platonic philosophy, and witchcraft.

The Smith collection alone gives the Hay the atmosphere of Lovecraft's Miskatonic University that holds one of the world's few editions of "the unmentionable *Necronomicon* of the Mad Arab Abdul Alhazred." But there's more. The Hay also houses the over one thousand volumes of the Damon Occult Collection, materials gathered of the former Brown professor S. Foster Damon. A William Blake scholar, Damon collected books and pamphlets on American Spiritualism but also sixteenth- and seventeenth-century works of learned magic, including work by the English necromancer John Dee—whom Lovecraft used as part of his history of the fictional *Necronomicon*.

Undergraduates sometimes use the Hay as a staging ground for Lovecraft-inspired Halloween tours. And so they should, as the Hay has become the center of Lovecraft studies since a series of bequests of his materials, growing over the years through sometimes peculiar circumstances. Barlow gave the library many of the materials when his older friend died in 1937. In the 1990s, the library received an original autograph of Lovecraft's *The Whisperer in Darkness* (1930), long assumed missing, found in the attic of one of Barlow's students after she died in Hawaii.

On my first morning of research at the Hay, I walked from the hotel district across the Providence River Canal, passing the First Baptist Church—where a precocious Lovecraft argued the case of the Romans against the Christians. In order to reach the Hay, you pass the site of Lovecraft's last place of residence in 1937, 66 College Street, and come to the western end of Angell Street. Angell continues its climb from the Hay up College Hill and toward the house Lovecraft spent his life yearning to return to (now an apartment complex) and to 598, the cramped quarters where he and his mother and aunts lived until 1924.

Walk the steep grade up the hill and you pass the oldest center of Brown's campus, collegiate gothic buildings amidst a green sward of open spaces. No one would mistake Brown for Lovecraft's shadowed Miskatonic U. on warm days in late spring like this one. Undergrads sun themselves, throw Frisbees, fall asleep studying for finals, hold yoga sessions, and look longingly at one another—just like every college campus with such a space in the country.

The Hay's Lovecraft collection contains almost six thousand pieces of material. It contains vast portions of his correspondence and more than a few quotidian items, down to the minutiae of electric bills. The massive pile of artifacts, correspondence, and monographs even includes the papers of his wife Sonia Greene and her second husband, eight boxes of material that held some surprising insights both into her life and the man she chose to marry after Lovecraft—an incredibly energetic and idealistic personality almost as different from Sonia's first husband as could possibly be imagined.

Lovecraft, despite some modest embarrassment, would take enormous pleasure in having his life's work preserved and cared for in this way, in a center of both scholarly and popular attention. In the spring of 2015 the archivist Christopher Geissler busily prepared the Hay for an exhibition that would coincide with that year's NecronomiCon, a gathering of Lovecraft fandom that's been meeting on and off in Providence for decades.

Lovecraft could never escape place, the America he dreamed even as it changed around him and motorcars invaded the somnolence of College Hill. His romance with Providence, and with New England, began to shape his fiction, Americanizing and historicizing his horror by bringing it close to home. In the early 1920s, Lovecraft's fiction began to move away from nameless cities to locales he named, clarified, and brought to unnatural life. By 1922, he had begun to use New England, the terrain he knew and fetishized, as the portal of horror. Edmund Wilson, doyen of American literary critics, would later mock him for this, writing that "outlandish gods . . . are always playing tricks with time and space and breaking through into the contemporary world, usually somewhere in Massachusetts."[29]

I don't mean to suggest a clean, bright line between Lovecraft's dream quests and his new emphasis on place. Instead, we begin to see his fiction maturing as his grasp of the world beyond Providence grew. Dreams of an apocalyptic intensity continued to play a role in his work till the end of his life. Increasingly, however, fantasy landscapes, tinted with darkness, tend to invade the world of the everyday in ways that are deeply disconcerting. One feels some of Lovecraft's own horror at life that this should be so.

His mind ventured outside of New England during this period and he tried writing of other places and times. His obsession with World War I showed itself once again in "The Temple," one of his deservedly lesser-known tales composed in the summer of 1920. Lovecraft comes up with a remarkable conception for the very short story, a crew of a German U-boat slowly driven to madness by some of the Deep Things hinted at in his 1917 "Dagon." The work fails in its execution and the uncertain, frazzled ending doesn't have the mysterious thrill found in his usual tendency toward climactic ambiguity.

However, in the winter of the same year, Lovecraft composed his first story set in the fictional Miskatonic River Valley, a tale well worth reading by anyone new to Lovecraft. "The Picture in the House" reveals the thirty-year-old beginning to work out all the possibilities of a New England gothic, how his own beloved landscape could become a landscape of horror.

"Searchers after horror," the story begins "haunt strange, far places." Such a sentence may have been hard to write for someone who would have little opportunity to see "strange, far places" outside of his dreams. There are, however, compensations, Lovecraft insists, since "the true epicure in the terrible . . . esteems most of all the ancient lonely farmhouses of backwoods New England. . . ." In such places, he assures us, we can find the "perfection of the hideous."

A traveller seeking shelter finds the "perfection of the hideous" in one such isolated cabin as he, like Lovecraft had often done, bicycled a lonely New England road in the bleak cold of the aging year. He took a path that snaked to Arkham, the first mention in Lovecraft's fiction of his favorite gateway of terror. As the shadows lengthen, he sees "an antique and repellent wooden building which blinked with bleared windows from between two huge, leafless elms." Although an unpromising place to take refuge, the hour is late, the weather cold, and the traveller weary enough to brave what he calls "the suggestive and secretive door" of a dwelling he assumes abandoned.

He finds inside a collection of books, indeed books the traveller confesses that he's shocked are not kept safely in a library or a museum. One of the leatherbound volumes with fitted metal clasps turns out to be a rare seventeenth-century edition of travels in the Congo while another contains early modern engravings of some of the allegedly cannibalistic peoples whom explorers first met in Brazil.

Explaining more of the events of "The Picture in the House" would amount to providing spoilers even if Lovecraft himself telegraphed the ending fairly early in the story. As with many narratives, it's knowing how we get there that really makes a tale work—and here Lovecraft superbly creeps us out.

This is American Gothic. In later years, the "cabin in the woods" became a staple of the American horror film, from the lonely homestead that only briefly hides its secrets of butchery and blood in *The Texas Chain Saw Massacre* (1974) to that other abandoned cabin that holds within it terrible books and terrible things in the *Evil Dead* series of the eighties and its excellent, and somewhat more frightening, 2013 remake. As Lovecraft writes at the beginning of the tale, the "epicure in the terrible" seeks strange places but America has no medieval castles or ancient ruins. It has the lonely cabin, the place where settlers mad for God or gold or a bit of both tried to carve out a refuge in the howling wilderness. These places, sites of murder and death, became our haunted house.

Aside from bringing his monsters home to New England, "The Picture in the House" introduces another important Lovecraftian theme. Throughout his work, the idea of the "Terrible Book" whose contents open doors to worlds of horror, plays a crucial role in plotting and narrative. He had this idea in mind as early as 1919, when he came across a story idea that Hawthorne had considered about a magical text that everyone fears to read.

The books his wandering traveller finds in "The Picture in the House" are actual historical works that suggest, rather than open doors for, otherworldly horror. The idea of magical tomes, the very reading of which can drive one to madness, became central to his mythology and even later to the mythologies we've made about him.

In 1922, his short story "The Hound" contains the first mention of "the forbidden *Necronomicon* of the Mad Arab Abdul Alhazred," the only really notable thing about that tale other than that it's the first of his work to appear in *Weird Tales* and the story most lampooned by critics of his style. The *Necronomicon* itself appeared again and again in his work, often as a crucial plot point.

"The Picture in the House" also reveals Lovecraft's complicated interest in Freud. Freudian concepts certainly enabled him to construct his theory that, as "The Picture in the House" puts it, Puritanism forced human instincts "to concealment above all else." It's not clear when he first read Freud. In mid-1921, he did assure an acquaintance in amateur journalism that "Dr. Sigmund Freud of Vienna, whose system of psycho-analysis I have begun to investigate, will prove the end of idealistic thought."

Lovecraft later agreed with Freud's argument in *Civilization and Its Discontents* that repression of instincts actually made civilization possible, preventing social relations from degenerating into a war of all against all. But he also believed, with Freud, that an excessive repression of the erotic could have dire consequences. He argued, as late as the 1930s—when it seems his reading in Freud had progressed from slight perusal to more serious engagement—that the "night-black Massachusetts legendary" and "macabre kick" of many of the tales, true and false, in New England grew directly from the "group neuroticism" of the Puritans. He made this claim in a letter to Robert E. Howard where, not surprisingly, he suggested that Howard read "The Picture in the House" for a fuller explanation of the point.

Lovecraft probably found in Freud ammunition in the unremitting war he waged against religion. Moreover, for someone given to powerful and highly affective dreams, Freud would have proven of natural interest. Freud's exploration of sexuality, on the other hand, Lovecraft could not have cared less about. Or so he claimed, whenever he had the opportunity.

Moreover, he sometimes contradicted his own interest in the new ideas coming out of Vienna. As he so often did, he chose to reject any idea that took the modern temper of the twenties by storm. This is perhaps why he damned Freud, or perhaps more specifically "Freudianism," to some of his correspondents even while he recommended him to others. Freud would have been fascinated with this profound inner conflict and undoubtedly would have delighted to write a case study of the peculiar young man of Providence.

However, unlike some commentators on Lovecraft, he never would have attempted an analysis of such a subject. In 1928, in an essay on Dostoyevsky, Freud admitted that when contending with writers and artists, "psychoanalysis must lay down its arms."

———

In the early fall of 1919, Lovecraft had written to Reinhardt Kleiner about the latter's impending marriage. At age twenty-nine, he confessed himself "unfamiliar with amatory phenomena save through cursory reading." We can only assume he means his early reading in medical encyclopedias or the romantic story lines he so heartily disliked in pulp magazines. He probably means both and, characteristically, he dismisses the rather large province of human desire and yearning with sarcasm. "I always assumed," he sniffed, "that one waited till he encountered some nymph, who seemed radically different to him from the rest of her sex, and without whom he felt he could no longer exist."

It's plain from his tone that he considers such matters beneath him and he quickly breaks off the discussion of matters romantic and erotic in favor of a discussion of his love of reading the epistolary output of eighteenth-century British authors and a list of his favorite Romans.

Clearly he did not wish to speak, just as he never really wrote directly, about "amatory phenomena." Other things stirred his imagination in the dark. In December of 1920, Lovecraft reported to Kleiner that he had written the first paragraph of a tale while still asleep, a believable oddment given his tendency to walk during liminal states of sleeping and waking in hopes of conjuring monstrous fictions. The story that he began in an altered state of consciousness, "Nyarlathotep," will likely join "Hypnos" as a new favorite among the next generation of Lovecraft fans. It in fact reads like a dream, a terrible dream of a world not unlike the one conjured by W.H. Auden in his "Shield of Achilles" (1955), a poem I've always thought would have given Lovecraft a more thoughtful appreciation of modernism and its fruits than he admitted in his lifetime.

"Nyarlathotep," which Lovecraft called a prose poem, reads today like the darker ponderings of the Beats, a frightening tale of a nameless place that might float to the top of some of William Burroughs's troubled waters of prose delirium. It imagines a world burdened by "a strange and brooding apprehension" where "out of the abysses between the stars swept chill currents that made men shiver in dark and lonely places."

This apocalyptic landscape Lovecraft immerses us in feels like all the dark desert places and cities in ruins that became the most common language for various prophets of doom on the political left and right for the post–World War I era. Eliot had his waste lands and his chambers of the sea where human voices wake us to drown, Oswald Spengler his ruins of value and meaning, and Freud his gothic tales of unleashed Ids tortured by sadistic super-egos in a world of suffering between the poles of sex and death. Lovecraft went to nameless cities and explored the fever dream territory where human experience collapses into the infinite spaces between what we cling to as reality and what we dread might be our true situation.

". . . Everyone felt that the world and perhaps the universe had passed from the control of known gods or forces to that of gods and forces that were unknown." Into this shadowy terrorscape comes Nyarlathotep out of Egypt, Pharaonic and "swarthy, slender, sinister." He's a sideshow barker for the darkest of carnivals, existential con man, antichrist in a universe with no Christ, a daimonic Nikola Tesla and Freud mash-up using "electricity and psychology" and giving "exhibitions of power which sent his spectators away speechless." All must see him, and in his dream state Lovecraft imagines the gathered multitudes of the sad and terrified world waiting to gaze upon Nyarlathotep, and yet they shudder to even speak his name.

The closest this nightmare comes to a clear narrative has the unnamed protagonist going to see this travelling show of horror when it comes to his unnamed city, "the old, the terrible city of unnumbered crimes." The narrator rejects the prophecies of horror he sees in the performance, a phantasmagoria part magic lantern show and part evangelical revival. This brief nod to linear narrative quickly descends into a tone poem in black, the universe imagined as a giant dead thing, Nyarlathotep becoming a wave of horror echoing across "this revolting graveyard of the universe" with "the muffled, maddening beating of drums and thin, monotonous whine of blasphemous flutes from inconceivable, unlighted chambers beyond time."

It's a story that makes you think of nothing so much as Edvard Munch. His 1893 "The Scream" conveyed the same sense of time collapsing on itself, a moment of horror so complete that it engulfed even the expression of it. Do we know the gender of the voice that screams in Munch? No, and it does not matter because it's the universal terror at the "maddening beat of drums," a moment on a bridge over a swirling abyss while above slants a red blur of scar tissue for sky. It's a new time and space and quality of human experience in which nothing can be saved or embraced or regarded. Munch, and Lovecraft the alleged antimodernist, gave us the modern moment in which the very conditions of mortality and experience are called into question and we hear the maddening drums. We can only cover our ears and scream.

A painterly element of Surrealist nightmare emerges throughout Lovecraft's work, an effort to create images that pull the viewer into an aesthetic atmosphere. This can be tough going in this age of putting a book down to read email or send a text or—worst-case scenario—send a text of oneself reading a book rather than reading a book. Lovecraft, as with every serious writer, demands a great deal more devotion than that. The longest of his works, short novels, can present special trials to contemporary readers used to interior monologues and conversational dialogues that pop novelists tend to use as exposition, getting you on your way through the story that will bring itself together, probably pretty dramatically, in a set piece confrontation of desires, worldviews, bodies, or manners.

Lovecraft ignored what he considered the trivialities of human conversation. Instead, he spent thousands of words on landscapes, either literal geographical landscapes or landscapes of time and experience. He could not care less for his characters and, for the most part, he didn't wish us to care either. They wander through his fictionalized New England, and dimensions of time and space, mostly becoming victims of forces they have unleashed or that have unleashed upon them.

Readers of weird fiction in the twenties and thirties didn't always find in Lovecraft the cracking good tale they found in his colleagues. Most other writers for *Weird Tales* simply took the conventions of the realist novel and placed the action in a haunted house or outer space. Lovecraft refused to write fiction where chains clanked or horror shaded off into space opera. He once wrote to a young August Derleth of the value of "precise rhythms and moods" that freed the writer from "the dragging responsibility of a plot." Exposition, to the degree it comes at all, drips like water torture on the reader's minds as slowly and horribly Lovecraft pulls us—both characters and readers—toward our inescapable fate.

New to amateur journalism and to Lovecraft's peculiar and original voice, Sonia Haft Greene really did not know what to make of "Nyarlathotep" and others of his earlier dark dreams. The summer after he finished the short piece and it appeared in an amateur journal (that Lovecraft himself edited at the time), he wrote to Kleiner that he "heard from Mrs. Greene" who "spoke of reading 'Nyarlathotep' and 'Polaris,' but confessed that both were incomprehensible to her mind." He tosses into this rumination a casually racist remark that her inability to grasp what he hoped to accomplish with the tales stemmed from the fact that "Teutonic mysticism is too subtle for Slavs."

He did add that, however, "Mrs. G. has an acute, receptive, and well-stored mind." He would soon be frequently dropping her name in his correspondence. In fact, his next letter to Kleiner praised her for a donation to the UAPA, adding that "she has a mind of singular scope and activity, and an exceptional background of Continental cultivation. . . ."

In Lovecraft's inability to talk about "amatory phenomena," comments such as this counted as being smitten.

They met in July of 1921. In that summer, Lovecraft attended the two-day convention of the National Amateur Press Association in Boston. Six weeks after his mother's death, he had begun to exhibit a bit of the wanderlust that characterized him the rest of his life. He appeared driven by a desire to find marks of the past, and see what we would call today historical sites. He would find this desire frequently frustrated by lack of funds. In the summer of '21, however, he made only the smallest concession to getting away from Angell Street. Boston is only about a half-hour train ride from Providence.

Sonia Haft Shafirkin had been born in a small village near Kiev in the czars' troubled Russia of 1883. Her father died sometime in the late 1880s. Sonia and her mother immigrated to Liverpool, England sometime around 1890. Ukraine had, and unfortunately continues to have, a well-earned reputation for an ugly and brutal form of anti-Semitism. A Jewish family had every reason to leave if at all possible. At some unknown date, Sonia's maternal uncle made his way to England. Sonia lived with him in Liverpool until 1892 while her mother went on to America.

Racille Haft, Sonia's mother, exhibited the extraordinarily independent streak that her daughter later showed again and again. She came to America alone though how she supported herself before, and indeed after her marriage to a "Solomon H——" (we actually don't know his full last name) in 1892 remains unclear. She brought Sonia, now nine years old, to the States.

Almost certainly for financial reasons and likely under her mother's direction, Sonia married the twenty-six-year-old Russian émigré Samuel Seckendorff in 1899 just as she turned sixteen. The marriage appears to have been an utter misery. They had a son almost immediately, who died at three months. In 1902, Sonia gave birth to her daughter Florence, with whom she later had a complete falling out. Samuel, who had changed his patronymic to Greene, apparently had a penchant for explosive rage and suffered severe depression, killing himself in 1916. In later years, she strongly hinted that he'd been physically abusive.

Sonia, despite brutal personal circumstances, always kept a lively intellectual curiosity she nurtured by following cutting-edge currents in continental philosophy and literature. Some of her earliest correspondence with Lovecraft concerned the work of Nietzsche, a still somewhat obscure taste at the time. She took extension courses at Columbia University and blossomed under some of the opportunities that New York City began to offer women in the 1920s. She worked in a managerial position for Ferle Heller's Boutique, what she called "a fashionable women's wear establishment on Fifth Avenue" (although, its location actually was just off Fifth Avenue). We know she secured her financial independence rather quickly after becoming a widow and managed to rent in what the early 1910s had the reputation of being a rather toney section of Flatbush in Brooklyn.

How did such an unlikely pair as Lovecraft and Greene become as enthralled with one another as I believe they did? The attraction does seem entirely mutual almost from the moment they met, despite the tendency of some biographers to view Greene as the hunter and Lovecraft the prey.

She did take some initiative, coming to Providence in September 1921 for a short visit to Lovecraft and his aunt Lillian. Lovecraft wrote to Kleiner of the visit in throwaway fashion. He calls her "the volatile and beneficent personage" and suggests she appeared more or less uninvited but also shows obvious delight in squiring her around what was apparently then the "cloistral hush of the Brown University campus" and, having shown her the best of College Hill, also let her experience what he describes as a "sensation of anticlimax" that attended a descent from the old hill and a sudden immersion in "the garishly modern." He added, in a comment likely to resonate with modern visitors to the city, that "The soul of Providence broods upon the antique hill . . . below there is only a third rate copy of New York." Or perhaps this is the feeling of the Lovecraft fan, myself in this case, unable to escape certain aspects of his prose when they regulate even an aesthetic response to the scenes he knew, lived, loved, hated, and turned into a finely tuned theremin of horror.

She led him to experience just a bit of the "garishly modern." Although Lovecraft had almost no experience dining out during his first thirty years, Sonia somehow persuaded both him and his aunts to leave College Hill and have lunch at the Biltmore Hotel. Certainly more respectable in the daytime than at night, the hotel's reputation as a favorite place for Providence to violate Prohibition must have been known to Lovecraft. Perhaps Aunt Annie and Aunt Lillian first developed their animus toward Greene on these outings, even as they dined out on her funds.

Sonia Greene probably represented the strangest and most interesting person Howard Lovecraft had ever met, a fact that goes a long way toward explaining his intense attraction to her. Most Lovecraft scholars would sacrifice a body part, at least one, in order to have the magnum opus of a correspondence the duet created between 1921 and the early thirties, the time of their complete separation from one another. They only lived together in something like a traditional relationship for part of two years but a library of letters crossed in the mail between them before and after that time. She seems to have been the only person that he, at one point, wrote to on a daily basis. At least a smattering of correspondence seems to have occurred even after she moved to California in the early thirties, correspondence stuttering and then finally ending a few years before his death.

But at the beginning, in 1921, and over the next three years, the two would engage in a strange, long, and certainly for Sonia, confusing sort of courtship. Lovecraft only let slip his feelings in his very occasional, although fulsome, praise of her in his correspondence.

Shocking everyone who knew him, the two suddenly married in

1924 and Lovecraft changed his world forever. His disaster of a marriage inaugurated the years that brought his work to maturity, years that made him fully into a dream-quester and monster-maker. This sometimes brutal process wrangled his mind, exuded a kind of psychic poison, ruined his relationship with Sonia, and helped raise Something that lay dead but dreaming in the ancient monoliths beneath the sea, a place that, whether he liked it or not, differed little from T.S. Eliot's dark chambers where even human voices make a noise of strangled horror.

The question of Lovecraft's sexuality, an uncomfortable one for many biographers, can't be ignored when describing his marriage to Sonia. Scholarship on Lovecraft has defended his heterosexual inclinations with vigor and, just as urgently, insisted that sex had very little meaning for him. In many descriptions of him by contemporaries, defenders, and apologists, he becomes ephemeral as a sexual being, abstracted from the desires that drive us, consciously or not, through much more of our lives than we'd like to believe.

Sonia Greene made opaque, in fact absurdly and almost satirically ambiguous, comments about this very private matter—private at least to her as his ex-wife if not to anyone who wants to make sense of the man and his work in historical context. Greene gives little away even as she provides a series of anecdotal remembrances written by someone still clearly in love with a strange man who had passed, wraith-like, in and out of her life.

She wrote a very sympathetic and kind description of their marriage in the late 1940s, almost ten years after Lovecraft's death and more than twenty years after they had lived under the same roof. The account she wrote, entitled "Howard Phillips Lovecraft as His Wife Remembers Him," appeared in the *Providence Sunday Journal* on August 22, 1948, a fact that would have horrified its subject. It comes framed with an introduction by Winfield T. Scott, that journalist and poet of extraordinarily limited gifts who saw a chance in the 1940s to gain some attention with the revival of interest in Lovecraft as a person and a writer. Scott calls Lovecraft's work "precarious and little known" and gives August Derleth, and himself, enormous credit for helping to resurrect this person of dubious worth to the larger world.

Frank Belknap Long, probably out of his own desire to seize an opportunity for his dear dead friend's fame to spread, put Scott in touch with Greene in late 1946. Scott used her written account while admitting that what he included in the newspaper accounted for "rather about half of what she put down." In other words, the article represents Scott's account of the marriage and not Sonia's.

Sonia, in this expurgated account, does say that she believed "he [Lovecraft] loved me as much as it was possible for a temperament like his to love." In describing his temperament, she does not allude directly to asexuality or homosexuality but, in context, to a general coldness. He apparently never actually told Sonia he loved her. "My dear, you don't know how much I appreciate you" seems to be as close as he ever came.

She expounded on these heavily edited comments in conversation and discussion with August Derleth. She called Lovecraft "an adequately excellent lover" obviously a bizarre and inexplicable collision of modifier and adjective that could only be used by someone who wanted to say little meaningful on the subject. De Camp had an exchange with Derleth in which he claims (and it's important to note that this is third-hand gossip) that Sonia told him that "Howard was entirely adequate sexually" but seemed not to care for such things.[30]

These shadowy comments do not allow me to assert that H.P. Lovecraft was a deeply closeted gay man or, as some have suggested in dated Freud-speak, "a latent homosexual." However, his sexual identity had plasticity to it, not at all unusual in any era and especially common in his own period, when sexual identity passed through a massive reorganization and reimagination in the first stirrings of the sexual revolution in the 1920s.

The 1960s are often seen as the beginnings of the sexual revolution, and it's true that in that era large segments of American society connected their sexuality to politics for the first time. However, most historians today insist the sexual revolution really began in the 1920s with the

1950s being a bit of a stutter step in an ongoing phenomenon. As early as 1916, women and men on the cultural left agitated for the legalization of birth control while "the rebel girl," a term as common as "flapper," insisted on her sexual freedom and autonomy as loudly as her counterparts in the 1960s.

Gay life, meanwhile, flourished in America's larger cities. New York City had a thriving gay subculture that emphasized flexibility in male sexual identities. In fact, the terminology of sexual desire by 1930 may have been even more complex than it has become today. George Chauncey, the leading scholar of this topic, has said that this "was not a world in which men were divided into homosexuals and heterosexuals." Terms such as queer, fairy, faggot, and flaming faggot, used as collective derogatory terms in the straight world, represented a veritable taxonomy of specific desires and self-representation for New York's vibrant gay community.[31]

I am not making the claim that any of these terms applied to Lovecraft's amorphous sexual identity. What's much more engrossing than such claims to me have been the efforts of various biographers and interpreters to ignore this interesting element of both his personality and the historical context in which their subject lived. De Camp, in 1975, wrote of "homosexuality" as an abnormal state and noted, without giving any specifics, that "Some writers have called him 'sexless'" and that "others have surmised he might have been a homosexual or at least a latent one." De Camp assures readers that such ideas can be "safely ignored," as if the possibility that we suffer from a terminal disease has been raised and then quieted so we can go about our day.

Joshi, writing much more recently, also accepts sexuality as a rather simple binary—you're either gay or not—rather than seeing sex as one of the most complicated aspects of the human personality, shaped in part by history and cultural change. In writing about the possibility of what he calls "gender confusion" in Lovecraft's early life, he simply notes that Lovecraft "displayed quick, unwavering prejudice against homosexuals." He sees this as definitive evidence that Lovecraft could not possibly have been gay. Moreover, Joshi insists that Lovecraft had a "sluggish" sexuality, a construction of his experience that, frankly, we have even less evidence for than his possible interest in men as romantic partners.[32]

Lovecraft did show entirely homosocial, if not homoerotic, tendencies in building his relationships. In fact, his attraction seemed specifically to very young men. Alfred Galpin, Frank Belknap Long, Robert Bloch, and, most significantly, Robert Barlow, all attracted his intense attention, devotion, and passion. He saw them as protégés and dear friends and clearly tried to defuse any sexual connotations that could be attached to these relationships by referring to them in correspondence, ad nauseum, as "my son" or "my grandson" or even affectionate titles like "Child" or "my little boy." Both Alfred Galpin and Robert Barlow were young teenagers when he began his voluminous correspondence with them. Barlow became perhaps the most important person in his life in his final years and he made months-long trips to Florida to visit the teenager in the 1930s.

I don't believe, by which I really mean I don't know, that Lovecraft's relationships with these young men proceeded to sexual activity. No such assertion can be made even in the suspicious case of Barlow. Lovecraft spent enormous amounts of time with Barlow who, later in life, had numerous affairs with young Mexican men, including his students, while holding a professorship in Mexico City. Barlow later committed suicide when one of his young male partners threatened to out him and destroy his career.

Why would we be shocked, and what exactly does it do to the image of Lovecraft or the meaning of his work, if we learned that he had a sexual experience of some sort with one or more of his male friends?

Anxiety about pedophilia, of course, lurks like a night gaunt in the shadows. This concept, and the terror it invokes, did not become current in American culture until the 1970s. Some might see this as presenting Lovecraft as a predatory homosexual. But that idea of the older, dangerous queen, a notion literally invented by conservative interests in post–World War II America, warrants no meaningful discussion. His relationship with men like Galpin and Barlow had intensity and a depth that cannot be encompassed by such culture-bound constructions. We might as well call Plato a pedophile.

No direct historical evidence has come to light about the nature of Lovecraft's sexual identity. But his life and fiction point to a period in American history that produced vastly original ways of talking about sexuality. Freudian readings of fiction often run aground on the premise that Freud's view of the world tells us something fundamental about human nature. In fact, his influence pushed writers and artists to take what we can only call the Freudian Mythos as a touchstone for their work. Surrealism did this very self-consciously. Other kinds of artists, Lovecraft included, may have worried around the edges of Freudianism in a less self-aware manner. Stephen King once noted, in a comment similar to Alan Moore's observation of Lovecraft's work, that when we consider "psychoanalysis as it existed in HPL's time" in relation to the author's slurping, sucking genitalia monsters "we're in a Freudian three-ring circus."

Lovecraft came to New York to marry and begin a life with Sonia in 1924. He gave up on all that in two years, really much less.

He seemed excited, delighted, embarrassed, nervous, and horrified all at once by his decision to essentially elope with Sonia, to marry without even telling his solicitous aunts, to move to New York.

Writing to Morton on March 12, 1924 from his new address at 259 Parkside Avenue, Brooklyn, it took him a full five paragraphs to work up to telling of their marriage at Saint Paul's Chapel, which, he assiduously notes, had been built in 1766. He was, he said, "eager to put Colonial architecture to all its possible uses."

He wrote an even stranger letter to his Aunt Lillian, taking twelve paragraphs to describe what's presented as simply a decision to move to New York City. He used up pages of spidery handwriting to explain his dislike of explaining things. He told her that New York would "electrify" him. He noted, bizarrely, that he had after all considered suicide as another possible option other than marriage or, as he put it, his "ancient plan of shuffling off to a Swan Point [cemetery] subterranean repose."

Finally this:

> *So epochal and stupefying as it sounds (pray don't faint or I shall feel that all the preceding paragraphs of artistic preamble have gone for naught!) the unbelievable is a reality. Old Theobald is a householder at last, and (hold in readiness the smelling salts) a bona-fide partner with that most inspiring, congenial, tasteful intelligent, solicitous and devoted of mortals and co-workers. S.H.G. in the venerable and truly classical institution of Holy Matrimony!*
> *(RECESS FOR RECOVERY OF POISE)*

The same letter announced to Lillian that she would come to "live permanently" in the city, and bring along his Aunt Annie. Neither had any intention of doing so.

Why did he do it? Some, notably Michel Houellebecq, have urged us to simply see him as being in love. I don't doubt this. But simple truths hide complex motivations, even if they are no less true for it.

He felt stultified. He makes this plain in his letter to Lillian, an incredibly honest one for all its meandering. He admitted to a "blind clinging to the hibernatory past" and saw in New York, and Sonia, "the magic spur of external inducement to active life and effective toil."

He did love Sonia. He also loved the narrative she gave him. The hibernating old young man who played at being a grandfather suddenly transformed into the published writer with a world of opportunities. A break with a past that for him held so many horrors: shame for his father; a conflicted and intense relationship with his mother now four years dead in Swan Point Cemetery; failures and regrets and never achieving what he'd been told, and had told himself, he could achieve. Suddenly, all of that became the past and the man who wrote horror stories about history crawling its way out of infinite abysses to gnaw at the present suddenly came to believe he could escape it all. Lovecraft, so stubborn in his assertions about the meaninglessness of human striving, succumbed to the illusion of meaning embodied in his attractive, brilliant, and adoring friend.

In 1921, he had confessed to Galpin that he found himself "unable to extract sufficient pleasure to make consciousness preferable to oblivion" while also asserting that his own lack of interest in life made perfect sense when "The cosmos is a blind vortex; a seething ocean of blind forces. . . ." But by 1924, his own life seemed to be falling into a happy pattern, personal circumstances that, it has to be noted, in no way changed his philosophical outlook. Still, he had in *Weird Tales* found a home for some of his early fiction, including "Dagon," "The Picture in the House," "The Hound," "The Rats in the Walls," and "Facts Concerning the Late Arthur Jermyn and his Family."

Opportunities came to him in a flurry when he moved to New York. In February *Weird Tales* requested that he ghostwrite a tale for Harry Houdini, who by 1924 had become one of the most famous living entertainers. Houdini had entered into a collaboration with the magazine, struggling financially at this time, that both found beneficial. J.C. Henneberger, the owner of *Weird Tales*, hoped that the name of the world-famous magician would pull in more readers. Houdini wrote columns for the magazine entitled "Ask Houdini," as well as contributing tales ghostwritten by various pulp writers.

Although some Houdini biographers describe the master of illusion as having "collaborated" with Lovecraft on the 1924 story, the truth is that Lovecraft wrote the entire piece based very loosely on Houdini's absurd claim that he'd been kidnapped by Arabs and imprisoned in a shaft known as "Campbell's Tomb" during a 1910 trip to Egypt. Lovecraft knew this to be a fabrication. In fact, we know today that while Houdini had been in Port Said in January of 1910, he may have stayed for less than a day before sailing through the Suez Canal on his way to Australia, where he arrived by the end of the month.

Lovecraft banged out the story rather quickly but lost the typescript.

He and Sonia passed their honeymoon retyping it. Despite a rushed deadline and the necessity of preparing the typescript twice, Lovecraft still managed to fill the story with enough about Port Said, Egyptian history, and topographical detail that it reads like a firsthand travelogue. He also took Houdini's fictional adventure and transformed it into his own vision of cosmic horror, of Ancient Ones older than the gods of Egypt led by "an unknown God of the Dead which licks its colossal chops in the unsuspected abyss, fed morsels by the soulless absurdities that should not exist."

"I know it was only a dream," says "Houdini" at the end of the tale. Of course, "it was all just a dream" has become a kind of metonym for bad storytelling but Lovecraft apparently felt compelled to include it since it allegedly represented the experience of the actual Harry Houdini, at that time embroiled in his war with spiritualism and other manifestations of belief in psychic powers and the occult. At the same time, it's worth remembering that only a porous wall exists between dream and reality in Lovecraft's tales, with some of his best driven by dreams, or occurring in dreamlands, that are all too terrifyingly real.

Lovecraft had evocatively entitled the story "Under the Pyramids," a title that the editor of *Weird Tales*, to Lovecraft's chagrin, changed to the more sensationalistic "Imprisoned with the Pharaohs." It appeared only a few months after his marriage to Sonia in the early summer issue of *Weird Tales*. Houdini pronounced himself pleased with it and invited Lovecraft to visit him at his New York apartment. The pair discussed a future "collaboration" on a nonfiction work that would seek to explode what both men considered the dangerous myths of mediums, séances, and psychic prophecy. In the spring of 2016, as I completed this book, about thirty pages of this proposed manuscript tentatively titled "The Cancer of Superstition" surfaced. The manuscript had been in the possession of Beatrice Houdini and then passed, along with a bundle of papers never examined, to a magic shop. The papers are not yet available to scholars as I write and are expected to fetch upwards of thirty thousand dollars at auction.

Lovecraft's plans to secure employment in publishing never came to fruition. He interviewed and submitted some of his material to The Reading Lamp, a literary agency and a publishing concern to which Sonia provided him entrée. Nothing came of this except possibly a book review he wrote for their in-house magazine. Lovecraft would have to depend on Sonia's income, though this proved more than sufficient while she continued her work at Ferle Heller's. The two even looked into purchasing land in Brooklyn with the idea of building a house of their own and presumably having Aunt Annie and Aunt Lillian come and live with them. What would likely have been an intensely uncomfortable situation was never to be.

Lovecraft wrote very little during his time in New York City. At first, his evident pleasure in being married, his circle of friends, and his early, surprising delight in the city itself account for the sudden drying up of his prose. He had found a life away from his writing desk. Soon, he would begin to write his Brooklyn and Greenwich tales—fascinating, sometimes brilliant, and just as often bitterly rendered fictions that end up entangled hopelessly in their author's rage and prejudice.

Lovecraft and Sonia seemed well matched at first. By her own account, she enjoyed making sure he ate regularly and dressed better. He appeared to fully embrace married life and provided her with the intellectual companionship that she craved. When they married, her income amounted to several times that of the average American family in 1924, so Lovecraft could play the gentleman of arts and leisure with no financial anxieties.

They sometimes seemed happy. Lovecraft seemed delighted with a visit they took together to Philadelphia. Sonia looked up to him to such a degree that they took "Socrates and Xanthippe" as nicknames for one another. In the early months, and really throughout their acquaintance, he's unfailing in his praise of her, even if it sometimes sounds as if he's speaking of a particularly bosom friend rather than someone with whom he's passionately in love. But who's to say that such feelings are really superior to what Lovecraft felt for Sonia? I find it impressive that he went as far as he did in expressing such affection for her, especially given how almost impossible the whole situation seems to have been for him.

A very intriguing, and never before discussed, memory of Sonia's suggests that the couple's private life had a more salacious element than we might think. In the Davis papers at the Hay, I came across one page of typescript in a stray document, in which she recalls that Lovecraft never especially cared for most highbrow music but loved it when she "turned on the record 'Danse Macabre' and danced to the music."[33]

Sonia's remembrance, and she may well have just been describing her own experience, was that she "at first danced a slow cake walk, as I had seen it done, slowly lifting my legs." "The Cake Walk" had actually originated in African American dance, a kind of satirical version of the Southern elite's promenade. By the 1920s, the dance had a hint of the bawdier corners of vaudeville, the savor of the sweaty dance hall.

Her pace increased with the changing tempo of the music. "At the end of my music and my dance, H.P.L. was enchanted."

Despite the sensual tone of Sonia's account, we'd do well to remember that "Danse Macabre" by Saint-Saëns essentially narrates a French folktale of corpses awakening to dance maniacally for their necromancer till dawn. Sonia herself notes that she calculated her movements to the narrative's pacing, the tales of corpses as "they came from their graves and started dancing" until driven back into their tombs by dawn.

Lovecraft's enchantment with her performance and the music itself fits with his fiction's tendency to employ dissonant sound as the acoustics of a malign universe. His terrifying mythology features Azathoth, one of the most powerful of the Great Old Ones who sits like "a demon sultan" amidst sounds of horrifying dissonance no human being could hear and keep their sanity. In "The Music of Erich Zann" (1921), often recognized as one of his best and most idiosyncratic tales, sounds can open portals to other terrible worlds—"a chaotic babel of sound . . . a pandemonium" that shakes the sanity of the narrator. Undoubtedly Lovecraft did find himself enchanted by "Danse Macabre" and Sonia's interpretation of it. But he also found himself weirdly enthralled by music played by a Syrian neighbor when he moved to his small apartment on Brooklyn's Clinton Street. The neighbor "played eldritch and whining monotones on a strange bagpipe which made me dream ghoulish and incredible things of crypts under Bagdad. . . . ." As if he needed help with his eldritch dreams.[34]

Sex, or rather its lack, certainly poisoned Howard and Sonia's connection to one another. Although boon companions of the intellect, it's plain from Sonia's strange references to sexuality that he barely expressed physical or even verbal affection. During their courtship, Lovecraft had shown so much enthusiasm for an outline of a horror tale she'd written that she felt bold enough to kiss him. She watched him "turn pale" and he admitted to her that "he had not been kissed since he was a very small child."

Lovecraft also slowly pulled away from her as he found male intellectual companionship that he clearly preferred to his wife's. By August of 1924, six months into his marriage, Lovecraft had begun to spend at least one evening a week with a group of literary raconteurs that included his correspondent friends Kleiner, Belknap Long, Morton, and, something of an oddity in the group, an elderly writer of boys' tales of adventure named Edgar McNeil. By the early fall, Samuel Loveman had moved from Cleveland and joined the group, along with another bookseller, George Kirk. Arthur Leeds, a former carnival worker turned writer for *Reader's Digest*, became a regular.

Soon, the men spent an enormous amount of their waking hours with one another. Most of the group, including Lovecraft, visited with Hart Crane in his Columbia Heights apartment, around the time Crane worked on his homoerotic poetry collection *Voyages*—inspired by his tormented love affair with merchant marine Emil Opffer. Lovecraft found Crane "despite his limitations . . . a thorough aesthete" and commented on how much he enjoyed his conversation and his "choice collection of modern books and some splendid small objets d'art." Oddly, the very same missive referred to Crane as an "egotistical young aesthete who has an unfortunate predilection for the wine when it is red." All indications are that Crane found Lovecraft a bit of a bore.[35]

They called themselves "The Kalem Club." "The gang," as they also referred to one another, took the name Kalem since "K," "L," or "M" appeared as the lead letter in the surname of each. Soon, their regular weekly gathering spilled over into many more evenings of book-buying expeditions and, under Lovecraft's guidance, seeking out colonial architecture or architectural points of interest around the city combined with discussion of all matters political, historical, philosophical, and literary. Lovecraft, and to a lesser degree James Morton, provided the group with its intellectual leadership.

Lovecraft blossomed in these friendships. He loved spending his time with Belknap Long, referred to by George Kirk as Lovecraft's protégé. Long affected an attempt at a moustache that he thought made him look like Poe, a bit of lip hair affectionately maligned by the other Kalems. Lovecraft and Morton continued their political and literary ambuscades. Morton, who lived in Harlem because of his commitment to African American rights, produced pamphlets during these years against racism and economic exploitation that Lovecraft found hopelessly utopian but that made Morton an ideal sparring partner.

Along with their regular discussions at Kirk's bookshop in Chelsea, the group explored the wharves of Red Hook in the middle of the night, scoured a colonial Dutch cemetery in Flatbush where Lovecraft contemplated stealing a red slate tile tombstone, and even frequented a speakeasy called Dominick's in the then-Italian section of Greenwich Village where, according to Kleiner, Lovecraft never drank the "sour wine" but remarked with pleasure that Dominick's "was quite the sort of place which someone of his more rakish forebears among the English gentry might have frequented."[36]

The interaction with the Kalems pushed Lovecraft in new directions. Perhaps encouraged by Morton, Lovecraft went with Sonia in September to see Eugene O'Neill's controversial drama *All God's Chillun Got Wings*. In Lovecraft's own description, the play dealt with "the marriage of a low Irish girl to an educated negro." The play had been partially censored by the city administration and Lovecraft noted approvingly that the director read the deleted scene from the stage "interspersed with appropriately sarcastic remarks . . . reflecting on the intelligence of mayors and other annoyances." Lovecraft, against all odds, liked the O'Neill play and obviously disapproved of the effort to censor it. It's possible that he may have had a different reaction had the marriage at the center of the drama been between a woman of "pure" Anglo-Saxon ancestry and an African American man.[37]

Sonia accompanying Lovecraft on such an outing appears in his correspondence as an oddity during these months as the Kalems took up more and more of his time. George Kirk, in a series of letters to his then-fiancée, describes not only the weekly Thursday meetings but Sunday gatherings, both of which seem to have gone to all hours. In the meantime, he notes dinners with the group, walks with Lovecraft, and Lovecraft simply coming by to snooze over a book on his couch. Meanwhile, Kirk informed his fiancée that he hardly ever saw "Mrs. Lovecraft" and made frequent snappish remarks about her, suggesting that the group considered her something of a rival for Lovecraft's time.

In late 1924, a bit of a crisis occurred in the Lovecraft household, if that's the term for the arrangement Lovecraft had begun to force on his wife. A failed effort on Sonia's part to start her own millinery business put increased pressure on Lovecraft to find work. Sonia later described her horror that someone as gifted as she believed her husband to be made "only a pittance" for revising "the atrocious" work of other writers. *Weird Tales* brought in little money and he had not done much writing at all for most of the year.

So, he attempted to find a job and failed rather disastrously. He worked for less than a week for a credit collection agency attempting to sell the company's service to retailers. His separation from the agency appears to have fallen into the twilight region of tendering his resignation and getting sacked. He tried and failed to get a job testing lamps. One letter of application he wrote in this period begins with a sentence the prospective employer undoubtedly had no idea what to make of: "If an unprovoked application for employment seems somewhat unusual in these days of system, agencies and advertising, I trust that the circumstances surrounding this one may help to mitigate what would otherwise be obtrusive forwardness."

He did not receive an interview.

He appears, now and again in this period, to make a serious effort to find employment. There's also more than a little self-sabotage in these efforts, an unwillingness to give up on his ideal of living as a leisured man of letters. When James Morton became the director of a local museum in Paterson, New Jersey, he attempted to secure a position for Lovecraft, who never followed up on the opportunity. Samuel Loveman tried to find him work as a book cataloguer, and Lovecraft apparently ignored this possibility. Even Houdini offered to help and Lovecraft never meaningfully responded. He continued to find ways to make himself unemployable.

He, for example, wrote a series of commercial blurbs as a kind of application to become a staff writer for a household goods trade magazine. They were never printed. The advertising copy he produced, if it can be called that, offers a series of disquisitions on American colonial heritage and polemics on the superiority of eighteenth-century design compared to the failings of "our mechanical civilization." It almost appears as if he's writing a parody, the tale of a Georgian-era gentleman baffled by modernity, a Rhode Island Yankee in Henry Ford's court. He probably was.

Financial strains arguably added more to Sonia's psychological burdens than to his. Shadows had lengthened over Sonia's life in the years leading up to her marriage. Florence Greene, her now teenage daughter from her first, horrific marriage, fell in love with a half-uncle and wanted to marry him. Sonia refused and the two began a cold war in the household with Florence leaving when she reached legal maturity in March 1923. Mother and daughter barely exchanged words and did not speak at all after Florence left New York for good in 1927. Florence went on to have a fascinating career as a journalist in Europe, indeed becoming the first reporter to break the story of Edward VIII's romantic entanglement with the twice-divorced American Wallis Simpson and his proposal of marriage that created something of a political crisis in Britain.

Sonia believed that in Howard Lovecraft she had found solace for her difficult past. But money worries, and Lovecraft's habit of spending his time on nocturnal wanderings about New York with the Kalems, began to take a toll. In October 1924, she began having stomach disorders apparently rooted in anxiety. Financial strains, and her husband's increasing lack of interest in being a husband, probably induced the illness.

She was admitted to the hospital and then ordered by her doctors to take a six-week rest. Lovecraft visited her each day although he never allowed this to interfere with his demanding schedule of male intellectual camaraderie. On Sonia's second day in the hospital, he spent the evening with "Kleiner and Loveman downtown for a tour of the bookstalls." He also reported to Aunt Lillian in the same letter that, four days into Sonia's hospitalization, he attended a discussion with "the boys at [George] Kirk's" that broke up at 1:30 AM but was followed by all-night rambling that included "considerable astronomical speculations," a brief stop at a cafeteria at 5:00 AM followed by yet more architectural expeditions well into the autumn morning. When Sonia began her rest at a farm in Somerville, New Jersey, Lovecraft stayed with her one night before taking a train jaunt to Philadelphia in order to stare at all things colonial.

Sonia did not stay the full six weeks in Somerville and returned to Brooklyn with a pronouncement. She had taken a job, apparently with a department store, in the Midwest. The household at 259 Parkside would be broken up, including the sale of furniture (though Lovecraft jealously guarded his own family pieces). Lovecraft would take a studio apartment at 169 Clinton Street, a fairly shabby single room with two alcoves where he sat with his books and a modicum of family furnishings from long-lost 454 Angell. Sonia left for Cincinnati on December 31, 1924, and Lovecraft went to a New Year's gathering with "the gang."

Although presented as a move made for economic reasons, both Sonia and Howard likely found their marriage untenable. Lovecraft simply did not wish to be married and Sonia had no intention of playing second-string to her husband's nerd circle. The Kalems likely made their disdain for her clear in their limited interaction with her. They certainly did so in their later writings.

She returned to visit whenever possible. But in her absence, if not entirely because of her absence, he grew wretched. He began to lose weight on a meager diet of canned beans, canned spaghetti, and a few sweets. More bad news came from Cincinnati as Sonia's health deteriorated. In the late spring of 1925, someone burglarized Lovecraft's apartment and gave him "a sickening shock." He let his Aunt Lillian know, though not directly, that he wanted to return to Providence as one who "had sampled the world and found that its dearest jewel was the hearthstone he left behind."

New York continued to keep him from doing any meaningful writing, with one striking exception. In October of 1924, he quickly wrote a tale based on a house he'd seen in Elizabeth, New Jersey during his very brief visit with Sonia. He set the house, however, not in its original location or in his fictional Arkham. Providence's Benefit Street, once much-visited by a soon-to-die Poe courting Sarah Helen Whitman and haunting the St. John's burial ground, became the location of a house locals called "unlucky." The house proves more than unlucky for the tale's two protagonists who find a terrible, noxious thing waiting in the basement.

"The Shunned House" offers Lovecraft's peculiar and brilliant take on the notion of both the haunted house and the vampire. In his hands, both commonplaces of horror took on stomach-churning dimensions and new, terrible meanings he wrestled out of a combination of historical atmosphere, thick description of place and a conjuring of absolute cosmic dread. Like all his best work, it doesn't wriggle up our spines in a shudder, it worms into our brains. The dread it created did not hover over a specific place, but rather over all places.

Farnsworth Wright, a new editor at *Weird Tales*, turned down the story when Lovecraft finally got around to submitting it in September 1925. Wright would make a practice of turning down Lovecraft's best works and then, seemingly perversely, suddenly deciding he wanted to publish them after Lovecraft resubmitted them with absolutely no changes. Meanwhile, he almost without fail snapped up Lovecraft's poorest efforts. He then published everything of Lovecraft's he could get his hands on after the author's death in 1937 and *Weird Tales* readers wanted more.

While sinking further and further into a miasma of depression and anger, Lovecraft wrote three other tales in 1925 including "In the Vault," "He," and one of his better known works, "The Horror at Red Hook." The latter doesn't deserve the interest it's received and, soon after writing it, Lovecraft came to agree it had failed as a story, without being very clear even to himself why.

"The Horror at Red Hook" secretes bile so poisonous it's as if its author is a wounded creature cornered in a lair. Lovecraft does create in it one of his more intriguing characters in the Irish police detective Thomas F. Malone. But, having created a promising protagonist, he does nothing with him other than traumatize him by the horrors he finds after "plunging into the polyglot abyss of New York's underworld." The story's hapless villain Robert Suydam, "the lettered recluse of an ancient Dutch family," dabbles in forbidden rites and mixes with "unclassified slant-eyed folk" and a leader of mariners described as "an Arab with a hatefully negroid mouth." These events coincide with an epidemic of kidnapped children and the raising of an unearthly horror. In the tale, Lovecraft even takes aim at the Kurdish sect known as the Yazidi whose theological eccentricity leads him to call them "Persian devil-worshippers." The Yazidi became well known to the world in 2014 as a religious minority in Iraq and Syria particularly targeted by the Islamic State for torture and murder.

Three things had happened to Lovecraft that account for his increasing penchant for racializing horror. First, the complexities of being an anti-Semite married to a Jewish woman revealed themselves rather quickly. They reached their apogee as the relationship soured and died. Sonia wrote of this and even her typical reserve reveals the degree to which his racial antipathies affected their relationship. She notes that he referred "to Semitic peoples as beady eyed, rat-faced Asiatics" and bitterly insisted "all foreigners were mongrels." Sonia would remind him—and let's note how bizarre it is that she had to do so—"that I, too, am of Hebrew people." He occasionally backed away from his racist pathology, apparently in an effort to console a woman he did seem to care for. Sometimes he even insisted to Sonia that he had been, in his word, "cured" of his prejudices.

But he wasn't. "Soon after our marriage," Sonia remembered, "he told me that whenever we had company he would appreciate it if 'Aryans' were in the majority." She remembered that walks through "the racially-mixed" streets of New York often prompted him to frightening fits of rage in which "he almost seemed to lose his mind."

Second, Lovecraft's intellectual limitations, largely enforced on him by his lack of an early systematic education, hobbled his understanding of race. Lovecraft's autodidactic abilities had run aground in his enthusiasm for Margaret Murray's witch-cult thesis, the notion ignored by serious historians of a secret lineage of fertility cults that had survived almost into the modern era. Worse than his ready acceptance of its unlikely argument, he conjoined it with his own racism in a way that Murray's own problematic work did not encourage.

Murray, respected for her early work in Egyptology, developed a theory that Neolithic fertility rites survived into the Christian era, though driven underground by the persecution of the Church. After the political triumph of Christianity in the west in the fourth century CE, the secret fertility cult survived through the Middle Ages. The European witch hunts of the fifteenth through the seventeenth centuries represented a final effort to stamp out an actual surviving cult rather than an outbreak of irrationalism. Her 1933 book *God of the Witches* took these ideas further, suggesting that the "Satan" created by the Christian Church grew out of "the Horned God" of the ancient fertility cult.

Professional historians mostly ignored Murray's speculations, essentially because they lacked any evidentiary base. Lovecraft swallowed them whole, both because they formed a useful background for horror tales and partially because they melded well with his fears—novelist Michel Houellebecq calls them outright phobias—of the atavistic savagery of racial groups he considered dangerous and subversive of Anglo-Saxon civilization.

He first made extensive use of Murray's theory in his 1923 tale "The Festival" in which an unlucky traveller finds himself taking part in the cultic rites in serpentine, shadowed caverns beneath the fictional Kingsport. Murray's influence on Lovecraft also appears in "The Call of Cthulhu" and "The Dreams in the Witch House," the latter making the assumption that in 1692 at least some of the accused in Salem had, in fact, been witches. The same idea appears in *The Case of Charles Dexter Ward*.

Lovecraft mentioned reading Murray in a letter to a new friend in California: the artist, poet, and writer of fantasy and horror Clark Ashton Smith. In October of 1925, he told Smith about "The Horror at Red Hook," which he described as his tale of "a nest of devil-worshippers . . . in one of the squalid Brooklyn neighborhoods." He then urged Smith, as he had apparently done before, to read Murray's book. He frequently discussed Murray with Robert E. Howard when they became bosom correspondents in the 1930s, raising the notion of the witch-cult in relation to various racially "degenerate stock."[38]

Lovecraft even felt compelled to allude to Murray in an important critical work that engaged him between 1924 and 1927, an essay called "Supernatural Horror in Literature" that has been praised by even his most astringent critics. Lovecraft both defines and explores the history of the weird tale from the earliest ruminations of "primitive" humanity through the age of the gothic novel and Poe, and on to some of his contemporaries' work in the field.

This praiseworthy piece of criticism, one of the best arguments for those who want to see Lovecraft as a comprehensive man of letters, unfortunately also drags us through the raw sewage of the author's racial theories. He suggests that the "power of western horror-Lore" grew from Europe's shadowy knowledge of "nocturnal worshippers . . . descended from pre-Aryan and pre-agricultural times when a squat race of Mongoloids roved over Europe. . . ." Lovecraft's New York days had fully convinced him of Murray's flawed history of witchcraft, a problematic schema he had twisted even further by injecting it with his racist hysterics.

Finally, he turned to racism's easy and dangerous comforts when New York City defeated him. He could not find employment, make his marriage work or do any satisfying writing. He had failed, he and his good Anglo-Saxon gentlemanly mien, in his struggle with the great city of immigrants, the gathering place of the world's cultures, a place he could only despise as a stew of evil. He'd truly come to hate the city, telling Belknap Long that "the New York mongoloid problem is beyond calm mention." Certainly it had become beyond calm mention for Lovecraft. Apparently the mongoloid hordes still roved across the western world.

The plot of his short story "He," the first Lovecraft tale I ever encountered, provides some insight into his hopes, growing disappointment, and ultimate terror at New York City. It's generally bad business to attempt to ferret out biographical details from fiction. But Lovecraft, like Thomas Wolfe, tended to make himself the protagonist of his tales. In "He" the narrator's interests, inclinations, and view of the city so completely align with the author's that it must have been a purposeful identification.

"My coming to New York had been a mistake," the narrator announces, explaining that "the disillusion had been gradual." He thought he had come to a great city of poets, a city like the heroes of his dream quests often sought, where his own art would flourish. Instead he found "squalor and alienage" and "throngs of people . . . squat swarthy strangers." These less than human denizens of the city "could never mean aught to a blue-eyed man of the old folk, with the love of fair green lanes and white New England village steeples in his heart."

The story further alludes to Lovecraft's nighttime rambles away from Sonia's bed, searching for antiquities with which he could ground himself. Wandering amid the side streets and courtyards of Greenwich Village looking for "curious arcana" brings him into contact with a world rather older and more horrifying than he had imagined. Lovecraft gives himself a happy ending, however, allowing his character to escape and return "home to the pure New England lanes on which fragrant sea-winds sweep at evening."

Lovecraft may not have noticed that his characters' love of colonial things and unwillingness to walk in the "garish sunlight" shows him a vision of terror and almost gets him devoured by his first description of the "Shoggoth" that he used again in *At the Mountains of Madness*. The story may have, on some level, been a criticism of his attitude as much as autobiography. Still, something very un-Lovecraftian creeps into this, one of his most autobiographical tales. It's possible to escape cosmic horror by going to New England? Don't his other stories suggest something horrid waits there, its terrible stench borne on the sea-winds?

By the time "He" appeared in *Weird Tales*, Lovecraft had moved back to Providence. W. Paul Cook wrote an admiring and frequently quoted paragraph about how Lovecraft left New York a better man than he arrived, that "the privations, trials, and testing fires of New York" had brought "his best to the surface."

This is not true. He left New York a better writer but a worse human being. Psyche poisoned by his sense of failure and a marriage turned bad, he spouted racist nonsense the rest of his days, in an era when fascisms of all sorts began casting their shadows across the western world.

He convinced his aunts to help him move back to Providence. Friends, especially "Sonny" Long, urged them to provide some aid as they feared for Lovecraft's mental stability. Some reports, thoroughly unconfirmed, have him carrying a bottle of cyanide with him during the worst of his New York days. His aunts consented to his return to Providence, probably pleased that this would mean the end of his relationship to Sonia Greene.

In April 1926, Lovecraft ended his time in Brooklyn. "GOD I AM ALIVE! And this is Home. . . . There is no other place for me. My world is Providence," he crowed in a letter to Belknap Long. He'd returned in triumph, or so all he said of the move proclaimed. But he'd really run from the actual world. He'd gone home with his tail firmly tucked between his legs.

⁓

Lovecraft believed, or claimed to believe, that Sonia would come to live in Providence, joining his aunts in caring for him. She did, in fact, make a suggestion, once, along these lines. It was never to be.

Number 10 Barnes Street on College Hill became Lovecraft's new home, his Aunt Lillian taking the second floor. He sent a note to Long, meant for all the Kalems to read, praising his new neighborhood, "all old Yankee homes with a good percentage colonial." He wrote to James Morton in May of his pleasure in escaping "the nightmare of Brooklyn's mongrel slums" and still referred to Sonia jokingly as "the missus." A steady flow of letters continued between him and his wife, a marriage by correspondence that perfectly suited Lovecraft but that Sonia found intolerable, at least after a three-year wait.

Wilfred B. Talman, a Brooklyn journalist who joined in with the Kalem (although missing the requisite KLM at the beginning of his surname), remembered that "When Lovecraft returned to Providence the gatherings sloped off promptly summoned now and again by Balknap [sic] Long into hasty conclave when HPL touched New York on one of his historical jaunts or to visit the Longs." Talman never mentions that these trips included visits with Sonia.[39]

Lovecraft and his friends from the Brooklyn years seemed to collaborate in an effort to erase her existence. August Derleth first wrote to Lovecraft—the man whose literary legacy he would devote his life's work to preserve, defend, and profit from—at his Brooklyn address. Lovecraft wrote back simply that the Brooklyn address "was temporary & is obsolete. I am 100 percent Rhode Islander by birth & upbringing." In a letter to Derleth in May 1928, he writes of being on "the alien soil" of New York—a place, he added, that "[I] hate like a poison." He notes visits to Long and that he'll be "damned glad to get back to colonial Providence." He goes so far as to report that he's staying in Brooklyn but not that he has an estranged wife he's visiting. Derleth did not learn of Sonia Greene's existence until 1931.[40]

Sonia, for her part, at first had an idea that would allow him his beloved Providence and keep his marriage to her at the same time. Specifically, Sonia suggested to Lovecraft and his aunts that she, using her own money, "take a large house, hire a maid, pay the expenses and we all live together; our family to use one side of the house; I to use the other for a business venture. . . . " This generous proposal, one that actually greatly benefitted Lovecraft's aging aunts Lillian and Annie, caused them to react with horror. The wife of a man from the Phillips line could not be a "businesswoman" or some such modern nonsense in Providence. Such things might go on, against their wishes, in a place like New York. But they'd not have it in their own town.

In Sonia's description of this incident, the only description we have, Lovecraft himself offered no opinion. Sonia never recorded, as far as can be known, her husband's feelings about the matter. His aunts had him well in hand and, as Sonia put it, "I knew where we all stood."

What lurked behind their refusal to accept this reasonable, indeed generous, proposal that might have saved their nephew's marriage?

Snobbery and the sheer stupidity of aristocratic pretension that worried over appearances and the family reputation while they could barely pay their own rent does account for some of it. But racial hatred could also explain it more fully.

Sometime between 1924 and 1926, they likely discovered that their much-pampered nephew had married a Jew. How and when they made this discovery we can't know, the story may be in "reams of paper and rivers of ink" Sonia and Lovecraft wrote to one another between 1927 and their divorce and final alienation. But Sonia set that pile of paper on fire and, with the same independence she'd always shown, moved to California to start her life anew.

Lovecraft did not wish to divorce although his reasoning must have cut her to bloody ribbons. He apparently explained to her that "divorce would cause him great unhappiness; a gentleman does not divorce his wife unless he has cause," and he had none. This cold, self-satisfied, and utterly infuriating reasoning finally pushed Sonia to file for divorce in 1929. Lovecraft never signed the divorce decree.

They kept up a desultory correspondence for several years. Lovecraft had always dreamed of a trip to Europe. He missed his chance when Sonia, whose finances had improved, visited England, France, and Germany in 1932. She had wanted to take Lovecraft with her but writes that "she knew he would not accept." How could a gentleman, his reasoning went, travel with a woman he was not married to?

Not long before her move to California, he did make a rather surprising visit to her in Farmington, Connecticut. Sonia was not well (she suffered from various gastric disorders, likely related to anxiety, for much of her busy, productive life) and had gone there to recuperate. Farmington had a great deal of colonial architecture and so she invited her now ex-husband to pay a friendly visit and pursue his antiquarian hobby. They took separate rooms. On the first night, after what seems to have been an enjoyable day for them both, Sonia asked him for a kiss good night. "No, it's better not to," he replied and they went to their own rooms. The next day they explored Hartford and that night Sonia didn't bother to attempt another kiss.

They parted and never saw each other again.

———

Ph'nglui mglw'nafh Cthulhu R'Lyeh wgah'nagl fhtagn.

Bodies of uncertain heritage and form dance in the firelight, the shadows casting ominous shapes, human only in the broadest definition of the term. The chant rises into the Louisiana night, sounds that no earthly vocal cords should shape. A bas-relief of insane antiquity sat at the center of these rites, a muscled and powerful winged Thing, gelatinous and rubbery, part demon of the sky, part horror from black ocean depths. The eyes, squint but enormous above powerful and mind-incinerating tentacles, are malign in their purpose.

The worshippers of the Thing's shouts are being repeated in similar scenes all over the world, unspeakable rites of sacrifice and blackest evocations in all the dark places of the earth.

"In his house at R'lyeh dead Cthulhu waits dreaming."

Weird Tales rejected "The Call of Cthulhu" when Lovecraft submitted it to them in the fall of 1926. He resubmitted it the next summer and, true to form, Farnsworth Wright accepted it with no substantial changes. Pulp readers loved it and Lovecraft's work suddenly had a degree of fame in the rather tiny world of *Weird Tales* aficionados.

Today, no Lovecraft story has been more frequently read by fans and advertised as the place for the curious to begin. No grotesquerie he ever created has become more recognizable. Tentacle terror has become a part of modern horror culture and Cthulhu may be as recognizable today as Bela Lugosi's Dracula.

Why?

Part of the answer relates to Lovecraft's own experience, what can only be described as the mental instability of his last year in New York. "The Call of Cthulhu" distilled his own insanities, some of which are intertwined with the nightmares of the twentieth century. "The Call of Cthulhu" is Lovecraft's "The Waste Land," a comparison he would have despised but is nonetheless true. Both became sprawling metaphors for the unspeakable horror of a century of fear, impending doom, and utter mayhem.

The story captured apocalyptic terror decades before fears of the apocalypse began to dominate the post–World War II world. He created a cosmic conspiracy theory early in a century that became a breeding ground of all manner of conspiratorial thinking. At a time when Freud proclaimed dreams "the royal road to the unconscious," Lovecraft turned them not into vehicles of self-awareness, but signposts to unspeakable terrors. Rustin Cohle, the nihilistic detective who spouts Lovecraftian philosophy in the first season of HBO's *True Detective*, puts it best when he says "like a lot of dreams, there's a monster at the end of it."

But the most compelling element of the story really isn't the monster. In fact, when Cthulhu finally appears, it's rather anticlimactic, not least of all because he's briefly popped like a balloon when rammed by a yacht piloted by an old mariner gone mad with terror.

What makes it possible to read this story over and over again is the slow, mounting horror of learning truths about the world that it's best not to know. The muddled if increasingly sinister research of a murdered professor, the terror-drenched dreams of artists and poets all over the world, the hints of a global cult seemingly devoted to the destruction of the whole human race all build toward a climax that's not the revelation of the monster, but the revelation that human civilization has a soon approaching expiration date, "that Loathsomeness waits and dreams in the deep and decay spreads over the tottering cities of men." Seldom has a more terrible poetry of nihilism been written.

Something even bolder at work here, something seldom noticed by those who, quite rightly, see in "The Call of Cthulhu" more examples of Lovecraft's racist obsessions, his infelicitous conflation of Murray's flawed witch-cult thesis with his own prejudice. He certainly imagines "the wooded swamps south of New Orleans" as the home of "a dark cult . . . more diabolic than even the blackest of the African voodoo circles." Professor Angell's research notes offer some of the first fragments of evidence that something terrible now threatens humanity and they mention "voodoo orgies now multiply in Hayti [sic], and African outposts report ominous mutterings."

Along with these frequently noted references to racist conceptions of peoples whose degeneracy makes them especially receptive to hearing Cthulhu's call, the story is also about the dreams of artists and how the boundary between reality and unreality collapses between dreaming and waking life, between art and reality. Henry Wilcox, a sculptor of "known genius but great eccentricity," first interests Angell in his investigation of the Cthulhu cult by crafting a bas-relief whose imagery, we're told, outdoes cubism and futurism in its ability to shock and confuse. Wilcox crafted the horrible thing, as Lovecraft often crafted his own tales, after a set of dreams both horrific and wondrous. The rumblings of Cthulhu's rise are also announced by the work of the "fantastic painter . . . Ardois-Bonnot" who "hangs a blasphemous 'Dream Landscape' in the Paris spring salon of 1926."

Lovecraft as an aesthete of dreams has attracted other dreamers. Indeed, the desire to replicate images of Cthulhu, and every other monster and terror he ever imagined, has proven inescapable. Make a quick image search online and you'll find all manner of tentacles and dread eyes, efforts ranging from paints to pen and ink to digital drawing to recreate the dreams about the dreams of Lovecraft's world of nightmare.

Independent artists are in some ways at the forefront of the Cthulhu rage. ZaPow! is a perfectly named nerdcore art gallery in Asheville, North Carolina. Paintings of the various incarnations of *Dr. Who* and pen and ink tributes to *Star Wars* jostle for your attention with sculptures of all manner of the fantastic, unearthly visions of dragons and rotting, if sometimes morbidly humorous, zombies. Not surprisingly, Lovecraft and his monsters are plentiful.

Lauren Patton, owner of ZaPow!, features some of her own art in the gallery, much of it dedicated to either images of Cthulhu or to her rendition of what the symbols of "The Ancient Order of Dagon" might have looked like, that cult of sex and sacrifice that holds congress with the Deep Ones in Lovecraft's 1931 "The Shadow Over Innsmouth."

Patton attended college in Providence, living less than a mile from the original location of 454 Angell. Living in Providence and having a lifelong love of Poe led her to what she calls Lovecraft's "hyper luxurious prose." But, as an art student, Lovecraft's emphasis in the "The Call of Cthulhu" on the "idea that artists heard rumblings of the Elder gods" enthralled her. Patton actually sounds a bit like Lovecraft when she describes how commercial America cares little for the artist, but that in his tales they become "high priests" who act as "interdimensional receivers" for all of the depths of the world and the cosmos.

Visual artists may seem to have a less mystical attraction to Lovecraftian themes. "Tentacles are fun to draw and look cool," Patton tells me, admitting that this doesn't get to the heart of his philosophy of "cosmic impotence" but reminding me that "sometimes the sheer visual joy of the thing is enough."

The popularity of "tentacle art" has in some ways become detached from Lovecraft. Another artist I talked to whose pen and ink drawings often feature monstrous characters in moments of ironic humor (Frankenstein and his Bride in couples therapy, a dinosaur and giant robot taking a moment out of their combat to gaze at the stars while a city dies in flames behind them) has included more than a few tentacles in her work over the years. The artist, who asked to not be identified, is actually not a Lovecraft fan and has no special interest in Cthulhu. But the tentacles that define the monster are everywhere in her work.

A bizarre but perhaps unsurprising sideline to the Cthulhu/tentacle obsession has emerged in so-called "tentacle porn," a fetish popular among many, including a number of fans who want to stretch the boundaries of what that much used adjective "Lovecraftian" can mean. They've succeeded.

A sex toy company calling itself Necronomicox sells Cthulhu-themed dildos. It's even possible to purchase Cthulhu-themed lingerie. Meanwhile, "tentacle porn" has become a recurring trope in Japanese manga, while a magazine called *Cthulhu Sex* published regularly 1998–2007 presented its audience with female nudes compromised by tentacles. And, at least a few Lovecraft-inspired porn DVDs have circulated, one with the perhaps inevitable title of *Booty Call of Cthulhu*. Filmmaker and founder of the Crimson Screen Film Fest Tommy Faircloth tells me that an indie film entitled *Call Girl of Cthulhu* has also circulated.

These are obsessions that have to do, as the director of Necronomi-Con Providence explained to *Vice* magazine, the "open source" nature of Lovecraft's work. If a writer has reached into realms of imagination that create tabletop role-playing games (imagine Hemingway- or Fitzgerald-themed RPGs or board and card games), then the sexual commodification of his work seems inevitable. It's the cultural logic of postindustrial capitalism; take art, at its most unruly, and package it for consumption.

Perhaps something a little more complex is at work in this niche market. This phenomenon not only challenges the alleged sexlessness of Lovecraft's universe, it reminds us that Thanatos and Eros are boon companions. Lovecraft's hymns to death—not merely of his individual characters but of the idea of a death of the cosmos itself—call forth the blind, primal sexual instinct, the intimations of immortality that are "the little death" in their raw assertion of throbbing life against the cold rationality of a universe in entropy, moving toward a steady state of nothingness.

Lovecraft showed humanity the carvings on its headstone. And, eventually, we turned his most perfect nightmare into a pop culture icon, an inspiration for art and even the world's most peculiar sex symbol. We did this because it's just possible that nothing has ever scared us so badly.

The friendship via correspondence that developed between H.P. Lovecraft and August Derleth became the most important professional relationship both men ever had. Derleth, still in high school and soon to enter the University of Minnesota, had already published stories in *Weird Tales*. He continued to do so at an astonishing rate, far surpassing the relatively tiny collection of stories Lovecraft saw in print during his own lifetime. By the time of his death in 1971, Derleth authored an innumerable number of horror, detective, and science fiction tales. He published 160 books, including well-reviewed regional literary fiction. And, he would be all but forgotten without H.P. Lovecraft. Lovecraft's legacy, meanwhile, owes much of its eventual commercial success to him.

A huge number of Lovecraft's letters to Derleth exist, although they are mostly very short in comparison to the novelettes he sometimes wrote his closest friends. S.T. Joshi and David Schultz, editors of two volumes of these letters, have pointed out that the exchange has a different quality from much of Lovecraft's correspondence. His letters to Derleth deal frequently with the more practical side of the writing business. They also show a side to Lovecraft almost never revealed in his correspondence; a decided interest in getting paid for his work.

Lovecraft denigrates commercial concerns in relation to art frequently in his letters and essays. It's also easy to find examples of him apoplectic with irritation at the "check's in the mail" attitude of *Weird Tales*, and often feeling harassed at the miniscule size of those checks. He refused to ever write again for Hugo Gernsback's now legendary science fiction magazine *Amazing Stories* because he received only twenty-five dollars for his now classic tale "The Colour Out of Space" when it appeared in 1927. Even that check was exceedingly slow in coming. Lovecraft forever after referred to the editor, today one of the legendary impresarios of American science fiction, as "Hugo the Rat."

There's absolutely nothing wrong in this attitude, indeed what's peculiar in Lovecraft is his frequent pose of being the eighteenth-century gentleman-artist above the pecuniary fray. He, of course, had every reason to expect remuneration for his work so that he could pay the rent and keep himself fed and clothed. He, after all, barely managed to do these things.

His letters to Derleth, always concerned with how many stories he had out there and when pay would be forthcoming, allowed Lovecraft a forum for his money worries. When Wright at first rejected "The Call of Cthulhu," Lovecraft groused that he "regret[ed] the check I shan't get for it." Though it never happened, he spoke of considering revision work that might take him briefly to Detroit rather than face "the danger of the poorhouse." He frequently envied Derleth's ability to buy so many books, though often took consolation in his own ability to acquire the same through the library or from generous friends, including Derleth himself.

The Derleth correspondence allowed Lovecraft to breathe, to let go of his pose. It also explodes one of the most persistent myths about him and his relation to his work.

The controversial French novelist Michel Houellebecq claims that H.P. Lovecraft's fiction contains no references to money or sex. On both points, he's wrong. Lovecraft wrote about sex and money all the time. His first protagonist, Jervas Dudley, gets to pursue his insanity because he had a wealthy legacy of the sort Lovecraft would have liked to maintain. The unlucky Charles Dexter Ward, whose occult experiences open him to possession and horror, begs money from his long-suffering parents to travel to Europe—where Lovecraft always wanted to go—and buy laboratory equipment. Purchasing a long-lost ancestral estate leads the narrator of "The Rats in the Walls" to hear terrifying scratching behind the ancient paneling, scratches that lead him to discover a terrible family secret suggestive of an even more mind-shattering revelation for the universe. The doomed antiquarian of Lovecraft's masterful "The Shadow Over Innsmouth" actually ends up in that place of illimitable horror because he's agitated over the high bus fares to his original destination, a problem Lovecraft often faced in his travels.

Houellebecq buys into the myth of H.P. Lovecraft, as told by H.P. Lovecraft. I don't think Lovecraft can be called a hypocrite for his frequent denial of interest in commerce and claim that a true artist sets such concerns aside while also having anxiety over money. After all, he refused to engage in the kind of hack work that others churned out for the sake of publishing more stories and receiving a few more checks in the mail. But he also saw the acceptance and ready payment of his work as recognition of the value of his stories.

Moreover, his own passion for his artistry always trumped his understandable financial worries. If waiting months for payment irritated him, so did the acceptance of work that he found below his own standards. Writing to Derleth in November 1926, he lamented that *Weird Tales* had so quickly accepted "The Horror at Red Hook," which he called "one of the poorest things I've ever perpetrated." Most interesting of all for the gentleman above the capitalist fray of the new commercial age, he confessed to Derleth that he'd written it with Farnsworth Wright's expectations in mind and it was "therefore pervaded by a cheapness & atmosphere of crude melodrama." He didn't like writing for money; but he did.[41]

Houellebecq is also wrong that Lovecraft never wrote about sex. He did, despite his assertions that he lacked interest in "amatory phenomena." In fact, he saw a place for the erotic in literature, at least when it told something true about human experience instead of providing masturbatory material. For example, he appreciated Joyce's *Ulysses*, with its unabashed celebration of eroticism—most pronounced in Molly Bloom's famous concluding monologue, her ecstatic "YES!" to sexual transcendence. Some question has arisen as to whether or not Lovecraft actually read *Ulysses* in its entirety, but he certainly confidently pronounced his opinion on it. In this, he joined the throngs of early–twentieth-century literati for whom not reading Joyce but having strong opinions about him became an avocation.

Romantic tales irritated him but not because of puritanical delicacy about sex. They reminded him of the Victorian sentimentality that he'd come to despise, a distaste for that world of sexual repression that swaddled him in his youth, made his desires seem intolerable or strange. He joined other modernists in seeing an animal drive and a mechanical directive in sex. Romantic notions, to his mind, simply hid the terrifying irrationality of desire while promising participants a false transcendence.

Sex in Lovecraft's tales had to be dangerous and decidedly weird, in fact it had to have mind-numbing cosmic implications. Lovecraft would have seen describing a sexual act, considered so astonishingly bold for modernist writers in his era and apparently for a current age that can be titillated by *Fifty Shades of Grey*, as about as interesting as describing the process of internal combustion when one of his characters drives a car. Eroticism was far more enticing, deadly, bewitching and savage. Why bother describing the plunging of erect penises and breasts bobbing up and down when you could evoke all the malignity of the cosmos instead?

Sex became a way for Lovecraft to mock the illusions that he held but did not believe. "Facts Concerning the Late Arthur Jermyn and His Family" actually destroys the notion of "Nordic superiority" that Lovecraft's letters sometimes touted. It tells a truly subversive tale of sexual hybridity that not only describes how bizarre sexual relations between a man and a woman/ape/thing destroyed Arthur Jermyn but explores the idea that humanity's origins are found in what Lovecraft's own era call miscegenation; indeed in racial mixing of a particularly startling variety.

Interspecies, perhaps interdimensional, sex forms the basis of some of his best works, stories that always make the list of "the great texts." In "The Shadow Over Innsmouth," almost an entire village has become the offspring of amphibious Deep Ones who first demanded of the town patriarch Obed Marsh human sacrifice and then wanted human women, apparently driven primarily by sexual desire. Alan Moore picked up on this element of the Innsmouth story in *Neonomicon* and used the idea of the sexually avaricious Deep Ones to gruesome effect.

"The Dunwich Horror" (1928) walks the earth because of a rather peculiar sexual liaison. The dread Yog-Sothoth, one of the most terrifying and powerful of the Great Old Ones, impregnates Lavinia Whateley in an intentionally scandalous parody of the virgin birth. Lavinia's grandfather, a delver into the dark secrets of the grimoire of the Elder things, acts as pimp and possibly as Yog-Sothoth's vessel. The offspring of this strange union include Wilbur Whateley, a monstrously tall hulk even at age ten, whose ill-fitting clothes hide various grotesqueries that Lovecraft describes with unconcealed delight and abandon. Worse, we learn that Wilbur has a brother, Lavinia's other son about whom the less said the better.

"The Thing on the Doorstep" represents a showstopper when it comes to imaginative kink. Written in 1933, it's a tale that begins with yet another featureless male character at its center. Edward Derby is a projection of Lovecraft's own wishes and fears, a young man living off an inheritance and not able to accomplish much of practical use. He spends his days studying and finally writing as a "fantaisiste and poet" whose "lack of contacts and responsibilities had slowed down his literary growth."

Then along comes Asenath Waite. She's child to Ephraim Waite, a reputed necromancer who hails from dreaded Innsmouth. Lovecraft describes Asenath as a dark beauty with "overprotuberant eyes" surrounded by some premature lines that are the outward expression of an intense inner will. Twenty-three and a student, she runs with a "wild" crowd from Miskatonic University and has her father's penchant for occult studies. When she meets Edward Derby, now an enervated thirty-eight, she seduces him with little difficulty. The couple marry. Derby appears to his friend who narrates the story as being under the "hypnotic" influence of Asenath, a barely symbolic nod to the sexual thrall she holds over him.

Asenath, the narrator learns, has been attempting to take over her weak-willed husband's consciousness. But there's more. Asenath Waite, Lovecraft's sexiest female character, shares her own consciousness with that of her father Ephraim, the old wizard of Innsmouth.

> *Just where the supreme horror lay I could not for the life of me at that moment tell; yet there swept over me such a swamping wave of sickness and repulsion . . . a freezing petrifying sense of utter alienage and abnormality . . .*

Maybe the narrator can't figure out the nature of this "supreme horror" but we can. Lovecraft makes sure we understand it even if he tells us without telling us. Asenath and Derby have been married for three years and the narrator has just discovered that Derby has been having sex with his own father-in-law through the conduit of sensual Asenath. Derby too is about to become swallowed whole by this genderless horror. Again, Lovecraft never feels the need to spell the situation out for us and never comments on it directly. But it's at the heart of the story, a man successfully having gay sex with a woman.

Aren't many of these examples also examples of misogyny? Of course they are. Asenath is somewhere between the silent film vamp and the images of Medusa/Circe/Medea that Lovecraft absorbed from his classicism. The small number of women who appear in his other tales are either victims or witches or some combination thereof.

But misogyny and erotica have always been bosom companions, even in high literary circles. De Sade notoriously reveled in raping and killing his female characters. His radical politics called for women's complete sexual liberation in the bedroom and utter subjugation everywhere else. Oscar Wilde, who scandalized with his thinly veiled homoerotic work before his own personal scandals sent him to prison, describes his female characters with venomous contempt in *The Picture of Dorian Gray*. Henry Miller, apostle of sexual libertinism, creates women who are merely obstacles to the narrator's sexual whims, "bitches," or more often "cunts," who refuse the control of his male characters' uncontrollable Id.

We could proliferate examples closer to the present day and not only in popular fiction like *Fifty Shades*. Did John Updike, whose characters have tremendous amounts of boring sex, ever write a female character who wasn't borderline schizophrenic, an object of yearning, or the ruin of his narrator (and often all three)? David Foster Wallace sometimes rose above these impulses in startlingly original ways, but often made women simply objects of desire who are simultaneously harbingers of death.

Although feminist critiques of Lovecraft are warranted, his critics stumble at the starting gate when accusing him of never writing a meaningful female character. Asenath Waite is sometimes written off since the character becomes the vessel of a male consciousness that possesses her. But, it's much weirder than that. She's transgender in a very literal sense, transcending the boundaries of both gender identity and performance in ways Lovecraft knew would unsettle the reader.

His other female characters are also finely drawn, even when making brief appearances as monsters or victims or a bit of both. They certainly don't pop off the page, but we'd do well to remember that none of his characters could be said to do so. He didn't care about characters and always made that plain.

Lovecraft hungrily sought the attention and admiration and occasionally the comradeship of men in part because he spent much of his life living with and being pampered by women, while holding overly idealized images of his long-dead grandfather and undoubtedly tortured by what he knew of his father's illness and death. His letters and time in the Kalem Club did introduce him to interesting personalities whose habits, ideas, and interests were as charmingly weird as his own: James Morton, aging political radical, devotee of Elizabethan drama and mineralogist; Frank Belknap Long, lover of metaphysics and decadent aesthetics; August Derleth, who seemed able to write tens of thousands of words a week on any and every subject while seemingly reading hundreds of books a month and using up whatever could have been left of his time in becoming an expert fencer.

And yet, Lovecraft could not write an intriguing male character to save his life. Almost all are rather flat gentlemen of New England ancestry, professors and antiquarians or seekers of occult knowledge who are poorly concealed versions of Lovecraft himself. Randolph Carter, a character whose adventures take up four short tales and a novelette, appears as part Lovecraft and part projection of what Lovecraft wanted to be, sometimes to a laughable degree.

Lovecraft's female characters seem to me to suggest a thorough-going and unrelenting misanthropy rather than simplistic misogyny. And no one can get away with ignoring the outré versions of sexuality that appear throughout his work. If you call him a Puritan, you have to do so because he never wrote a close description of two or more bodies performing various physical acts on one another. But to say that he never wrote about sex, and indeed in some of the oddest configurations imagined before Burroughs wrote *Naked Lunch*, is to never have paid attention to his work.

The man who so unabashedly identified with Providence got himself on a bus and a train any time he could possibly afford it during the last decade of his life. In 1928, he spent a full six weeks in New York City with his estranged wife, or at least staying with her while he wandered the town in all night discussions with "the old gang."

In the same year, he spent two weeks with correspondent pals in Vermont and then made an extended trip south that took him to Baltimore and Virginia, including an excursion to "The Endless Caverns" at New Market that impressed him with "grotesque formations [that] lee'red on every hand . . . buried areas—submerged civilizations—subterranean universes and unsuspected orders of beings and influences that haunt the sightless depths—all these flitted thro' an imagination confronted by the actual presence of soundless and eternal night." An imagination that wandered ancient dreamlands and horrifying vistas at every opportunity could find its way to such things in a place that for many tourists offered merely an interesting attraction for the kids.

He returned to Virginia in 1929, visiting Jamestown, Yorktown, and Williamsburg, the colonial restoration of the latter only recently begun with the cash of John D. Rockefeller, Jr. In 1930, he visited what became, other than College Hill, his two favorite places on earth: Quebec and Charleston. He wrote an enormous travelogue of the former in eighteenth-century diction, the longest work he ever wrote, for circulation among his friends rather than publication.

Charleston he called "the only thoroughly civilized city now remaining in the United States." He appreciated the slow pace of commerce in the Southern town where business hours ran short and dinners long and most every lawyer, landowner, politician, and layabout in town had a name that dated to the colonial era. Charleston, like Williamsburg, had also only recently begun its campaign of historical restoration as its cash-poor but politically powerful gentry began to ponder the possibilities of a tourist trade that would pull the once significant seaport out of its post-Emancipation economic doldrums.

Lovecraft found plenty of Georgian architecture and other antiquities to stare at even in 1930 and frequently expressed, surprisingly given his attachment to Providence, a desire to make Charleston his home. In the last six years of his life, he returned to his other favorite seaport city as often as he could.

Architecture, history, and the affectation of a non-commercial, even anti-commercial, ethic certainly attracted him to the city. Unfortunately, Charleston's miniscule number of immigrants, a few Irish and Germans with a smattering of Italians, also attracted him. The city had an interesting and vibrant Jewish community for a Southern town but it remained tiny, composed largely of families that came to South Carolina before the American Revolution—a fact that would have impressed Lovecraft.

Maybe most significantly, Charleston brutally enforced Jim Crow segregation, both de facto and de jure. Ordinance and tradition forbade African Americans from using most public spaces and Lovecraft would never have to encounter an African American who was not a stevedore, shoe shiner, or one of the "crab men" who Lovecraft found picturesque, singing their mournful-sounding appeals for custom as they guided their pushcarts down Charleston's broken and uneven lanes.

Charleston's attraction for Lovecraft dovetailed with his frequent praise for the practice of segregation, praise that continued to flow even as his politics took a sharp turn left in the thirties. Not long after his return from his first visit to Charleston, he wrote two combative letters to James Morton. Morton had lived for a time in Harlem as a personal statement of commitment to ending segregation and Lovecraft couldn't help but launch into a tirade against such ideas, arguing for the absolute necessity of Jim Crow since "the black is vastly inferior. There can be no question of this among contemporary and unsentimental biologists."

Of course, Franz Boas, a Columbia University scholar widely regarded as founding modern anthropology, more or less undercut white supremacist cultural conceptions during Lovecraft's lifetime. Lovecraft knew this was happening and makes mention of Boas (and insults him) without the least deployment of a rational argument in a letter to Morton. "There's no more sense in trying to prove a nigger a white man's equal," he wrote, "than in trying to prove a Neanderthal Man's corresponding equality." He never wrote sensibly about this issue and always simply asserted that African Americans, and Asians and Arabs and Persians and most everyone outside of England and Germany, were inferior because they were inferior and therefore must be treated as inferior.[42]

Following his death, Lovecraft's circle of admirers sought to downplay his fairly systemic, if stupidly circular, racist philosophy of history and culture. In some ways, it worked. Now and again, in both formal and informal conversations I've had with young Lovecraft fans, most have dodged my question about how they deal with Lovecraft's attitude toward race. A few make the case that they disregard it because what they care about are the stories, not his personal prejudices, and the two are distinct. Some assert that his attitudes changed before his death, that he realized he'd been mistaken in his ideas about race.

Sadly, they are catastrophically wrong on both counts. He infused his fiction with racism, indeed attempted to use conceptions of "mongrelization" (a favorite word of his) to induce a sense of terror among his assumed readership of white, male Anglo-Saxons. And he never changed his mind. He died in a decade when the use of notions of racial superiority had begun to manifest political horrors and he held on to the concept of "Aryan supremacy" years after Hitler came to power in Germany.

Of course, it's not that the young are easily fooled. I once included an extra credit question on an exam that asked my undergraduates to describe Lovecraft's philosophy. I was looking for "cosmicism" or "indifferentism" or I'd even take "nihilism" and "materialism" (although the former probably isn't technically accurate). The majority who answered the question simply wrote "racism." We had not looked at the Lovecraft letters in class. They had simply read "The Call of Cthulhu" and drawn their own conclusions.

Asheville celebrates its hipster bizarrerie as central to its appeal. Nestled in the sublimity of western North Carolina's green forested mountains, it's a haven of pop art, hip bookstores, record shops, microbreweries, vegan restaurants, and bong palaces that senses its own deep peculiarity. In a single day you can eat a vegan doughnut, drink a beer soured in old wine casks, enjoy a kimchi taco from a Korean/Latino food truck, screen-print a T-shirt acknowledging your love of the Adam West *Batman* series from the 1960s, and shop at Malaprop's, perhaps one of the two or three best independent bookstores in the United States. "Keep Asheville Weird," a T-shirt and bumper sticker that shares a self-aware sense of the outré with Portland, Oregon and Austin, Texas, tells you all you need to know about how the town contemplates itself.

One morning I found myself in Asheville enjoying a chai at a coffee shop called Battle Cat named, delightfully, in honor of a character from the 1980s Masters of the Universe toy line and TV series. Reading Lovecraft's "Pickman's Model" on the front porch led me to a conversation with a young man who wanted very much, and somewhat against my will, to talk Lovecraft. Heavily tattooed and wearing a Tony the Tiger Frosted

Flakes cereal T-shirt, he sported a standard hipster runaway beard that you associate with ZZ Top and Orthodox Church fathers from the fourth century. He wore a bowler.

These conversations are, as I've noted before, not uncommon for me. I asked my standard question: "So, what's your favorite Lovecraft tale?" I waited for the lean, hirsute face to tell me "The Call of Cthulhu."

"'The Silver Key,'" he said. "All you need to fucking know about the world is in 'The Silver Key.' It's a dream, man, a dream in a dream in a dream. And we just gotta get back there."

I was astonished.

Lovecraft wrote "The Silver Key" in 1926 soon after his return to Providence and not long after completing "The Call of Cthulhu." This became an incredibly prolific period and his work on this short story/essay coincided with beginning work on two short novels, *The Case of Charles Dexter Ward* and *The Dream-Quest of Unknown Kadath*.

The latter functions as a companion piece to "The Silver Key." Both stories feature the further adventures of Randolph Carter, first introduced in the 1919 short tale "The Statement of Randolph Carter." *Unknown Kadath* takes the reader on a journey through Lovecraft's dreamlands and encounters with almost every creature in his menagerie: zoogs, ghouls, gugs, night gaunts, and, the objects of Carter's quest, the Old Ones themselves.

"The Silver Key," so beloved by my coffeeshop interlocutor, is not a dream quest, it's about the failure to find the world of dreams once it's been lost. "When Randolph Carter was thirty he lost the key of the gate of dreams." It's a tale about the loss of certain kinds of knowledge and Carter's longing for the dreamlands he visits in *Kadath*, the place where truths about the cosmos hide.

Carter, like the narrator of "He," acts as Lovecraft's avatar. Lovecraft, however, used the tale for satire rather than to describe a mystical journey of self-discovery. He didn't believe in mysticism and there's no question he creates Carter's dilemma to mock some of the paths his contemporaries travelled in search of transcendence. T.S. Eliot's conversion to Anglo-Catholicism comes in for a drubbing in Carter's turn to "gentle churchly faith . . . the outgrown fears and guesses of a primal race confronting the unknown." He also goes after political and cultural radicals he knew from his New York days, Greenwich Village bohemians who, in his mind, had a lot in common "with their cast-off priestcraft" and "could not escape from the delusion that life had meaning apart from that which men dream into it."

I'm afraid my Tony the Tiger T-shirt–wearing friend missed Lovecraft's point. He was clearly having a memory of Poe's famous and much overused line about life being "a dream within a dream." But that's not Lovecraft's message. What Carter had to find, the real silver key, was the knowledge that no difference exists between the world of dreams and the world of reality . . . both are material phenomenon, both are chemical reactions, molecular combinations, phantoms being conjured by electrons in the brain. In the closing line of the tale, the narrator tells us that "the great silver key" primarily stands as a symbol for "all the aims and mysteries of a blindly impersonal cosmos."

Spend your time with C.S. Lewis if you want to find the door to Narnia or J.K. Rowling if you're waiting for the train to Hogwarts. Lovecraft leaves you alone and yearning with your dreams, chemical reactions as false as the promises of religion, mysticism, bohemianism, and utopias of both mind and politics. The universe could not care less.

———

"I am very glad to hear you like my stuff. . . . I rather liked Cthulhu myself . . . [and] as for the matter of an autograph—something of very little value indeed as connected with an obscure non-entity like myself— if the following signature won't do, I'll be glad to sign any old thing except cheques on my largely non-existent bank account. . . ."

Lovecraft wrote this in Charleston in the summer of 1931. He was responding to a letter his aunt forwarded to him that came from a thirteen-year-old fan named Robert Barlow, though Lovecraft had no idea at the time of his correspondent's extreme youth. Hundreds of lengthy, affectionate, and revealing letters passed between the two over most of the next six years. Long visits would make for some of Lovecraft's happiest and most carefree times. Barlow, self-consciously gay, utterly isolated, and living with parents who suffered from depression and mental instability, found in Lovecraft much more than a mentor and became closer to him than anyone else in the older man's life, perhaps closer than Sarah Susan and Sonia had ever been able to come.

Lovecraft apparently only learned of Barlow's age when young "Bob," as he affectionately called him, picked him up at the Deland, Florida train station in the early summer of 1934. Lovecraft spent seven weeks that summer with Barlow, his mother, and the housekeeping staff. Barlow's father, probably luckily for everyone, was away during Lovecraft's visit. A former military man, he suffered deeply from social anxiety, debilitating depression, and, at one point, the delusion that he knew the date of his own death.

Living with these shadows on him, Barlow nevertheless stunned Lovecraft with the breadth of his interests. Lovecraft called him "a writer; painter; sculptor; printer; pianist; marionette designer, maker and exhibitor; landscape gardener; tennis champion; chess expert; book-binder; crack rifle shot & manuscript collector and heaven knows what else!"

Meanwhile, Bob seemed hardly able to contain himself that Lovecraft had come for such a lengthy visit. Lovecraft, to his shocked delight, discovered that Barlow had been making a bas-relief of Cthulhu "from common Florida clay," in imitation of the statuette that plays such a prominent role in the story.

The two friends saw one another again briefly in late 1934. Frank Belknap Long struck up a friendship with Barlow through Lovecraft and invited him to come up and stay for a New Year's visit. Lovecraft took the train to the city he hated, and he and Barlow waited out the first wee hours of 1935 together, talking till three in the morning.

Lovecraft returned to Florida in the following summer of '35, this time staying ten weeks in isolated Deland. He came close to accepting Barlow's seductive offer of wintering there to enjoy the company and the warmer weather. But Lovecraft needed his books and Providence. He stayed until the middle of August and headed back north, making a stop at his much-beloved St. Augustine. Barlow surprised him there on the twentieth, showing up to celebrate Lovecraft's forty-fifth birthday.

Almost a decade after Lovecraft's death, Barlow wrote a deeply moving elegiac piece about his time with him in Deland. Picking him up from the bus station he saw a "tall, stooped figure with grey-brown hair and a protruding jaw." He noted that "at another bus station I was to see him for the last time, but this was the first time and there were hundreds of things to say, and opinions to ask as I drove him homeward with his tiny valise."

Talk they did . . . about Houdini, about what made for a good—and a great—horror story. Barlow showed his friend a closet full of collectible magazines and books, a bureau he nicknamed "Yoh-Vombis" after a mysterious vault in a tale by Clark Ashton Smith. As Yoh-Vombis yawned open, it spilled out treasures any contemporary geek would sell away their loved ones to own: an almost complete file of *Weird Tales*, books autographed by H.G. Wells and Jules Verne, and, of course, the letters and signature of Lovecraft himself.

The days passed and the pair wrote stories with half-seriousness. Barlow, with more concentrated intent, wrote tales for Lovecraft to offer an opinion on. A blueberry expedition ended with Lovecraft hilariously falling into the water and then apologizing to his hosts, as he stood soaked and dripping, for losing the blueberries. They took out a rowboat onto a pond on the Barlow property and composed doggerel by contesting with one another over what might rhyme with pretzel and Schenectady. Lovecraft befriended every cat wandering about the cypress woods, naming one Alfred A. Knopf.

They talked, and talked, and talked . . . according to Barlow about history, chemistry, the New Deal, and—always—horror and fantasy. They discussed these things until late in the night when Barlow's mother insisted that young Bob get to bed. Sometimes Lovecraft entertained Barlow by reading his tales "with sinister tones and silences." One morning at breakfast he told of a dream in which "he was a magician sending balls out into space and guiding them back, some of them returning with the scars and mosses of seas and spaces unknown."

Barlow called his memoir, a piece an editor cajoled him to quickly prepare for a volume of reminiscences of Lovecraft in the forties, "The Wind That Is in the Grass." By then, Barlow, a professor of Mesoamerican studies, had become enmeshed enough in Mexican culture to know the poignant saying that "the wind that is in the grass cannot be brought into the house." You don't get to keep the moments, or the people, you love.

Barlow's tumultuous family situation continued and in 1936, his mercurial father decided on a move to Leavenworth, Kansas. Barlow convinced his parents to allow him a detour to Providence, where he stayed with Lovecraft and his surviving aunt at Lovecraft's final place of residence, 66 College Street. Lovecraft affectionately complained to one of his editing clients, Anne Tillery Renshaw, that the young man proved "a constant responsibility." It's an echo of how he sometimes described Sonia's visits and there's a subtext of sheer joy in having his beloved Bob in his beloved Providence.

Barlow stayed for three weeks. At one point the inseparable pair ventured a midnight visit to St. John's graveyard for a poetry-writing contest. This had been Poe's favorite place to lurk about during his visits to Sarah Helen Whitman. They took a trip to Salem on Lovecraft's birthday and Barlow got to drink in the inspiration for "witch-haunted Arkham" with his closest friend by his side.

R.H. Barlow was more than a little in love with H.P. Lovecraft. In later years, Barlow became much more open about his own sexual identity, or at least as open as one could be in the intense and heavily politicized homophobia that ravaged American society by the 1940s. His completely fascinating and utterly tragic life receives more attention later in this book, in part because of the important and odd role he played in the preservation of Lovecraft's work and legacy. He passes out of Lovecraft's life at this point, however. On September 1, 1936, they parted at the Providence bus station and never saw one another again.

Lovecraft wrote *At the Mountains of Madness* in February and March of 1931. It's a masterpiece. He simply never wrote a story that, unwinding deliberately, so imperceptibly creeps up on the reader. Mounting horror emerges in the accretion of small details about geological time, Antarctic exploration, archaeological discovery, the sublimity of an alien-seeming landscape that in fact resides in the unknown places of the earth and then, rather suddenly, the appearance of a thing that delivers a nearly unbearable shock to the nerve endings.

Lovecraft opened his tale, as he so often effectively did, with a warning from the narrator of terrible knowledge lying in wait, a secret that once revealed might cause even the hardiest souls to loosen their grip on agreed-upon illusions. "Men of science have refused to follow my advice," Professor Dyer, a geologist at Miskatonic University, writes despairingly. Dyer importunes the human race to stay away from "those mountains of madness" in the Antarctic where he and his colleagues discovered a "nightmare city," one that tends to terrify contemporary readers more than all the other ancient, sunken, dreaming, hidden cities that Lovecraft's mind ever mapped.

The Old Ones that once ruled the city tens of millions of years before Dyer discovered it lived amid "cubes and ramparts," strange labyrinths stretching for miles that test even Lovecraft's prodigious powers of description. But those powers don't fail him in his terrifying evocation of the monsters that still can be found there, the unruly servants of the Old Ones known as the Shoggoths. S.T. Joshi told me, and it's hard not to agree, that he considered one particular revelation in the story "the single most terrifying passage in all weird fiction."

At the Mountains of Madness came to 115 typed pages and, a few years later, Lovecraft called it "the longest thing of mine I have not repudiated." Due to its sheer length, Lovecraft had imagined it appearing in *Weird Tales* in two installments. Wright rejected it immediately, perhaps because he felt it verged too much toward what the thirties called "sciencfiction" rather than the "weird tale." Whatever his reasoning, the rejection came as a serious blow to Lovecraft, increasingly prickly about criticism of his work.

The rejection of *At the Mountains of Madness* helped trigger, though does not fully explain, the bitter irony of Lovecraft's final years. Convinced that he had produced nothing of lasting value, frequently facing rejection of some of his most well-wrought stories from *Weird Tales*, and sometimes even receiving some shortsighted criticism of his work from his circle of correspondents, his quantity of literary output wavered at a moment when he had begun to break new ground with tales like "The Shadow Over Innsmouth" and the supremely odd "The Thing on the Doorstep." In 1930, "The Whisperer in Darkness" made use of a compelling narrative device to tell of the horrors from Yuggoth, a world of weird terror Lovecraft created with some inspiration from the recent discovery of Pluto. His 1935 "The Shadow Out of Time" introduced a dizzying conception of the cosmos, humanity's tiny place in it and one of the oddest and most inventive conceptions of time travel ever imagined.

Numerous rejections from various major New York publishers soured him on the possibility of ever seeing a published collection of his tales. He seemed on the verge of giving up altogether on his fiction. He felt a bit put upon when his fellow *Weird Tales* contributor Edgar Hoffmann Price suggested the pair collaborate on a sequel to "The Silver Key" that Price drafted, with the title "The Lord of Illusion." Still, Lovecraft more or less rewrote the whole story anyway, telling one of his correspondents that he "scrapped almost all of it" and renamed it "Through the Gates of the Silver Key."

We owe much to a young correspondent and hopeful writer named Donald Wandrei and the typewriter of Robert Barlow for preserving some of the groundbreaking material Lovecraft created in these years. Lovecraft continued his intense hatred of typesetting his stories and Barlow offered to bang out the tales in exchange for being able to keep the original manuscripts. Meanwhile Wandrei convinced *Astounding Stories* to publish *At the Mountains of Madness* in three installments in 1936.

By 1935, Lovecraft became so convinced that his fiction had deteriorated that he didn't bother to submit "The Shadow Out of Time," now considered one of the "great texts," to *Weird Tales* and simply circulated the handwritten manuscript to some of his correspondents. During his summer visit to Barlow in Florida, his young friend delighted Lovecraft by typing it for him on the sly (and with plenty of errors) from the handwritten manuscript that eventually made its way to the Hay Library in the 1990s. Donald Wandrei, again without asking Lovecraft for permission, passed the story along to *Astounding Stories*, whose editor proved pleased enough with *At the Mountains of Madness* to buy this next tale without reading it.

Even when encouraged by his correspondents' circle, he remained recalcitrant about attempting to publish his work. In 1934, E. Hoffmann Price more or less begged Lovecraft to submit a copy of "The Thing on the Doorstep" to *Weird Tales*, suggesting that he might be willing to send it along for him. In late summer of 1935, he suggested that they collaborate on a revision of the story and use the resulting check to go visit Clark Ashton Smith in California. Lovecraft said no.

His refusals to submit his work seem at odds with the financial worries that clawed at Lovecraft. "If I could ever be sure of $15 a week—or even $10 a week—through some honest employment outside of the writing field, I'd never think again of the commercial side of authorship," he complained.

Perhaps he'd simply decided that the concerns of art and the demands of the pulp market couldn't overlap.

He wrote one more tale after "The Shadow Out of Time." Although "The Haunter of the Dark" has nothing like the literary power of most of his work in the 1930s, it's an immensely entertaining story that grew out of his friendship with the young Robert Bloch. Bloch had published a story called "The Shambler from the Stars" in which a character, rather obviously based on Lovecraft, dies in a suitably horrific manner. *Weird Tales* readers loved the inside joke and one wrote in to the "The Eyrie," the pulp's letter column, to suggest that Lovecraft write a story that would "return the compliment."

"The Haunter of the Dark" features a writer and painter named Robert Blake who lives in rooms "of a venerable dwelling in the grassy court off College Street." Lovecraft chooses Providence itself, not his mythic Arkham, Kingsport, or Innsmouth, to set what became his final tale. It references Brown University, the Memorial Hall of the Rhode Island School of Design, and places its horrors in a ruined church on Federal Hill, loosely based on St. John's Roman Catholic Church that—while not a ruin—had had its steeple destroyed in a 1935 storm. The description of place and architecture that plays such a prominent role in the story becomes a love letter to Providence, an altogether fitting final statement of the author's romance with the city.

The story itself involves Blake in an ever-growing obsession with "the vacant church" with "sooty gothic windows," an ill-rumored place feared by locals. Blake feels compelled to explore it, finding evidence of a dread cult that had taken over the abandoned church and the notes of a dead man that warn of what the so-called "Church of Starry Wisdom" had raised with its rituals. Like so many of Lovecraft's characters, Robert Blake must find out more, must pursue the secret. The discovery of Blake's diary entries suggest to the police, and to the reader, cosmic horrors beyond imagining. Though far from his best tale, "The Haunter of the Dark" has one of the more memorable, and chilling, endings.

The relationship between Bloch and Lovecraft that became the impetus for the tale tells us much about the universes that Lovecraft created and the ones that would grow from them. Bloch began the fifteen-year correspondence with his much older friend in 1933. Bloch later recalled that the man who referred to himself as "Grandpa Cthulhu" very quickly developed "a sincere regard for . . . even so brash and bumbling a teenager as myself."

Bloch became so thoroughly entranced with Lovecraft and his monsters that he not only began writing imitative tales of the master but also made some chilling drawings of Lovecraft's various creatures now kept at the Hay Library. They deserve recognition as some of the first efforts to illustrate Lovecraft's Yog-Sothery, his organic mythology of monsters and meaninglessness.

Bloch drew for us the mad Arab Abdul Alhazred transcribing the dread *Necronomicon*. Alhazred's flowing black robe contrasts with the nauseating green Bloch chose for the color palette, including the horrible thing that inspires Alhazred to write his dismal and dangerous tome. What appears to be a blood-red Shantak bird, a creature that plays a central role in Randolph Carter's dangerous journey in *Unknown Kadath*, appears in another drawing. The indescribable thing from "The Lurking Fear" gets a finely detailed finish from Bloch that's hard not to unsee when you reread the story.

The letters between Bloch and Lovecraft are a delight, two nerds at play in shadowed, whispering fields of their own dreamland. Bloch often drew weird art on the outside of his envelopes and referred to his mentor as Luveh-Keraph, as if he wrote to some mage of the hyperborean age. In a letter to Lovecraft in the early summer of 1935 (while Lovecraft visited Barlow), Bloch announced with delight that he would soon have a new story appearing in *Weird Tales*. In the language of mythic fantasy he and Lovecraft both loved, Bloch praises "Algol, the daimonic star of destiny" for his good luck and signs off, "Yours by the seven stars of Eplidus the Learned."[43]

Bloch, arguably as much if not more than August Derleth, became essential in spreading Lovecraft's influence. His early short stories are well wrought but slavishly imitative of the master's own work. Ludwig Prinn, the protagonist of many of these tales, became something of Bloch's double (and indeed Prinn became Lovecraft's affectionate name for him). Prinn, a Flemish knight fighting in the Crusades, discovers terrible secrets from Syrian magi, secrets that he writes down in *De Vermis Mysteriis*, or *Mysteries of the Worm*. This fictional, forbidden book joins the Lovecraftian library beside the *Necronomicon*. In "The Fane of the Black Pharaoh," a terrible sacrifice is made to Lovecraft's terrifying Nyarlathotep. Even a tale such as "The Eyes of the Mummy," with no direct references to Lovecraft's universe, features Bloch's mentor's ideas about the deadly nature of time and the insanity that comes with facing what Bloch calls "the ecstasy of horror."

Bloch expanded his repertoire, and his apprenticeship to Lovecraft became just that: journeyman attempts to learn his craft rather than creative plagiarism or high-order fan fiction. He turned increasingly to science fiction, fantasy, and horror suspense. Before his death in 1994, he won five Bram Stoker awards and even wrote several very strange, horror-themed episodes for the original *Star Trek* series. Indeed, in the second-season episode "Catspaw," the crew of the Enterprise must contend with two powerful aliens who are the last of a race of "Old Ones." Lovecraft, Bloch ensured, could even appear subtly in the high-gloss, futuristic world of Gene Roddenberry's United Federation of Planets.

Of course, Bloch is best known for a 1960 adaptation of one of his novels that changed film forever. Alfred Hitchcock based *Psycho*, perhaps one of the top ten cinematic classics of all time and of any genre, on Robert Bloch's work. Many have heard the story that Hitchcock had copies of the novel purchased in huge quantities, essentially trying to take it off the market so that he could deliver audiences the utter shock he intended.

Less well known, in part because the reference does not appear in the film, is that Bloch's novel makes Bates a collector of books on the occult as well as corpses. Bates owns a copy of Murray's *The Witch-Cult in Western Europe*, a book he learned about from Lovecraft and included in *Psycho* as a small homage to his long-dead mentor. Horror fans, at least those who have never read the novel, claim that Norman Bates actually owns a translation of the *Necronomicon*.

———

On January 27, 1937, H.P. Lovecraft typed, instead of penning, a letter to R.H. Barlow.

Lovecraft's use of what he referred to as "the hated machine" represented such an astonishing event that he felt compelled to comment on and explain it. "This goddam grippe or whatever the hell I've got," he wrote, "has left me so Yuggoth-cursed weak that my script can't be depended on." Letters to other friends echoed his sense of increasing ill health and complaints of "the grippe," a generalized term once used to explain flulike symptoms.

Even when alluding to his correspondents of his health troubles, he often only briefly mentioned it and moved on to subjects of mutual interest. In his last letter to Bob Barlow, he teased about his young admirer's conversion to Communism.

Lovecraft's final letter to Derleth in February of 1937 largely dwelt on his plans for catching up with the current state of astronomical study. He had, a few months prior, attended the meeting of a group of amateur astronomers in Providence calling themselves "The Skyscrapers," and the gathering seemingly delighted him. October 1936 had cheered him up more generally. He saw Roosevelt, his new political idol soon to be reelected for his second term, at a rally in Providence.

A final unfinished letter to James Morton, of enormous length, also covered his renewed interest in astronomy, a discussion of the New Deal, a description of what he considered some of the "libels" against the character of Poe, and concluded with a reflection on the Surrealist movement and what he thought its "aesthetic decadence" signaled for the age. The letter breaks off in praise of the artist Nicolas Roerich and how his work evoked "alien landscapes . . . fantastic carven stones . . . precipitous slopes & edging upward to forbidden needle-like peaks." He was back at the mountains of madness in their grotesque sublimity.

He did not have problems with his indigestion as he sometimes suggested, nor the passing symptoms bundled together as grippe. He had cancer of the small intestine. Lovecraft hated going to the doctor and so, only when his pain became unbearable, did he make his way to Butler Hospital. This was about one month before his death and at a point when the only thing to be done was to treat his pain with morphine.

Harry Brobst had been a fan of Lovecraft and Clark Ashton Smith during the twenties. He moved to Providence to become a psychiatric intern at Butler Hospital and he and Lovecraft saw one another occasionally in a cordial, if not especially close, friendship. It's from Brobst that Robert Barlow learned of his love's death.

On March second, Brobst wrote to Barlow to tell him that "our old friend is quite ill and so I am writing this letter for him." Lovecraft, we know from a diary he kept during the last month of his life, drifted between intense pain and morphine-induced oblivion. But he encouraged Brobst to write Barlow and playfully inform young Bob that he fully intended to write him soon, perhaps about politics. He, Brobst joshed, plans to "demolish your arguments when he can." But, despite the levity, Brobst made the state of things clear. "I am honestly worried about his condition . . . the poor fellow is certainly in intense pain."[44]

About one week later Barlow received another, more distressing message, "that the great sage has been removed to the James Brown Hospital." Brobst described him as suffering from "a severe kidney condition" while adding that "he remains in continual agony and nothing but morphine will soothe his pain." Brobst noted that when his wife went to visit Lovecraft, she was distressed by his state but "his mind is still clear" and "he spoke to my wife very beautifully."

On March fourteenth, Bob made plans for the then-enormous trek from Kansas to Providence. He telegraphed Lovecraft's Aunt Annie Gamwell to say he was coming. Lovecraft died in the early morning hours of March 15, 1937.

Barlow arrived a few days after Lovecraft's burial in Swan Point Cemetery. Aunt Gamwell, who always found Bob delightful, took out a piece of paper that, Barlow remembers, "She had been horrified to see him [Lovecraft] write by chance a few months before." Written in pencil, the document bore the title "Instruction in Case of Decease."

He knew.

The paper distributed books and effects to various friends, including some of the family's colonial book collection to James Morton. But it began very directly with the following sentence: "First choice of all my books and manuscripts is to go to R.H. Barlow, my literary executor."

Barlow sounds broken in everything he writes about Lovecraft's passing. Derleth, on the other hand, sounds immediately like he's come to understand the meaning of his very busy life. *Weird Tales* readers demanded more Lovecraft tales, surely some unpublished material must be out there? It's as if Lovecraft's death touched off some turning of the mental axis of the twentieth century, created new genres in the mass culture that he claimed to despise. And, it created a cult of Lovecraft that puts his own fictional esoteric cults to shame in its intensity.

Why this obsession? Why did they care so much about a man who simultaneously loved and hated the world, who believed in nothing and yet seemed able to assert his will, his passions, even his dreams into fantasy worlds no one had ever visited before, so much so that we can now visit them with his help? How did it happen that more than a century and a quarter after his birth, western popular culture—especially its triumphant realms of geekdom—is in some special sense the creation of this very enigmatic man, this conservative decadent who hated the twentieth century and helped to create some of its essential obsessions all at the same time?

We'd do well not to try and answer these questions by too close a look at his end.

There's an immense sense of futility connected to these final days. Lovecraft himself did not express it. The diary records only intense pain. But he writes neither with complaint nor with a sense of injury incurred from the universe he never trusted anyway. The diary of his death reads almost like a combination daybook and set of astronomical observations, as if he has stepped away and rationally separated himself from his agonies to become the oddest sort of objective observer.

He died in a narcotic blur and we're curious if he dreamed and what came upon him in those dreams. We hope cities beyond all antiquity and the sound of black wings, the beautiful grotesqueries that first came to him lying in his room at his beloved 454 Angell. Sublimity, fear, and wonder, all.

PART III.

CTHULHU RISES

The hierophant intones a dread liturgy, words first spoken in dark tongues. These are prehuman and nearly unutterable sounds from the *Necronomicon* itself. A black-robed choir sings a blasphemously evil hymn, meant to replicate what Lovecraft described as pulsing horrors that surround the "ultimate void of chaos that wherein reigns the mindless daemon-sultan Azathoth."

A bleary-eyed mob waits expectantly as the bearded old wizard calls up the Names of Things not to be uttered and it seems as if the stars at last are right. Great Cthulhu will rise from his watery slumber in the sunken city of R'lyeh. Humanity's short and troubled tenure on earth is at an end.

The setting is not Lovecraft's fictional universe, at least not exactly. It's NecronomiCon Providence's famous "Cthulhu Prayer Breakfast," the tongue (or perhaps tentacle) in cheek celebration of the cultish aspects of the Lovecraft universe that have been growing since his death eighty years ago. The crowd is bleary-eyed, not from partaking in the orgiastic worship of the Great Old Ones but from being up a bit too late the night before drinking more than a few of Rhode Island's famous microbrews after several days of panels, walking tours, marathon RPG gaming sessions, and a general celebration of all things Lovecraftian. The berobed choir's chants are less the terrors at the center of Lovecraft's bleak universe and something more like parody and pastiche of the worship of the terrible Great Old Ones.

There's also a breakfast buffet, a bit out of step with the allegedly dark rites at work but somehow perfectly suited to the affectionate whimsy of the proceedings.

Robert M. Price served as celebrant for the Cthulhu Prayer Breakfast held, of course, on Sunday morning and the last day of the Con. Price is one of the most interesting people I came across in my pilgrimage to understand Lovecraft and the world he made—quite a statement given some of the personalities who hover around the dark light of Providence.

Price is a biblical scholar who rejects Christianity, and is part of the scholarly organization called the Jesus Seminar that uses textual criticism to determine what can, and cannot, be known about the historical Jesus. Price is something of an outlier even in this group in that he doesn't believe a historical Jesus ever existed and holds to the notion of the "Christ myth." He calls himself "an atheist who loves the Bible, religion, and theology" and has written innumerable works of biblical criticism with titles that challenge the reader with élan and a wink and a nod: *Inerrant the Wind: The Evangelical Crisis of Biblical Authority*, *Deconstructing Jesus*, or, more directly, *Jesus is Dead*.

He's also been an important figure in the Lovecraft renaissance, creating and editing the 1980s fanzine *Crypt of Cthulhu* and working with Chaosium Press in bringing out the Lovecraft-inspired tales of Robert Bloch. He has also edited forthcoming Cthulhu Mythos titles for Chaosium tentatively entitled *The Yith Cycle* and *The Yog-Sothoth Cycle* as well as a five-volume set of Lovecraft's work. He's even tried his hand at a fair amount of Cthulhu Mythos fiction of his own and has been working to collect a group of stories called *Tales of the Derleth Mythos*.

Price seems a kind of whirlwind of Lovecraftian lore and good humor, a human explosion of ink who dearly loves pulp fiction of all kinds as much as he enjoys rattling the cages of the orthodox with his peculiar mixture of theological acuity and a firm, unbending atheism. The Cthulhu Prayer Breakfast finds him robed, complete with a mitre, in what seems a good imitation of a high priest of the Esoteric Order of Dagon, the mystagogical vestments of the "degraded cult" that keeps alive the terrors of Obed Marsh's horrible bargain in "The Shadow Over Innsmouth." He described to me how he "brandishes" a fake *Necronomicon* and delivers what he calls "something of a serious or semi-serious homily." Author Cody Goodfellow, a profane, irritable, and irresistible author of Lovecraftian tales, joins him in the profane liturgy. Fantasy author and critic Darrell Schweitzer writes the satirical hymns to the Old Ones and leads the black-clad choir.

What would Lovecraft make of this? His letters to friends, admirers, and protégés frequently make numerous references to the mythology he had created. "By Yuggoth," he would swear, referencing the alien world from which the horrific fungi come to trouble an old Vermont farmer, and the world, in "The Whisperer in Darkness." Near the time of his death, he signed off a letter to an admirer, "From Still Sunken R'lyeh, Grandpa Cthulhu." He would play at writing to his correspondents "From Kadath in the Cold Wastes" and date the note "The Hour of the Night Gaunts" or "The Hellish Sabbat."

In other words, the idea that fans of all ages would come and play in this dark and drear universe that spilled out of his dreams would have delighted him to no end. The devotion that a young, indeed a very young, generation of fans gives his work would have made him especially content. While seemingly playing the old man in his teens and calling himself "Grandpa" by the time he reached thirty, he reserved his deepest affection for young friends and, in the case of Long, Derleth, Bloch, Barlow, Fritz Leiber, and numerous lesser-known, aspiring weird writers, he drew enormous inspiration from their fanboy love of his creations and their personal devotion to him.

As my earlier story about the hipster who found the meaning of his life in a Lovecraft tale suggests, it's almost impossible for me to walk into a bar or coffee shop carrying a book of Lovecraft tales, or a book with his name somewhere on the cover, without someone telling me how much they are into him, or how they just bought a collection of his stories after meeting him through a film or a video game.

They all want to tell me their favorite Lovecraft story if they've read one, or to talk about the stories they've heard they need to read. So far it's a race between "The Dunwich Horror" and "The Call of Cthulhu"—with Cthulhu having a pretty fair margin of victory. I find the deep delvers into the dark want to talk about "The Colour Out of Space" and the "The Shadow Over Innsmouth." Few seem aware, as was my bowler-wearing friend in Asheville, of his more bizarre flights of fantasy or much of his early work.

These Lovecraft enthusiasts are never aging professors with an acquired taste in obscure writers. They are twentysomethings, usually with more than one tattoo, and so self-consciously hip that they've learned to seem unselfconscious about it and probably are.

Sometimes they raise a T-shirt (or even lower some skinny jeans) to show off their Cthulhu tattoos. In one case, Lovecraft's long face, complete with his easily recognizable lantern jaw, decorated a well-developed bicep. Do a quick online search for "Lovecraft tattoos" and you'll be more than a little surprised at their ubiquity and variety . . . and perhaps at how often they employ the writer's easily recognizable if not conventionally attractive visage.

Some of them are sitting at the bar or at the tiny table next to me writing their memoirs at age twenty-four because of Lena Dunham or working on an app thanks to Mark Zuckerberg. I'm pretty sure one tweeted the experience of talking to some old guy writing about Lovecraft. Another, permissionless, took a picture of me with my nose stuck in one of the Penguin Classics Lovecraft collections, sending it into the cyber-ether on Instagram or SnapChat or Yik Yak, likely with the exclamation "LOVE-CRAFT! WTF!" Or, maybe, "Some old dude, into Lovecraft. Cool."

The awkward young man pretending to be a distinguished old man at age thirty did not have this audience in mind when he began his exploration of worlds of horror. He struggled to make the art and not the audience. He wrote primarily for himself and for a group of eight to ten admirers of his work who became his friends, his critics, and frequent correspondents. I can't begin to imagine what he would have made of his current admirers, of their willingness to put his images, his words, and sometimes even his face on their bodies. I picture him taking as much delight in this as in the Cthulhu Prayer Breakfast while writing a seventy-page missive to someone bemoaning the whole trend.

It's a trend that, while moving in definite cycles within the world of literary reputation and the entertainment industry, shows no sign of abating. The path his work took to get to the apex of American popular culture's current fascinations form a story as peculiar as his own life. Perhaps more interesting, it's a story that showed the tentacles of Cthulhu tangled around the very roots of contemporary geek culture, no longer an isolated world of fanboy (literally, mostly boy) enthusiasts but a multi-billion-dollar entertainment juggernaut that has transformed terms like "geek" and "nerd" from insults into compliments about cultural aware-ness, into a new version of being hip.

August Derleth had special affection for Lovecraft's tale "The Outsider," possibly because its odd structure and conclusion yields itself to several competing interpretations and, more likely, because he thought it auto-biographical.

Lovecraft, as Derleth makes clear in the first collection of stories issued by Arkham House in 1939 entitled *The Outsider and Others*, repre-sented the ultimate outsider, on the margin of modernity and even the normal spectrum of human emotion and experience.

More recent interpreters of Lovecraft have tried to fight this image and suggest a basic normalcy to Lovecraft. They challenge the picture of him as reclusive, obsessional, and odd. Mostly they have succeeded in underscoring just how peculiar he was, indeed, how he put significant effort into being out of step with his times.

Derleth wanted to do more than prescribe a specific image of his mentor that the world would remember. He moved amazingly quickly in putting together a publishing house devoted, at least at first, only to Lovecraft's fiction. In fact, according to his own account, the idea occurred to him immediately upon hearing of Lovecraft's death. He writes of receiving the letter bearing the news "on my way into the marshes of Sauk City" where he frequently did his reading. Walking to the outskirts of the small town that would become the headquarters of Arkham House press for the rest of his life, he read a letter from Howard Wandrei, the brother of Donald Wandrei, who worked to get Lovecraft to publish his stories outside of *Weird Tales*. The letter told of Lovecraft's recent, somewhat horrific, death.

Derleth doesn't record what would be his understandable grief at his mentor's passing. Instead, he says, "I sat at a railroad trestle beside a book and thought of how Lovecraft's best stories could be published in book form."

He actually wrote to Donald Wandrei on the very day he received the news to suggest that "something should be done to keep Lovecraft's fine stories in print." In the next two years, both men took out liens against their homes and used insurance policies as collateral in order to get a press up and running. Mortgaged to the hilt, they began work on the first collection of stories and, rather miraculously, had the *The Outsider and Others* in print by 1939.

Derleth and Wandrei kept at it, continuing to finance Arkham House with their own funds. Copies of the *The Outsider and Others* moved rather slowly and it took four years to sell out the original printing. Derleth, in a move somewhat inauspicious given the literary routes he later took, put out a collection of what he considered his best fiction in 1941 after his own publisher, the New York house Charles Scribner's Sons, suggested Arkham House as a better venue for tales of the supernatural. Derleth thus released *Someone in the Dark* through his own press, admitting that he had succumbed to what seemed to him "vanity publishing."

Derleth shouldn't be understood simply as a hack imitating his mentor, though he certainly did not consider hack work beneath him in the effort to keep both the press and his own finances afloat. Lovecraft himself had written to friends that he suspected that Derleth's real gifts lay in the direction of his realist, if sometimes heavy-handed elegiac, regional fiction.

Derleth must be recognized for his business acumen. Donald Wandrei departed for a four-year stint in the U.S. Army during World War II and, during this time, Derleth successfully secured the American publishing rights to numerous classic authors of the weird, living and dead, including Sheridan Le Fanu (famous for the seminal lesbian vampire tale *Carmilla*), Lovecraft's onetime inspiration Lord Dunsany, and two authors who became very dear to Lovecraft—though I see only slight direct inspiration in his work—Arthur Machen and Algernon Blackwood.

Derleth also quickly sought to acquire the copyright to the work of Californian Clark Ashton Smith, Lovecraft's much loved friend on the west coast whom he never had a chance to meet but whose tales, poetry, and drawings of cosmic horror are both influenced by Lovecraft and in some respects inspired Lovecraft's last productive years of work. In 1942, Arkham House published a collection of Smith's stories. Many of them, such as "The Vaults of Yoh-Vombis" and "The Dark Eidolon," are essential for the modern Lovecraft fan today, given that they frequently pantomime Lovecraft's vision, offering snappy, pulpy versions of his own stories.

August Derleth took a shadowy turn in the mid-forties—perhaps because of his anger at how some mainstream, and highly influential, critics like Edmund Wilson had responded to Lovecraft's work, and some friction with his Arkham House partner Donald Wandrei. In 1945, he took the fateful step of publishing *The Lurker at the Threshold*, the first volume of his "collaborations" with Lovecraft that helped build the idea of what Derleth christened "The Cthulhu Mythos."

Derleth's "Cthulhu Mythos" held that Lovecraft had intentionally set out to create a mythology that involved all his Beings from "outside" and various forbidden tomes such as the *Necronomicon*, the less well-known *Pnakotic Manuscripts*, and other books of ancient terror invented by him and his friends. Moreover, Lovecraft had obviously placed many of his stories in a fantasy topography of the author's own beloved New England landscape in which Arkham, Kingsport, and Innsmouth became settings of cosmic horror.

Had Derleth stayed within the bounds of this definition of the "Cthulhu Mythos," it would never have been especially controversial—excepting perhaps the notion that Lovecraft intentionally sought to create a mythology. However, he went much further. Derleth rather oddly blended some of his own Catholic Christian beliefs into his allegedly Lovecraftian tales, transforming the idea of a universe indifferent to humankind into one populated with Beings interested in aiding the human race and other creatures seeking to harm it.

A 1969 essay by Derleth entitled "The Cthulhu Mythos" detailed this fascinatingly absurd co-option of Lovecraft's mantle for fiction that never would have interested him and a worldview he would have found repugnant. Derleth claimed that "As Lovecraft conceived the deities or forces of his mythos . . . Elder gods were benign deities" while the "powers of evil were variously known as the Great Old Ones or The Ancient Ones." In other words, Lovecraft's tales added up to a simple struggle between good and evil.

Derleth may have been partially confused, as some have claimed, by some misquotations of Lovecraft from their mutual correspondent Harold Farnese. But Derleth's own correspondence with Lovecraft make this "misunderstanding" truly peculiar. He knew of Lovecraft's atheism and, though it's a topic they mostly avoided in their correspondence, his rather intense dislike of Christian theology.

In one of his earliest letters to Derleth, written in October 1926, Lovecraft asserted that "There's nothing more flat than the pitiful seriousness of those who actually believe in the supernatural." Responding to Derleth's youthful surprise that his friend could reject the possibility of everything from God to ghosts to telepathy, Lovecraft replied that while he did not consider himself a "crusader" on such topics, he had little doubt that once anyone set out to "investigate the illusion-forming and memory-twisting qualities of the human brain . . . one finds it impossible to continue in supernatural faith."

Although they mostly avoided the controversial topic over a decade of fairly continuous correspondence, Lovecraft always made clear his own views and rejected Derleth's willingness to believe various forms of theology and parapsychology. "The process of shedding supernatural explanations for things," Lovecraft wrote him in the fall of 1932, "has really been going on ever since man began to emerge from the total savage ignorance which gave birth to the original conceptions of 'spirit,' 'deity' & other forms of primitive pseudo-explanation. . . ." This straightforward rejection of religious claims makes Derleth's later attempts to transform the Lovecraftian universe into a Christian allegory especially risible.

Efforts to baptize Lovecraft's terrifying cosmology aside, I strongly doubt even Derleth's notion that Lovecraft set out to create a cycle of stories. Much of Lovecraft's correspondence with friends and admirers about their expanding universe of malign Beings and forbidden books has a playfulness rather than a purposefulness about it. Now and again, Lovecraft and his comrades sound as if they are putting together an especially intricate and intense Dungeons & Dragons scenario rather than crafting "a Mythos." Much of the time, they simply mentioned one another's fantastic creations rather than making them a central part of the narratives they sought to construct. In other words, we find in Lovecraft and his circle simply a collegial sense of mutual allusion to one another's work.

How much or how little thought Lovecraft put into the creation of a mythology will likely never be fully known. We do know that after a brief flurry of writing in 1926–27, some of which Lovecraft later disavowed, his output became torturously slow, with none of the energy of someone eager to build a new literary cosmology. He put an enormous amount of time into the craftsmanship of each individual tale rather than worrying over cycles of stories. He sought out advice from friends for improvement and worried over the prose of each tale over many months. Meanwhile his writerly confreres, including Derleth, began to churn out story after story for a wide variety of pulp magazines, often carefully targeting their fiction for maximum profit and in order to, in the language of contemporary corporate-speak, "create a brand."

Compare Lovecraft's work to Clark Ashton Smith and Robert E. Howard in order to fully grasp Lovecraft's view of himself as an artist. Both Smith and Howard created more than one cycle of tales and, in relatively short periods of time, shaped detailed and multilayered mythologies. They, not Lovecraft, became Mythos-makers before Tolkien took the concept to an entirely new level by creating whole languages for his races and expansive histories for his fantasy cultures.

Smith wrote two important story cycles, the Zothique series and the Averoigne tales. The first takes place in a future that in Smith's hands becomes something of a reimagined deep past, a world of sword and sorcery that has emerged on earth as the light of the sun slowly dies and civilization as human beings have known it begins to collapse.

Smith's Averoigne tales occur in an imaginary medieval France and are perhaps the closest he ever comes to social and historical realism. They also contain a hefty dose of the invasive supernatural thrown in; some of the dark proceedings made use of ideas loaned by Lovecraft, including an archaic spelling of Yog-Sothoth.

Howard represents an extraordinary case of massive, and massively uneven, systemic output. His popular Conan cycle of stories aside, he developed an entire mythology around the monster-hunting English Puritan Solomon Kane, the Atlantaean hero Kull, and a boatload of stories of historical fiction, horror, and a significant number of sports tales usually centered on prizefighting. Although his Conan tales have had a lengthy life in popular culture, even these are often aesthetically challenging for many readers today. Patrice Louinet, certainly a fan of Howard's who wrote the introduction to Del Rey's 2002 compendium of his original Conan stories, admits that the author's financial difficulties in 1932 and 1933 pushed him to churn out the frequently substandard Conan tales that had become his "meal ticket."

But none of Lovecraft's circle departed quite so radically from his virulently anti-commercial attitude as did August Derleth. Derleth's own constant, restless, ever unsatisfied search for checks resulted in numerous rejections that eventually turned into acceptances through his sheer persistence. His correspondence with Lovecraft sometimes suggests he simply did not comprehend his mentor's slow, methodical, and anti-commercial sense of what writing meant. We're left to wonder if this is why their correspondence becomes almost the only place Lovecraft opens up fully about the challenges of producing for a market when he allegedly rejected market values.

Derleth unfailingly viewed publishing as a business enterprise and went after markets, as lean and hungry as the founder of a modern-day Silicon Valley tech start-up. How could he grasp even a little of what Lovecraft described in February 1932 as the desire for "a rest from the rebuffs and restrictions of external agencies" and a desire to produce material in secret without having to worry about "suiting this or that commercial standard . . . what I must do is get the whole loathsome picture of tradesmen and hagglers out of my head."

Derleth's obsession with publishing as many words as possible perhaps explains his willingness to later exploit Lovecraft's style, plots, and narrative tropes. In fact, during his mentor's own lifetime, Derleth seemed determined to publish "Lovecraftian" tales if Lovecraft wouldn't do it himself. One of his submissions to *Weird Tales* in 1931 received a rejection letter from Farnsworth Wright because, in Wright's words, Derleth had "lifted whole phrases from Lovecraft's work." Unfortunately Wright's wholly correct assessment proved a portent for what came to fruition in 1945 when Arkham House published *The Lurker at the Threshhold*.[45]

In what became a short novel, Derleth took two fragmentary pieces of Lovecraft's writing and added something on the order of 30,000–35,000 words of his own. He chose not to tell readers about this and instead simply referred to this, and later stories, as "posthumous collaborations." This left the impression that he had access to large unfinished works of Lovecraft that he merely edited and filled in some of the missing gaps.

The stories that appeared in the 1957 collection, *The Survivor and Others*, show Derleth taking his efforts to co-opt Lovecraft's reputation to new lows. By this time, Derleth began selecting the kernel of ideas contained in Lovecraft's daybook, and even parts of his correspondence, and writing stories of his own based on these fragments. Often readers, and worst of all reviewers, believed that they had just read an original Lovecraft tale edited and polished by Derleth, when in fact they encountered only Derleth's purple prose.

An episode in Lovecraft and Derleth's correspondence makes these "posthumous collaborations" appear as especially egregious betrayals of Lovecraft's wishes. In early 1932 Derleth offered, unnecessarily, to revise one of Lovecraft's masterpieces, "The Shadow Over Innsmouth." Derleth inexplicably disliked the story now much beloved by Lovecraft fans, and believed it needed more action. Lovecraft politely refused this offer, telling his impetuous young friend that "you doubtless realize yourself that a second person's changes cannot help destroying something of the homogeneity of a piece of writing. No other person can quite duplicate the mood of the original author."

Lovecraft politely added that, in any case, "the trouble for you would be enormous" and then dropped the matter. Lovecraft never submitted the story to *Weird Tales*. Derleth, in 1933, submitted it without Lovecraft's knowledge. Farnsworth Wright rejected it because of its length.

Derleth's proprietary attitude toward Lovecraft's work took on epic proportions after his mentor's death in 1937. The confusion that Derleth created, along with a more general attitude of professional disdain for genre fiction, accounts for some of the literary establishment's attitude toward Lovecraft. Derleth's "posthumous collaborations" are, frankly, boring and sometimes just silly.

Two collections of these stories, printed previously in various pulps, appeared in quick succession in the late fifties and early sixties, entitled *The Mask of Cthulhu* (1958) and *The Trail of Cthulhu* (1962). Both collections attempt to imitate Lovecraft's style and fail rather stupidly. They include flashy and often absurd characters and plots that borrow more from the alien invader obsessions of the American 1950s than the world of Lovecraft. Nuclear weapons are actually used against Cthulhu in one of these tales, reminiscent of the increasingly popular *Gojira* (Godzilla) sequels, remakes, and revisions that began to flourish in America during this era—often themselves heavily redacted versions of the original Japanese *kaiju* films.

Part of the problem had to do with Derleth's own sense of writing a Lovecraft imitation. By including a few of Lovecraft's favorite adjectives like "eldritch" or "shadowed" or "witch-haunted," he thought he successfully captured the essence of his friend's style. Readers who come to Lovecraft after encountering "Cthulhu Mythos" tales, whether by Derleth or others, are often pleased and surprised to learn that Lovecraft's admittedly baroque prose did not have the addiction to adjectives that his work has been accused of displaying.

Moreover, unlike Derleth's failed efforts, you'll never find in Lovecraft the tedious lists of extraterrestrial monsters and taxonomies of forbidden books that became Derleth's special practice. In other words, when you read Lovecraft you step out of the world of fan-fic and into the world of original creation powerful enough to generate fan-fic.

Although simultaneously doing his reputation some harm, Derleth certainly played an essential role in keeping Lovecraft's name alive. Indeed, he allowed—though legally the publishers could have done it anyway—the mass distribution of Lovecraft's work in paperback.

However, there's an interesting paradox at work. Once Lovecraft's work made its way outside the limited bounds of Arkham House and into the mass market, it started a popular boom that began to build toward his current fame. Few would know the name of August Derleth or many of the writers of Lovecraft's circle, without Lovecraft's own fame. Lovecraft's own work would have remained forever a parochial taste had it been left to August Derleth.

———

Derleth and those he managed to influence tried, fairly successfully, to cut R.H. Barlow out of the public process of preserving Lovecraft's work. The reasons for this are complex, ranging from an inability to understand the depth of Lovecraft's relationship with Barlow to simple jealousy that the young man had been granted the status of Lovecraft's literary executor.

Derleth believed, apparently to the end of his days, that Lovecraft had given him this honor, based entirely on a single stray, joking comment in one letter written in April of 1932. Derleth, along with Donald and Howard Wandrei, worked to make sure that others in the Lovecraft circle saw Barlow as an interloper and proved highly successful in this malicious endeavor.

Barlow had done anything but play the role of usurper. Aunt Anne Gamwell had Lovecraft's 1936 "Instructions Case of Decease" probated in the Providence courts. The note made Barlow "literary executor" in a definitive, legal sense even if Derleth fanatically claimed the title for more than three decades. Other than a few volumes gifted specifically to Morton, Lovecraft gave Barlow first choice of 2,000 volumes and "all files of weird magazines" along with "all original manuscripts." Barlow gifted most of these materials immediately to the John Hay Library.

Barlow's life took a series of dramatic and fascinating turns. He came into conflict with both Donald Wandrei and August Derleth, both of whom became convinced that he had seized Lovecraft's library because he'd been at the right place at the right time to do so. When Barlow moved to California to live in San Francisco, he wrote his long-time literary hero Clark Ashton Smith in an effort to visit him. Smith had apparently been convinced by the Derleth and Wandrei gossip and wrote Barlow a nasty, two-sentence letter saying that he "had no wish to hear ever again from a person who had acted so dishonorably in the estate of his dear friend." The letter came as a terrific shock to the sensitive Barlow, who described its emotional impact as the same as "cutting my entrails out with a meat cleaver."

He became a poet in San Francisco, writing gorgeously strange free verse that stands up well today. Under psychoanalysis, he came to terms more fully with his gay identity and, in an autobiographical note written when he was twenty-six, spoke openly of "the gorgeous blond boy" he'd been "infatuated with" at eighteen. He took pleasure in the "nice prick" of a young man he shared a rooming house with on his arrival to the west coast.

Barlow enrolled at Berkeley and studied Nahuatl, the language of the Mexica (better known as the Aztec) Empire. Deeply learned in the Aztec culture and language by 1942, he moved to Mexico City to teach, under a Guggenheim Fellowship. Over the next decade, he produced more than 150 academic papers, pamphlets, and monographs on Meso-american culture. He became chair of the anthropology department of Mexico City College in 1948 until his death at his own hand in 1951.

By the time of his death, he'd given the overwhelming majority of his Lovecraft collection to the Hay. He did hold onto a few pieces. He kept the original manuscript of "The Shadow Out of Time" that eventually made its way from an attic in Hawaii, where Barlow's student had retired, back home to Providence in 1994. Thus, though S.T. Joshi is technically correct that Barlow "systematically deposited" materials at the Hay, including his copies of *Weird Tales* that completed the library's collection, his gifting of these materials did include some clever negotiation that allowed him to pursue his own curious and fascinating work in the 1940s.

The Hay holds an intriguing and at times unintentionally hilarious exchange of letters between Barlow and various frustrated librarians in the 1940s. Beginning in the spring of 1937, Barlow began delivering Lovecraft's books and papers, including with them typescripts of Clark Ashton Smith. Well into the 1940s, he would continue to ensure that the library received anything related to Lovecraft, at one point even requesting the manuscripts for *The Dream-Quest of Unknown Kadath* and *The Case of Charles Dexter Ward* so that he could prepare a proper typescript.

Some Lovecraft scholars have suggested that at first the Hay had limited interest in receiving Lovecraft's books, manuscripts, and other papers. Barlow's correspondence tells a different story. Barlow had a number of exchanges with Professor S. Foster Damon and the library's administrative assistant in the late 1930s that suggests that Damon's interest in all things occult encouraged his own desire to add Lovecraftiana and related materials to the library's special collection.[46]

By the mid-1940s, as interest in Lovecraft began to grow, Barlow began to bargain with the press for his entire collection, the contents of Yoh-Vombis. He would give them all his "fantastic journals" along with fan journals and manuscripts of other *Weird Tales* writers. He also had come across, apparently during his time in Mexico City, "Lovecraft items (including some pirated Spanish-language editions of interest)."

In return, Barlow asked that Brown University get him "a printing press neither to print Spanish (except incidentally) nor English" but specifically one that could print a paper in Nahuatl or, as Barlow explained in his letter, "the ('Aztec') tongue." He gave the Hay precise specifications, down to the size of the motor the press should contain. He wanted the Hay, in turn, to have the entirety of his fantasy and horror collection that he had "assembled with such pains and enthusiasm, unconsciously building it around Lovecraft's personality." He added that he didn't know how much "haggling" Brown University could do.[47]

F.G. Martineau, one of the Hay's librarians, did his best. In an internal memo in early July 1946, Martineau inquired about whether or not the University could get its hands on a printing press that could print Nahuatl. Although he apparently was told that this was impossible, he did write back to Barlow in early August, pleading that the University had "no printing machinery or no particular facilities or know how [sic] about getting any" but that they would offer him the cost of the press in return for the materials.

Barlow apparently received his press and continued his work in Mexico City for the next five years. By this same time, he had apparently at least placated Derleth. He contributed to two Arkham House publications, although Derleth heavily edited both contributions given that some of the material did not suit the image of Lovecraft he wanted to present and some of it would prove embarrassing to Derleth himself.

By a peculiar chance, William S. Burroughs took courses in Meso-american archaeology from Barlow, feeding his own fascination with ancient cities that would result in some of the Beat mentor's more Lovecraftian works, especially his 1981 novel *Cities of the Red Night*. Burroughs and Barlow never got to know one another personally. When the scandal that threatened Barlow's seemingly productive and happy career led him to take his own life, Burroughs did take note. He wrote to Allen Ginsberg in January 1951 that his former professor at Mexico City College "knocked himself off a few days ago with overdose of goofballs. Vomit all over the bed. I can't see this suicide kick."

———

Sonia Greene also became, at least for a while, a focus of Derleth's rage for control over the Lovecraft legacy. In an account printed by Wilfred B. Talman in his booklet "The Normal Lovecraft," she describes how Derleth contacted her regarding her plans to put her own memories of her husband into print.

By 1947, Sonia lived in Los Angeles, having remarried to a man of equal peculiarity to Lovecraft—if at the opposite end of the spectrum of oddity—and arguably significantly less brilliant. Nathaniel A. Davis, a former economics instructor at Berkeley, founded a tiny movement he called the Planetaryans that devoted itself to the worthy ideals of world citizenship. He lectured widely on topics as diverse as venereal disease, harbor development, and the dangers of fascism.[48]

In that year, she wrote to her old friend Samuel Loveman, part of that original circle of amateur journalists that had included Morton and Kleiner and the group in whose company she had fallen in love with Howard in the early twenties. Now, she found herself being chased, much against her will, by the legacy of that love.

"Enclosed is a letter from Derleth," she wrote to Loveman. "Do you think he's 'shooting in the dark'? Bluffing?" Her concern over Derleth's extraordinary letter is more than understandable. He managed vaguery and threat all at once, and apparently mailed the letter so that it arrived in the midst of the December holidays. Greene claimed he wrote in the letter that he "hoped you [Sonia] are not going ahead regardless of our stipulations to arrange for publications of anything containing writings of any kind, letters or otherwise, of H.P. Lovecraft." He then raised the specter of Arkham House seeking to "bring suit." He then made the off-handed claim, utterly without legal foundation, that any material of Lovecraft's had to pass through "our office" (Derleth's house, in other words).

Then, ending this already harsh missive with a dreadful flourish, Derleth noted that he, from Lovecraft's letters, had "a complete and detailed account of how things went during his [Lovecraft's] married life."

She had replied to the letter curtly, telling Derleth that since he claimed he had in possession letters that might prove embarrassing to her, perhaps he had all the information he needed. In essence, she asked that he leave her alone.

What the hell was he even talking about? It appears that Derleth had developed an obsession with preventing the tale from circulating that Greene had "subsidized" Lovecraft between 1922 and 1929. The reason for Derleth's fascination with the question probably needs the attention of a psychiatrist rather than a historian. Nor do I think it accomplishes much to try to quantify the amount of financial support that Lovecraft received from Sonia as opposed to what remained of his legacy and that of his aunts. Either way, he certainly wasn't supporting himself with his revision work and the very occasional check from *Weird Tales.*

"It was an evil hour when I met him," Sonia wrote Loveman concerning Derleth in a later letter. In it, she made clear her own lack of interest in gaining notoriety from her late ex-husband and worried mostly over whether Derleth had managed to turn some of her old friends against her, friends from days she clearly remembered as a bright moment in her life.

Sonia did not back down easily from this challenge and her unwillingness to let Derleth browbeat her tells us something about the role of women in Lovecraft's personal life and indeed in the expanded universe of his stories. Lovecraft-inspired fiction long remained dominated by men. Women stayed notably absent from some of the earlier stories that sought to expand the Lovecraft canon. One of Ramsey Campbell's early, and arguably one of his best, Lovecraft imitations, "The Tower of Yuggoth," follows the basic formula of a male protagonist acquiring forbidden knowledge, though his doomed investigator shows a bit more complexity than many of Lovecraft's characters. Robert Bloch's early Lovecraft-inspired tales had a deeper interest in character and plot than Lovecraft himself ever did. But, for the most part, his work contains troubled men facing the horror alone, often in tales like "The Brood of Bubastis" that seem to be sequels or prequels to some of Lovecraft's own tales (in the case of "Brood," there are some rather clear connections to "The Rats in the Walls").

I suspect some readers will delight in the reevaluation of women's essential role in his life. Other readers will actively dislike discussions of sexism, or even gender, entering Lovecraft's world. A few will respond to such a discussion in a fashion not dissimilar to the amazingly hostile reaction by many male geeks toward women interested in comics, video games, or tabletop RPGs.

These attitudes become especially sharp in defense of the fandom of Lovecraft who did, after all, create something like the original pop culture boys' club. When writing about the women in Lovecraft's life, biographers and Lovecraft scholars sometimes seem unhinged in describing the influence his mother had over him and, at other times, simply get unnecessarily, indeed weirdly, nasty when talking about Sonia Greene.

De Camp, for example, rather bizarrely feels the need to tell us, apropos of nothing, that as Sonia Greene "aged she put on weight and she dressed and did her hair more plainly." This aside appears in a passage where he's supposed to simply be telling us about her life after Lovecraft, a rather rich one that included foreign travel, her move to California, and remarriage. We've already seen the sheer tonnage of abuse heaped on Sarah Susan Lovecraft.[49]

I do not think it possible to write about H.P. Lovecraft without establishing his connections with women in his life and the enormous influence they exercised over him. I also do not think it possible to write about these women, just as I cannot write about Lovecraft himself, without describing the world that made them, frustrated them, offered them new opportunities and other times stripped them of those same new options.

The period of Lovecraft's youth featured what one historian has called an attempt to "create sexless men as well as sexless women." Victorian culture saw the respectability of the middle-class family as a triumph over barbarism, a mark of progress rather than a reactionary set of ideals embedded in social relations. This accounts for an aspect of the late nineteenth–early twentieth century that became an important part of Lovecraft's fiction: the idea of a highly developed and seemingly secure civilization under threat by all kinds of dark things, including dark people.

Such a view of human domesticity required the denial, indeed the repudiation, of certain aspects of human nature. Cultural historian T.J. Jackson Lears says this middle-class ideology of safety and security in prescribed class and gender roles shaped literature that relied heavily on sentimentalism to maintain the fiction of the happy family. He sees in this what he calls a "process of evasion," an unwillingness to face the darker sides of family life, gender relations, and what it meant for people to spend their lives trying to imitate these roles.[50]

The women of Lovecraft's world betrayed the era's dominant ideals. We've learned that his Grandmother Robie, born in an even earlier moment of Victorianism's bourgeois epoch, nurtured some interest in astronomy rather than baking and mending. Both of Lovecraft's aunts, for differing reasons, ended up living as independently as their limited incomes allowed.

And Sarah Susan? In a society that glorified achievement and indoctrinated young boys with the notion of the "self-made man" at every opportunity, she let his imagination run in its wildest directions, ensuring he had the books, chemistry sets, telescopes, and role-playing materials that allowed his mind to roam across endless and ancient cities, through time and space, searching barren landscapes for chasms into unknown places. There would have been no H.P. Lovecraft, and the world he created for us, without her.

On top of all that, both Sarah Susan Lovecraft and Sonia Haft Greene are incredibly interesting people. Who can blame a writer for wanting to tell their story? And, why wouldn't you want their story told?

Ironically, Victorianism had no greater enemy than the cold-water temperance man in wing-tipped collars with an upper-crust Providence legacy.

But, without the influence of his intellectually inclined mother or the wife who seems to have helped him understand Nietzsche, Lovecraft may not have been so committed to ripping out the still-beating heart of Victorian sentiment. Under their influence, and the influences that flowed into his life because of them, he created art that combined Nietzsche's nihilism, gods of the ancient world, alternative histories, and monsters no one knew existed. This gave life to an art form that constitutes at least as much a cry of agony as Eliot's "The Waste Land" and a repudiation of the hopefulness, the inveterate optimism about American possibilities that appeared in the experimental prose forms of writers like Dos Passos.

He demanded of his work something more visceral than the modernist poetry and prose that depended on a fictionalized populist realism, the language of the streets clashing purposefully with pedantic allusions to history and undefined yearnings. In a letter to Frank Belknap Long, he called T.S. Eliot "an acute thinker" but denied him the status of artist. He had forgotten the world of dreams, that reality must be seen by "moonlight" and not excavated out of random snatches of conversation and lines in Sanskrit (for the rest of his life, it became a running joke with Lovecraft to mock the famous "Shantih! Shantih! Shantih!" postlude of "The Waste Land"; "What does that damned Shantih mean anyway?" he quipped to Long).

Horror, however, could destroy the pillars of optimism, bourgeois or utopian, in a way that realism could not achieve. To paraphrase Nietzsche, Lovecraft believed an author must write fiction with a hammer, accomplishing Nietzsche's task of pursuing truth with the same blunt and savage force. The women who shaped his life helped to put that hammer in his hand.

By the 1940s, Arkham House had sold enough volumes of his material that Lovecraft's work reached cult status, indeed a fairly expansive cult status that brought his tales the undesired attention of Edmund Wilson. In an especially brilliant move by Derleth, he had Lovecraft thrown into the hopper of cheap "Armed Services Editions" of paperback stories from the pulps. Lovecraft went to the battlefields of Europe, North Africa, and the Pacific and then came home, roughly-used copies of his tales for a new generation to discover on their fathers' shelves. In 1945, Derleth worked out a deal with World Publishing Company to publish a Lovecraft compilation. Within four years, almost 80,000 hardback editions had been sold.

In 1948, Lloyd Briggs of Altamont, New York wrote to *The Providence Journal* to find out how to get in touch with Arkham House. He had read "The Dunwich Horror" and although he noted, apparently after reading Winfield Scott's "tribute" to Lovecraft, that "the fellow was a bit of a screwball," he was sure a Lovecraft collection would make good reading "up here in New York State when the winter wind blows."[51]

A larger fandom had begun to grow that went beyond an appreciation of Lovecraft's stories and thought of him as anything but a screwball. Pennsylvanian Andrew Clark found his way to Lovecraft as a high schooler in the 1960s. He recalls sitting up late at night "with the only light being the one on the table next to my chair. Bach concertos and partitas for harpsichord played on the phonograph to create atmosphere." Lovecraft opened "a new world" to him.

Early fans of Lovecraft revealed the same sense of devotion, and utter absorption, in Lovecraft's world that soon made interest in his work the haute cuisine of geekdom. A friend of horror scholar Victoria Jackson had been a teenage fan of Lovecraft in 1965. He remembers being moved to walk out onto Montauk beach in the middle of a summer's night and pray to Cthulhu to rise across the darkened horizon. Luckily for the rest of us, nothing listened.

The claim has occasionally been made that Lovecraft's work stands alone in creating the need for writers, filmmakers, and even game designers to build on and extrapolate his mythology. Certainly at midcentury, only Arthur Conan Doyle's Sherlock Holmes managed to gain a fan base avid enough to want to further explore the Baker Street detective's exploits, an exploration that continues today in television and film.

It's not exactly true, however, that Lovecraft is truly singular in the felt need among gifted fans to expand his dark vision. However, Lovecraft's influence has grown more organically than other ever-proliferating modern mythologies. The Tolkien estate maintained tight control over *The Lord of the Rings* but that has not prevented the explosion of epic fantasy that borrows, sometimes rather heavily and directly, from Tolkien's worlds of quests among elves, dwarves, orcs, and, that new kid on the block in most fantasy worlds, humans. Moreover, the six Peter Jackson films, particularly his extended retelling of *The Hobbit*, introduced all manner of new elements into the Oxford philologist's original creation, as have more than a dozen officially licensed video games that involve new characters and scenarios far removed from anything that came from Tolkien's pen.

Star Wars offers another example. Although George Lucas long ruled the "galaxy far, far away," he did allow the growth of an intricate mythology around the original trilogy and the later additions. Since *Star Wars: A New Hope* appeared in 1977, a mind-boggling number of comic book series, novels, role-playing games, and computer and console video games have emerged under the guidance of Lucasfilm, with animated television series joining into the mix in more recent years and, of course, a whole new series of films helmed by Disney Studios and J.J. Abrams.

These are, obviously, heavily commodified mythologies, very much under the control of the entertainment conglomerates that now hold their licenses. Disney can plan a "Star Wars" land to compete with Universal Studio's "Harry Potter" world in Florida. Video games give players the opportunity to play on the margins of the events of the War of the Ring. These products can be good and bad, entertaining or indifferent, but they are going to have significant success because they join a popular myth with the sorcerous powers of modern advertising.

Lovecraft's mythology has grown without the aid of mass culture's most powerful players. The language used to describe these different worlds of fantasy is striking. Fans have denominated Lovecraft's work as a "mythos" and not a franchise in the manner of *Star Wars*, *The Lord of the Rings*, or *Harry Potter*.

The elaboration of Lovecraft's mythology began even before his death. Robert E. Howard and Clark Ashton Smith both borrowed gods and monsters from their friend. It's worth noting that Lovecraft, in turn, used his friends' mystical tomes and horrific Old Ones, creating a kind of milieu and atmosphere of dark fantasy that helped to turn *Weird Tales* into one of the first outposts of geek culture. Eventually millions of people would participate in horror, science fiction, and fantasy worlds, landscaping them with fan-fic, cosplay, and an ongoing conversation that owns large portions of Internet real estate. It began with camaraderie among the authors of *Weird Tales* that, through letters to "The Eyrie," became a connection with fans who collected the magazine and, as was the case with R.H. Barlow, collected authors' autographs as well. Frequently, as was the case with Derleth, Bloch, and Barlow, fans then became writers themselves.

Smith, perhaps Lovecraft's closest correspondent friend that he never met, decided to try his hand at fiction largely under Lovecraft's influence. The poet, artist, and sculptor saw in Lovecraft's work the possibility of creating a new kind of art through the medium of the weird tale. Whether he accomplished this himself remains an open question. One of his best stories, "The Vaults of Yoh-Vombis," borrows directly from the basic plot idea of *At the Mountains of Madness*, which Smith had read in manuscript form early in the summer of 1931, before writing "Yoh-Vombis" early that fall. Notably, it succeeds in creating a true visceral terror, featuring bat-like creatures that dig their claws into the minds of their unlucky victims. The story fails to awaken any meaningful sense of cosmic terror or panic over the meaningfulness of human experience in an indifferent, occasionally hostile, universe that Lovecraft excelled in invoking.

Efforts like Smith's aesthetic leaps in the dark have made possible the expansion of Lovecraft's influence. Derleth's efforts to bully and browbeat anyone who attempted to publish anything related to Lovecraft arguably helped to strangle a vestigial fame that might have come to full growth earlier. What makes this even more unfortunate is that Derleth never held a meaningful claim to copyright. In 1947, Derleth had purchased, or at least thought he had purchased, the rights to Lovecraft's stories directly from *Weird Tales*. However, beginning in 1926 (the year he began to write the works later thought of as canonical), Lovecraft wisely began to reserve the rights of second printing to himself. Therefore, it's questionable whether *Weird Tales* could have legally sold the rights to the stories to Derleth.

As late as 1969 and 1970, when a year before his death he penned a commemorative essay on the first three decades of Arkham House, Derleth managed to exude continued malice toward suspected interlopers. He seemingly notes philosophically how envy constitutes "the basest emotion of which man is capable" and then launched into a tirade against "self-serving fans who wanted to print without fee or without any copyright protection material by Lovecraft." He claimed that some of these "self-serving fans" then had attempted to "weaken confidence" in Arkham House.

American popular culture passed Derleth by, especially in the 1960s. He claimed that Arkham House had "many imitators" who had "spewed forth many books of little or no merit, cluttered the limited market." In truth, horror and fantasy had quickly proven to have an unlimited market in a rapidly changing America.

By the late sixties, a vibrant and exploratory counterculture shifted the center of cultural gravity in American life. Student groups like Todd Gitlin's Students for a Democratic Society (SDS) consciously sought to break the stranglehold of the neo-domesticity of the 1950s over their own lives while also confronting the terrifying realities of American foreign policy that had resulted in military adventurism in Latin America and Southeast Asia and what amounted to an apocalyptic arms race with the Soviet Union.

African Americans, weary of court decisions that seemed to change little, took up the slogan of "Black Power." Older organizations like the SNCC (Student Nonviolent Coordinating Committee) began to demand economic and social power that went beyond the right to use the same water fountains and lunch counters as whites. The Black Panther Party, from its modest beginnings in Oakland, California, grew into a mass movement that J. Edgar Hoover called the greatest danger facing "the internal security of the country," an extraordinary admission to make during the Vietnam War.

Lovecraft would have found this new world bewildering. His vaunted conservatism had undergone a rather radical change by the 1930s. Seeing himself as a Tory of the eighteenth century rather than a twentieth-century Republican, he seems to have been revolted by the corruption and failure to govern that characterized the Harding, Coolidge, and Hoover administrations in the 1920s. The coming of the Great Depression and the dwindling state of his own finances pushed him to become an ardent supporter of FDR and to hold views slightly to the left of most of the policies of the New Deal. Some of his young protégés, particularly Barlow and Frank Belknap Long, moved hard left in the "red decade" of the 1930s and declared themselves Communists. Lovecraft himself could never embrace what he called simply "Bolshevism" but began openly describing himself as a Socialist in the years before his death.

This sharp political turn, however, would not have prepared him for the 1960s and it's easy to see him taking another swing back to the right had he lived into his seventh decade or beyond. He esteemed order and stability above all and the revolutionary aspects of the 1960s, from the sexual revolution to the success of integration and the rise of the Black Power movement in the latter part of the decade, might have sent him into paroxysms of reactionary and racist rage greater than what we hear out of him in his New York days.

Whatever he would have thought of the counterculture, they, especially white college students, came to love horror and fantasy and eventually Lovecraft in a way that seems surprising, perhaps at first even contradictory, given their stated political program. The hip nature of Marvel comics, leading to posters of *Spider-Man* and the *Fantastic Four* decorating many a dorm room, seems a bit out of touch with weed-fueled debates about Johnson's escalation of the war in Southeast Asia or the new, revolutionary free speech movements that swept college campuses across the nation. No doubt the counterculture's love for fantasy had elements of escapism, the perennial critique of genre fiction. But more is at work than such a simplistic interpretation suggests.

Before Lovecraft became beloved of the counterculture, they met the very different work of J.R.R. Tolkien. Tolkien's *The Hobbit* and *The Lord of the Rings* trilogy became, as an essay entitled "Hippies and Hobbits" penned by Jane Ciabattari claims, "required reading for the nascent counterculture." Graffiti proclaiming "Frodo Lives!" and "Gandalf for President!" began to appear on abandoned buildings and subway trains.

Why the appeal of the rather old-fashioned seeming Tolkien? The novels, although written by a conservative Catholic, suggest a nostalgic, agrarian message in which the industrial war machine of Mordor seeks to destroy the natural pleasures of Middle Earth. Nixon easily looked like Sauron to the antiwar generation.

Perhaps more practically, Tolkien's tales celebrated the hallucinogenic and healthful benefits of "halfling weed," enjoyed by both Gandalf and the inhabitants of the Shire, a premodern paradise that seemed an environmentalist dream. Indeed, rumors circulated, as they did with Lovecraft, that Tolkien had written his stories under the influence of hallucinogens. Both sets of rumors are almost certainly false, though I'd not be surprised to learn that either one of them sampled some of the chemical possibilities their era offered as a path to the boundaries of imagination they both sought.

Rock music, the very soundtrack of cool, took plenty of notice of Tolkien. Well-attested rumors suggest that the Beatles considered, and then in a decision probably good for all concerned, dismissed the idea of a rock opera based on *The Lord of the Rings*. Led Zeppelin consistently alluded to Tolkien's imagery, most famously in "Misty Mountain Hop" and "The Battle of Evermore." Ciabattari concluded that the "tweedy" Oxford professor "was once so square he was cool."

Lovecraft, it might seem, offered much more of a challenge to countercultural tastes. In Tolkien's world, a clear, an absurdly clear, division existed between good and evil. This idea, ironically, appealed to members of the counterculture as much as to their parents, despite serious differences of opinion over which side was which. Lovecraft of course has no use for notions of good and evil. He terrifies us with his "cosmic indifferentism" that leads to no particular politics since such terrestrial matters are pointless against the backdrop of his bleak universe of malign entities that, if we are lucky, simply leave us be.

Lovecraft's work may not have fueled political action (and he certainly would have been horrified had it done so) but it's his dysmorphic visions of reality in which "the angles are all wrong" and "non-Euclidean geometry" opens portals into other dimensions, that attracted the psychedelic side of the counterculture in much the same way that William Burroughs's sometimes horrific visions and hallucinogenic dream quests opened the doors of perception for an experimental generation. Indeed, Lovecraft's work began to disseminate slowly beyond the bounds of the Arkham House readership just as the famous "acid tests" in San Francisco began.

The cultural exchange between Lovecraft and the counterculture took an even stranger turn. Tolkien may have received a name-check from some of the most important bands of the late 1960s and early 1970s but Lovecraft got a band that both named themselves for him and developed portions of their set list in his honor, titling their most widely distributed album in homage to one of his most obscure stories. A group of musicians led by George Edwards, heavily influenced by the Chicago blues and folk scene, banded together in 1967 under producer George Badonsky—such a Lovecraft aficionado that he had named his Yorkshire Terrier Yuggoth. Before deciding to take the name H.P. Lovecraft, the band checked in with the aging August Derleth, probably having heard of how frequently he threatened litigation. Perhaps not being entirely clear what he was giving permission for, Derleth agreed (it's unclear if he demanded a fee).

Although the group eventually disintegrated from internal dissension, substance abuse, and a mixture of the two, their album *The White Ship* included the eponymous song that paid tribute to Lovecraft's little-known 1919 allegorical tale, a story that represented something of an early practice sketch for his novel *The Dream-Quest of Unknown Kadath* and, to some degree, the dark mysticism of "The Silver Key." Dour harmonies, feedback, strains of a harpsichord thanks to classically trained keyboardist David Michaels, and even the gentle tolling of an 1811 maritime bell set the stage for a psychedelic trip that actually makes for a perfect soundscape for the story.

A second album in 1968, called simply *H.P. Lovecraft II*, featured a trippy tribute to *At the Mountains of Madness* that one music critic called "one of the better musical approximations of a lava lamp." The rhythms meander and menace in ways much more sinister than any lava lamp I've ever met and, perhaps owing to their increasing drug use, the band's groove takes a dark turn less suggestive of the flower power music the group started out to make and much more in line with the gloomier prog rock of Pink Floyd. In other words, like *The White Ship*, it conveys something of the feeling of the story from which it took its name.

Lovecraft's dread shade hovered over another emerging musical culture he most certainly would have eschewed. By the 1970s, working-class English teenagers turned increasingly to heavy metal, music constructed of angry dissonance that echoed the industrial sounds of their childhoods against the bleak landscape of unemployment and economic disaster.

In 1968, Birmingham, England decayed into a cityscape whose economic woes not only resulted in abandoned factories and buildings but in whole blocks of wreckage and rubble as mortgages collapsed and homes and businesses became abandoned. It also became the home of a band that called themselves Earth and played a harsh, heavy blues that incorporated the morbidity of the tritone, regarded since the Middle Ages as the "devil's fifth" for its gloomy and dread-inducing sound.

The original line-up of Earth—Ozzy Osbourne, Geezer Butler,

Tony Iommi, and Bill Ward—needed something new, even as they became more popular on the pub circuit. They wanted to differentiate themselves from the psychedelic sounds of the hippies and, in fact, another popular pub band in England already called themselves Earth. Geezer Butler's interest in horror films and the occult inspired their new direction and they took the name Black Sabbath when the cinema across from their rehearsal space revived the 1963 Boris Karloff film of the same name.

Their self-titled first album featured a tribute to "Beyond the Wall of Sleep," a title taken from a 1919 Lovecraft tale of the same name. The lyrics themselves have little to do with the story. Gary Hill, who has written at length about Lovecraft-inspired music in *The Strange Sound of Cthulhu*, asked Butler about this but received a somewhat muddled answer in which the bassist noted that he remembered little about the circumstances of the song's creation, though he made clear that what he knew of Lovecraft came largely through the popular British writer on the occult, Dennis Wheatley. It's worth noting, however, that Butler's memories are often a bit fuzzy from those days. He is, in fact, unable to recall the woman who appears as the famous figure in black on the cover of Black Sabbath's first album.

Heavy metal came to the United States in the 1970s and created an enormous subculture that called themselves "headbangers" or simply "bangers." It also touched off a wave of experimentation with the sound Sabbath created.

Speed-metal band Metallica, whose style became known as thrash metal, became the largest musical behemoth to let their fascination with Lovecraft make its way into their catalog. Their 1984 album *Ride the Lightning* features a song called "Call of Ktulu" with guitar riffs that spin spasmodically until the listener feels engulfed in an acoustic cloud at a dizzying height. All in all, the song's a perfect aural soundscape from which to contemplate "the corpse city of R'lyeh" and its dead but dreaming inhabitant.

Since the 1980s, so-called extreme metal, death metal, or black metal has made frequent use of Lovecraft and his themes. Joseph Norman closely examined this phenomenon and found no fewer than 227 groups the world over who have used Lovecraft or elements of Love- craftiana in their music. He came across bands named Yog-Sothoth, Azathoth, Dagon, Arkham, and quite a few who couldn't resist calling themselves simply Necronomicon.

Cradle of Filth, the best-known black metal band in the U.K. in the early twenty-first century, has incorporated both the work of Lovecraft and modern horror author and filmmaker Clive Barker into a frightening mythological universe that structures their albums. The 2000 album *Midian* and their 2004 *Nymphetamine* make frequent mention of Cthulhu and the apocalypse. In their interesting read- ing, Cthulhu is female and represents every alluring, dark goddess in human mythology. Only squishier.

Lovecraft hated noise and very much enjoyed a brief loss of hearing in his youth. The cacophony of crowds constituted part of what troubled him in his New York days. It's doubtful that a man whose musical taste never got much beyond popular tunes of the early century and Gilbert and Sullivan musicals would have subjected himself to Cradle of Filth.

Or, at least not more than once. On the level of the artistry of the weird, he would have understood what such bands are about. He's the one who, after all, imagined in "Nyarlathotep" a dread cosmos that resounded with "the muffled, maddening beating of drums and thin, monotonous whine of blasphemous flutes from inconceivable unlighted chambers beyond Time." The cultists of Cthulhu "whipped themselves to daemoniac heights by howls and squawking ecstasies that tore and reverberated through those nights' woods like pestilential tempests."

Even the most conservative devotee of Lovecraft has to admit that such passages are undeniably metal.

⌣

H.P. Lovecraft would have hated Hollywood. First of all, there are no antiquities to visit unless you count the nine-mile slow and sun-baked drive east of downtown L.A. that takes you to Spanish missions like San

Gabriel Archangel or the signs in town that tell you only where things used to be located.

Some of the city's "historical monuments" actually date to Lovecraft's own time and it's inconceivable that he would have considered them historical, had he lived a somewhat longer life. So I imagine him making his way around contemporary L.A. and hear him grumbling about a place that has no meaningful past, that only exists in a vast, heavily commodified present where the new Chick-fil-A on Sunset—angrily puffing out exhaust that's supposed to smell enticing rather than nauseating—has become a weird contemporary landmark. This is, after all, a city where Grauman's 1920 Chinese Theatre (opened the year Lovecraft turned thirty) counts as history in a world where the building of permanent human settlements dates back 14,000 years.

Moreover, for a committed pedestrian of Lovecraft's caliber, the City of Angels would prove more than daunting. He could not have actually seen very much of it using his preferred mode of transport. I see him walking the length and breadth of West Hollywood, the only part of town a dedicated urban hiker can conceivably hoof it. But he would have hated it. It is everything about modernity he did hate.

Impossible as it is to see Lovecraft, in wing-tipped collar like a banker from the 1890s, lumbering his slumped frame up the Sunset Strip past the Viper Room, peeking in on Book Soup to look for new critical editions of Dryden and Pope and walking—undoubtedly in a black rage—past the line of teenagers waiting outside the Whisky a Go Go to hear a Mastodon cover band; it's an image that makes a bizarre kind of sense. He would not have loved the town and, as I've suggested earlier, might have agreed with those trendy postmodern writers who speak of contemporary America, and L.A. in particular, as a "desert of the Real." But the town has not returned his disfavor.

In fact, as much as Lovecraft would have hated Hollywood, the factory of dreams has loved him. Since the 1960s, his work has inspired most modern horror films either directly or indirectly. In fact, it's impossible to imagine modern horror without his small, once unloved, body of work.

Lovecraft's great contribution to the modern horror film has not come in either adaptations of his stories or direct references, although there have been plenty of each. His influence over a generation of horror film directors appears most compellingly in what these films began to do to us. The "new horror" that emerged in the late sixties (with projects such as George Romero's *Night of the Living Dead*) had the rejection of human values of comfort and personal happiness as the goal of their narrative. These movies did not care about us. They wanted to make us suffer.

But is it scary? That's all most viewers want to know about a horror flick. The proliferation of every subgenre of horror imaginable, and the incredible profitability available to directors willing to churn out dreck because a cheap horror film is almost predestined to make money, would seem to make it an adolescent's playground. You can be forgiven for thinking of horror movies as the ultimate cheap thrill, somewhere between the roller coaster and circus in important cultural phenomena.

You'd be wrong. Some of the great achievements of late–twentieth-century film came from a generation of directors, coming of age with the counterculture and doing their best work amid the Lovecraft renaissance of the same era. *Rosemary's Baby* and *The Exorcist* started the craze for the possession film, with the latter being called by film historian Tony Williams "one of the great aesthetic documents of the twentieth century." George Romero's 1968 film *Night of the Living Dead* may have had its start on the drive-in theater circuit but has since been recognized as a masterpiece. Film school students closely study the claustrophobic, bleak little tale that represents the beginning of the modern zombie craze.

The late Wes Craven proved you could use the horror genre to make a deeply political film fueled by rage against the middle class in 1972's *Last House on the Left*. Then he brought nightmares to the quiet streets of Reagan's "morning in America" with Freddy Krueger, a dream demon I suspect Lovecraft would have understood as one of many ghouls and ghasts of his own dark dreamlands, perhaps Nyarlathotep the Crawling Chaos in one of his many guises. Craven, before he was done, reinvented horror again in *Scream*, the self-reflexive horror film about horror that terrifies with its own supreme certainty of our hearts' devices and desires.

Given Lovecraft and Craven's interest in what lurks in dreams, it's natural that the famed writer/director/producer drew inspiration from the twentieth century's first master of horror. Near the time of his death in 2015, Craven began collaboration with director Daniel Knauf on a film called *Sleepers.* Details are very sketchy but they seem to have had in mind a series of tales by Knauf that drew inspiration from Lovecraft's novella *The Dream-Quest of Unknown Kadath,* one of the many Lovecraft tales that has been labeled "unfilmable" over the years. Who knows what it could have been, but for Craven and Lovecraft fans, the world is surely a poorer place without his vision of one of Lovecraft's oddest fantasies.

Gallons of ink have been spilled by thinkers as diverse as Immanuel Kant, Edmund Burke, and Freud trying to make sense of the meaning of terror. Why do we need to be scared and why turn our minds over to directors who want to hurt us on some level, even as they entertain us and take our money? Why should we decide to expose ourselves to that which, in the context of the narrative, could destroy us?

The truth is, most who have thought about it claim that these stories can't actually destroy us. That's the point. We love the thrill of terror but only insofar as it remains at a safe distance. Horror movies and weird tales are not about creating terror. They are about controlling terror, channeling it, being glad it's not happening to you.

Aren't they? Perhaps the horror tale would have only ever been this without Lovecraft. His stories broke those rules and his filmmaking disciples did the same. John Carpenter, more than any of the other directors of the new horror, speaks frequently of his debt to Lovecraft's work. His father first introduced him to Lovecraft with "The Rats in the Walls," Lovecraft's homage to the gothic tale with a sort of male "heroine" who becomes trapped with family secrets in a crumbling castle in England. Carpenter remembers reveling in the character's search through hidden chambers beneath the castle, an ill-fated quest that becomes a kind of devolution of the protagonist's personality, a peeling back of the layers of civilization until a terrible confrontation with ancestry, a notion that both obsessed and horrified Lovecraft.

Carpenter's films have themselves questioned the lines between civilization and savagery, making use of many of Lovecraft's themes of unstoppable cruelty, the attractive and deadly power of the past, and a profound sense of alienation between human beings and the universe they find themselves inhabiting. Carpenter has described his work as, in part, an effort to explore the idea of "the Dreaded Other" writing that during these explorations he's found "the footprints of someone who passed the same way before me—the footprints of Howard Phillips Lovecraft."[52]

Although his break-out film *Halloween* (1978) may seem the seminal, simplistic slasher rather than a foray into Lovecraftian horror, the terrifying indifference of Michael Myers (called "The Shape" in the script) replicates the utter contempt for human values and human life that all of Lovecraft's monsters exhibit. Moreover, the inability to kill the Shape, its unstoppable nature, suggests that we are dealing with Something other than a simple serial killer. Even the fact that—unlike Rob Zombie's 2007 remake—Carpenter chose to make the Shape's true nature and motivation ambiguous, reveals Lovecraft's touch.

Carpenter's 1982 *The Thing*, although ostensibly a remake of Howard Hawks's 1951 classic *The Thing from Another World*, also shows the heavy influence of Lovecraft. Hawks himself had based the script of the 1951 film on a 1938 novella called *Who Goes There?* by John W. Campbell, longtime editor of *Astounding Science Fiction*. Campbell's book ripped off Lovecraft's ideas in *At the Mountains of Madness* so egregiously that we would have to call it plagiarism if not for the sorry state of the writing.

Carpenter's interpretation of Hawks's film gave us an inhuman Antarctic landscape, perfectly pitched with a spare soundtrack, and offering some sense of what a cinematic adaptation of *At the Mountains of Madness* might be like. A bleak message, that humanity lies at the mercy of indescribable things that come from somewhere out there and that the basic human values of civility and compassion break down in the face of such horror, broods over the film.

Carpenter, who only half-jokingly noted of Lovecraft that "few authors claim the distinction of becoming an adjective," used "The Shadow Over Innsmouth" as an atmospheric inspiration for his classic film *The Fog* (1980). His 1994 film *In the Mouth of Madness* makes direct references to the Old Ones and the unlucky horror author at the heart of the tale writes novels that directly reference Lovecraft's titles, including *The Thing in the Basement* (instead of on the doorstep) and *The Whisperer of the Dark* (instead of in darkness). More importantly, Carpenter used the film to play with the idea of dread knowledge, gained from books, that drives us to madness.

What had Lovecraft exposed, what tumors did his work biopsy in twentieth-century American life? What made it possible for auteurs like John Carpenter to bring the monster so close, into our homes, our dreams, our beds, our bodies?

Gothic literature in the eighteenth century emerged from the shadows as a literature of secrets. Authors wrote of the ruined rooms of crumbling fortresses that hid manuscripts turning to dust with age. The novels told stories of madness and mayhem, the secret in the castle walls, the story no one wanted to know, or at least tell. Poe had taken the sensationalistic conventions of gothic in works like "The Fall of the House of Usher" and transmogrified them into art. Lovecraft went further.

He told the secret, a secret not of the graves but of humanity's mass grave. The beginnings of the tales of terror in the eighteenth century had played with the idea, rationalized it sometimes. In one of the most famous of the early gothic novels, Anne Radcliffe's *The Mysteries of Udolpho*, corpses appear that aren't corpses at all, people seemed to die but, we later discover, they were alive all the time and everything's fine. The reader preserved their distance from the final horror. In fact, many writers who explored the supernatural before Lovecraft seemed to seek to guard their readers from the secret, or to turn the final revelation into something less macabre than they at first expected.

Lovecraft understood that our own final extinction is the story we won't tell. The thing that is most true—that we will die—is the thing we avoid, or ignore, or—like any good horror film viewer—pretend to sit at a safe distance from the reality of it. Lovecraft refused to stop staring at this horror, interrogating it, making it the closest thing to a lover he ever had.

Guillermo del Toro, the greatest aesthetic genius of the fantastic creating film today, understands Lovecraft and understands horror as a sentiment about death. His first feature, the 1993 film *Cronos*, offers a vampire flick that I guarantee plays with the genre in ways you've never seen before. Scarabs intertwined with clockwork, forbidden occult objects from a distant past, and a vision of vampirism as a desire both overpowering and nihilistic all come directly from his lifelong engagement with Lovecraft's tales.

Since the surprise success of *Cronos*, during which del Toro found himself the toast of Cannes, he's kept up a seemingly impossible work schedule that's led to independent efforts such as a ghost story from the Spanish Civil War and big-budget studio productions like his two-part *Hellboy* series. *Pan's Labyrinth* shows the influence of Lovecraft in its use of horrific monsters that come to us at the borders of dream worlds, worlds that are dimensional portals rather than simply veils between waking and sleeping. Moreover, these monsters come intertwined with the realism characteristic of Lovecraft, appearing in the life of a young girl surrounded by the violence of modern war and totalitarian militarism.

Hellboy, based on a character from a now-legendary comics series by Mike Mignola, drew del Toro because of the material's roots in Lovecraftian horror. Mignola has said that Hellboy came directly from his discovery of Lovecraft, telling an audience at the West Hollywood Book Festival that he wanted to create a hero that fought not in a world of good versus evil, but one in which "an ignorant humankind faced a vast alien cosmos."[53]

Both of del Toro's *Hellboy* adaptations did all but make Cthulhu a main character in their use of Lovecraft's universe. In the first film, a resurrected Rasputin uses a mixture of turn-of-the-century technology and the occult (something of a nod to Lovecraft's "From Beyond") to open a portal to horrific Things from outside. These creatures, the "Ogdru-Jahad" or "The Seven Gods of Chaos," are great tentacled Things waiting for the chance to return to earth and destroy the human race. The film opens with an epigraph directly from Lovecraftian fiction, a fabricated quote from Robert Bloch's fictional forbidden book *Mysteries of the Worm*.

In *Hellboy II: The Golden Army*, an ancient race that predates all human consciousness threatens to rise out of its slumber in an ancient city easily recognizable to Lovecraft fans as an iteration of the City of the Great Race or that terrible "Nameless City" where, early in Lovecraft's career, one of his many unlucky characters discovered terrifying waiting Things.

Lovecraft, racist and deeply xenophobic, could never have guessed that his work would become the obsession of a talented Latino writer, artist, and filmmaker who grew up in Mexico. A twelve-year-old del Toro discovered Lovecraft one hot Guadalajara summer's day while leafing through his older brother's lit class textbook on a drive with their family. Derleth would have been pleased that "The Outsider," translated into Spanish, became del Toro's introduction. In fact, del Toro became so entranced with what he calls Lovecraft's "mannered, convulsive prose" that, after his family reached their destination, he sat behind in the unbearable heat of the car in order to finish the tale that some have seen as Lovecraft's zombie story, one of his earliest dark fairy tales of grotesque dreamlands or just his worst imitation of Poe.

Whatever the merits of that first tale, it became del Toro's silver key to a new world of terrible wonder. "Starting that afternoon and for the rest of my life," del Toro later wrote, "I have devoted more time to Lovecraft than virtually any other author in the genre." Discovering *At the Mountains of Madness* in his mid-teens, he became enthralled by what he sees as Lovecraft's ultimate vision of "the cold indifference of the cosmos." Ever since del Toro finished the last sentence of the disorienting tale, the shrieks of a man driven insane by the Thing he saw among the ruins of the Old Ones' citadel, he made it his life's goal to film the tale. As of 2016, he's still trying.

He wrote a first draft of a script right after the success of *Cronos*, a version that set the story in the midst of the conquest of the New World by the Spanish. Fragments of his notebooks published in 2013 suggest that more recent versions hew closer to Lovecraft's original vision of a scientific expedition.

Del Toro continues to explore the Lovecraft's ideas even as he awaits the chance to do a direct adaptation of his work. His television series *The Strain*, based on his novels of the same name, takes place in a recognizable Lovecraftian universe in which humans are swept aside by a vampiric "Ancient One." Lovecraft fans are even treated to various Easter eggs, including a plot point that revolves around the search for a Forbidden Tome, and much of the action in season two taking place in Red Hook, Brooklyn—a nod to "The Horror at Red Hook."

———

"Know, O Prince, that between the years when the oceans drank Atlantis and the gleaming cities. . . . Hither came Conan, the Cimmerian, black-haired, sullen-eyed, sword in hand, a thief, a reaver, a slayer, with gigantic melancholies and gigantic mirth, to tread the jeweled thrones of the Earth under his sandaled feet."

Robert E. Howard wrote these words in 1932 as part of his fictional "Nemedian Chronicles" that appears in one of his early Conan stories in *Weird Tales* entitled "The Phoenix on the Sword." Unlike his close correspondent Lovecraft, Howard did spend a significant amount of time creating a backstory, indeed world-building a new history of the human race, in order to give his fictional Conan the Barbarian a sense of deep realism and a broad mythology. Lovecraft's inventions of a few gods, fictional towns, and a very brief history of his facetious *Necronomicon* seem like vestigial efforts beside Howard's *The Hyborian Age*, a long essay on the faux history of the period, and efforts to draw detailed maps of the geography of his world of 10,000 BCE—what he later called "a 'history' as a guide to all the stories in this series I have written."

But I, and most of my generation, did not meet Conan the Barbarian in the stories of Robert Howard. Indeed, I first read the paragraph quoted above in the October 1978 edition of Marvel Comics' *The Savage Sword of Conan*, a black-and-white magazine that accompanied Marvel's enormously successful full-color comic. I would have been a tad too young for Conan in 1978, so I suspect that I somehow convinced my likely dubious mother to purchase it at a rummage sale sometime in the early eighties.

The cover of the magazine features the muscled barbarian wielding a giant phallic sword at a fearsome, equally phallic, serpent. Behind Conan cowers a Nordic beauty, apparently nude and undoubtedly chilly as she sprawls on the snowscape. Unfortunately, for a hetero male's adolescent eye, the artists strategically covered all her most interesting parts with long, flowing red hair. Conan must face THE LAIR OF THE ICE WORM promised on the lurid cover.

Savage Sword affected—usually badly—a self-consciously literary style that sometimes borrowed directly from fragments of Howard's plots and other times departed from them substantially in order to churn out new Conan tales. In fact, on the credits page Robert E. Howard is noted as "soul and inspiration" for the series, not exactly the description we'd expect for the creator of the character and the ethos behind him. Indeed, many of the tales, including "Lair of the Ice Worm," came from L. Sprague De Camp and Lin Carter's Conan stories, their version of August Derleth's "posthumous collaborations."

The Marvel adaptations of the Conan tales do substantially follow the spirit of Howard's contributions to *Weird Tales*. This was relatively easy to achieve since, other than a few early Conan stories published in the early 1930s, few depart from a basic formula. Conan confronts a menace that combines monstrosity, racial degeneracy, and sorcery, defeating it with a combination of native guile and brute force, the epitome of the Aryan barbarian in Howard's view of the world. He's accompanied by a scantily clad female companion, one that's often described as skilled in cunning swordplay but whose primary attribute seems to be to get into trouble that only Conan can rescue her from, while her clothes fall off in the midst of combat.

Sadly, what became almost the paradigmatic Conan tale became Howard's last. Cobbled together out of his interest in pre-Columbian Mexican–Texas history and a recent visit to the site of the Lincoln County War, his Conan story "Red Nails" appeared in October of 1936, after Robert E. Howard killed himself following the long illness and quickly approaching death of his mother.

I read this story many years ago, but had the chance to read it again more recently with a group of scholars interested in horror and the uncanny. The gathering included an interesting cross-section of backgrounds and expertise with knowledge of everything from medical history to the history of the pulps to Russian literature to a grasp of the recent theoretical discussions of gender and sexuality.

They had little interest or admiration for Howard. Who can really blame them, with sentences in "Red Nails" like this one introducing the supposedly fully capable female hero, a formerly successful pirate, we're told, as "tall, full-bosomed and large limbed with compact shoulders. Her whole figure reflected an unusual strength, without detracting from the femininity of her appearance. She was all woman, in spite of her bearing and her garments."

Howard's character, Valeria, also gets a once-over when she meets Conan whose "fierce blue eyes" predate her "magnificent figure, lingering on the swell of her splendid breasts beneath the light shirt, and the clear white breeches displayed between breeches and boot top."

Howard's often seen as the creator of the genre of "sword and sorcery" and perhaps, along with lesser known names among *Weird Tales* writers, he deserves the credit. But in granting this, any objective observer of the subculture of geekdom has to admit that it's a genre that quickly became its own dead end. Only so many strapping barbarian warriors could tangle with so many wizards and creatures from oblivion before the template became depressingly boring. It's an adolescent wet dream of a genre and would have likely disappeared without two things: a heavy transfusion of cultural DNA from epic fantasy in the style of Tolkien and his many imitators, and the terrifying cosmic horrors of Lovecraft.

Hardcore sword and sorcery produced only a few films in the 1980s, including two Conan films that have become cult favorites. By the nineties, the genre had passed into self-parody, with collections of stories appearing with titles like *Chicks in Chainmail.* An attempt at a reboot of the Conan films failed at the box office in 2011.

Howard and Lovecraft made for unlikely pen pals as they differed very much in their conception of fiction and shared few interests. They both wrote for *Weird Tales* though the speed of Howard's production, both for this and a number of other magazines, far outstripped Lovecraft's. Their exchange began when Howard wrote to Lovecraft in 1930 about a Gaelic quote he had used in "The Rats in the Walls." Lovecraft answered his query and the correspondence began, often dwelling at length of pedantic topics like that one that initiated it.

Howard wrote to Lovecraft in sycophantic fashion early in their relationship. He tells Lovecraft how "highly honored" he feels to receive a letter "from one whose works I so highly admire." He then told a probably overpleased Lovecraft that he had done a "close study" of the work of Poe and Arthur Machen and concluded that neither had "reached the heights of cosmic horror" attained by Lovecraft.

I first dove into this correspondence expecting the letters making their way back and forth between Providence, Rhode Island and Cross Plains, Texas to brim with insights into the making of modern American popular culture. Here we had the doyen of horror and an original master of magical wizards and sword-wielding heroes writing one another letters of enormous length. I found myself sorely disappointed.

Occasionally, one of the pair provides some insight into their understanding of their work. Lovecraft writes to Howard in an early 1930 letter that "the basis of all true cosmic horror is violation of the order of nature and the profoundest violations are the least concrete and describable." Perhaps no better short description of the chills Lovecraft administered to his readers has been written. We learn in a brief aside from Howard that a warrior, and a character completely unknown in pop culture today, named Gottfried von Kalmbach actually may have been the character he most loved, even if Conan brought him a more reliable income.

Unfortunately, most of their letters are unrelievedly boring. Both are contemptuous of immigrants and African Americans and pour into their missives venomous indignation about the "mongrel hordes" allegedly swamping the United States. Making matters worse, Howard clearly found Lovecraft's self-taught erudition daunting. This leads to an odd kind of contest, that Robert Howard always felt he was losing, to recreate the pseudo-scholarly dissertations on the origin of various "racial stocks" that many would have read as reactionary even in the 1930s, given the recent advances in genetics and anthropology.

So, rather than hearing about the craftsmanship, philosophy, and aesthetic possibilities of sword and sorcery and the weird tale, we get from their correspondence painfully detailed discussions about the historical moment the Jews fell irrevocably behind other races in their inability to prosper without subterfuge and fraud . . . was it perhaps in the Phoenician period or when "native Egyptians expelled the Hyksos" that the Jews became a slave race? Lovecraft wonders why the Slav and Italian sank into degeneracy given their "Aryan" background while insisting, in what's supposed to represent a historical argument, that clearly the Jews are not able to rise above "their offensive rattiness."

The pair never became close enough friends for Lovecraft to share anything like personal details. Howard apparently never knew that his correspondent had been married to a Jewish woman of Ukrainian descent just two years before their regular correspondence began. It's simply not a fact that fit with the image Lovecraft wanted to present to his fellow *Weird Tales* writer.

On June 29, 1936, Lovecraft received a letter from I.M. Howard, Robert's father. "It is barely possible," the letter began, "through some other source that you may have heard of the death of my son, Robert E. Howard." Although clearly distraught through the course of the lengthy letter, he writes with almost forensic precision that "on the morning of

June 11, 1936, at about 8 o'clock, he [Howard] slipped out of the house, entered his car which was standing in front of the garage, raised the window and fired a shot through his brain." His mother had become gravely ill and entered her final coma when Howard shot himself. Howard's father explained to Lovecraft that his son had made it plain he had no desire to outlive his mother. He did not, even though he lingered in unconsciousness for eight hours. His mother lived, never knowing of Howard's death, another thirty-six hours.

Lovecraft wrote a laudatory, if somewhat impersonal, memoriam for Howard for the August 1936 issue of *The Phantagraph*. This new breed of pulp magazine carried stories but also signaled the beginnings of horror, fantasy, and science fiction fandom through creating a medium for the discussion of genre tales and the people who wrote them.

"A major blow" had been dealt "the phantasy world" in the death of Howard, Lovecraft wrote. He details Howard's creation of a "prehistoric world" and highlights "the memorable hero Conan the Cimmerian." Lovecraft called Howard's death "an incalculable loss," though he seems to be describing the loss of Howard's vigorous style rather than his own sense of loss over the friend and sparring partner he'd never met.

In a letter to James Morton soon after hearing the news, Lovecraft called it "a hell of a blow" but saved most of his sentiment for Howard's father. He referred to his correspondence with Howard, not in the terms of affection he often used with his male friends, but as "our six year long debate."

It's impossible not to wonder how it must have felt for Lovecraft to discover that his friend had done what he had so often contemplated. It's also impossible, if unfair to the dead and their secrets, for me not to think of Lovecraft's reaction to his own beloved mother's death, the despair that drove his heart and intellect to open itself ever so slightly to the world rather than turning inward and letting himself crumble like the decayed House of Usher.

Why have Howard and his Conan tales not come in for the same kind of criticism that Lovecraft has just received for his work's racist assumptions? Howard celebrates Conan as a kind of Aryan Superman, slaughtering mountains of foes that are often, as in "Red Nails," portrayed as racial inferiors. Certainly the sheer popularity of Lovecraft has led to critics and scholars digging up his foulest prejudices and finding them, clearly recognizable, in some of his best, and also his worst, tales.

Ironically, Robert E. Howard put forward a vision of a seemingly invincible hero in mortal combat with degenerate races that much more closely approaches the fascist ideal of the 1930s. In Lovecraft's cosmos, weak human beings, most of them from good New England stock, are driven insane or killed or even revealed as monstrous themselves by the cthonian forces they confront. The forces of the universe, as Lovecraft time and again emphasized in his letters, are utterly indifferent to human notions of civilization and, indeed, even race. We are all food for Cthulhu. This is a kind of human equality.

Howard's tales, on the other hand, imagine a world in which a powerful blue-eyed, muscled barbarian of the north can subdue various supernatural and racial grotesqueries. It's hard not to see in his most well-known creation a kind of Death's Head SS commando in a loincloth, treading the jeweled kingdoms of the earth beneath his jackboots.

———

An archaeologist opens a tomb emanating waves of cosmic power. An ancient entity awakens, a Being aeons old called Nabu that exudes such extra-dimensional power that it kills the unwary scholar. Nabu, regretting what has become of the explorer, takes the archaeologist's orphaned son and raises him as his own, teaching him powers of wizardry and black arts already old when the human race was young.

Rather than being an imitative tale with a twist written for the pulps by one of Lovecraft's many admirers, this story appeared in DC Comics as the 1940 origin of Doctor Fate, in his original incarnation a somewhat short-lived superhero that ultimately proved little competition for Batman and Superman. Doctor Fate, the orphaned boy that learned the dark arts, uses these powers to protect humanity from a variety of

Lovecraftian threats. Gardner Fox, a contributor to *Weird Tales*, created Doctor Fate out of his admiration for Lovecraft.

Doctor Fate essentially battles the threat from "The Shadow Over Innsmouth" in issue #65 of a DC series called "More Fun Comics." The otherworldly sorcerer faces "The Fish-Men of Nyarl-Amen," the title suggestive of Lovecraft's Nyarlathotep, the Crawling Chaos. Doctor Fate also once faced "an entity from the seabed of the Nile," an octopoid creature that vaguely sounds like Cthulhu. In his struggle against Nyarl-Amen, the threat posed is the raising of an ancient city, with shades of both R'lyeh and the island that extrudes from the ocean floor in "Dagon." In another allusion to "The Shadow Over Innsmouth," the action centers around an attack on a U.S. navy base, a somewhat inverted description of the Navy torpedoing "Devil's Reef" outside of Innsmouth.

Although never one of DC's A-list heroes, Doctor Fate has been a recurring character, frequently dying and being replaced by a new iteration. These reimagined Doctor Fates subsequently drifted far from their Lovecraftian roots, one of them actually joining the standard pantheon of DC do-gooders in the Justice League of America.

He (sometimes a she has taken on Doctor Fate's rather literal mantle) still represents a significant point of departure, arguably as significant as the founding of Arkham House, for the influence of Lovecraft over American popular culture. Comic books, a medium that certainly would have delighted the young Howard Lovecraft, have become a primary conduit for Lovecraftian themes into popular culture.

Comics have not always had the level of cultural respectability they hold today. I once asked S. T. Joshi if he had ever read the now rather large pile of comics series and graphic novels directly inspired by Lovecraft's work. He somewhat briskly responded that he had not, since, much like tabletop role-playing games inspired by his favorite writer, they seemed to him "crude and juvenile." He confessed, however, that he'd come to see what a wide influence they had and understood that, for many, they become an entrée to the writings of the master himself.

Joshi's changing opinion of the influence of the comic book reflects larger changes in their importance. Since the 1980s, more and more critics have come to see the graphic novel as a literary art form deserving of significant respect. Art Spiegelman's 1991 *MAUS* has become almost a standard text in many university classrooms that discuss the Holocaust. Two recent graphic novels, the first two volumes of a trilogy entitled *March*, have served to increase interest in the civil rights struggle in Selma, Alabama.

Comics receiving rave reviews in *The New York Review of Books* would have been unimaginable in the 1950s, when artists adapted a small number of Lovecraft tales for a controversial company known as EC (short for "Entertaining Comics" but usually only known by their initials). EC, guided by publisher William Gaines, believed that comic books could find an adult market if they moved beyond superheroes and simplistic struggles between good and evil. The company's line of horror and mystery comics, most prominently *Tales from the Crypt*, became enormously popular and controversial in post–World War II America.

EC adapted Lovecraft's "The Outsider" for issue 23 of *Tales from the Crypt* in 1951, though bearing the title "Reflection of Death" and breaking the plot up substantially. Al Feldstein, the company's Lovecraft aficionado who penned "The Outsider" adaptation also reworked "Herbert West—Reanimator" and gave it the unintentionally hilarious title "Experiment . . . in Death." Feldstein also adapted Lovecraft's "Cool Air" into a story for EC's *The Vault of Horror* title called "Baby It's Cold Inside."

Feldstein would also be responsible for a 1950 tale called "The Black Arts" that, while not referencing any single Lovecraft story, becomes one of the first productions of pop culture—outside the novels and short stories written by the master's own circle—deserving the adjective "Lovecraftian." The story references "secrets stolen from the ages of darkness" and unfortunate mortals who attempt to wield the power of dark cosmic forces by making use of "a loathsome volume" that the last page reveals as the *Necronomicon*. The revelatory nature of the final panels shows that Feldstein assumed his readers know this book already. The fact that Feldstein could provide a twist ending for EC readers by unveiling the book as Lovecraft's dreaded manuscript illustrates how knowledge of his work had already, by 1950, begun to percolate throughout the subculture of Americans interested in horror, fantasy, and science fiction.

EC, and the entire comics medium, attracted much unwanted attention during the nervous 1950s. The United States went through a neo-domestic revival in the postwar period after several decades of rapid cultural change. Advertising, official government publications and films, the medical establishment, politicians and religious leaders all urged white middle-class America to huddle with their children in the safety of their suburban homes, possibly building a fallout shelter that replicated some of the comforts and values of middle-class domesticity.

The imagined ideal of the fifties came under direct criticism during the decade itself and represented an aspiration rather than a social reality. For example, it became the first decade in the history of American labor that the number of married women employed outside the home caught up substantially with the employment of young single women. Still, the creation of the image mattered a great deal to an atomic age America that perceived itself as under siege by a Communist threat, a threat many believed an America weakened by "juvenile delinquency" or, indeed, any evidence of social alienation.

Lovecraft's work, or adaptations of it, arguably had little cultural oxygen to breathe in an era when even comic books as a threat to the young became something of a cultural obsession. Horror comics, the ultimate expression of social alienation in the eyes of the censorious, came in for special criticism. Psychiatrist Fredric Wertham's best-selling book *Seduction of the Innocent* proposed that comics numbed young minds to all forms of depravity and even contributed to delinquency. EC essentially stopped producing its horror comics after the industry adopted a comics code under the pressure of congressional hearings in 1954. The code, largely created by EC's competition, did not allow any mention of supernatural horror.

The 1980s became, due to a handful of creators, a rebirth of the comic book for adults, and often only adults. Frank Miller led the way by placing traditional heroes in a darker world, including a brutal reimagining of Batman in *The Dark Knight Returns* that ultimately influenced Christopher Nolan's cinematic vision. Alan Moore changed comics forever in 1986 with *The Watchmen*, a series that represented Moore's lifelong obsession with deconstructing the superhero genre.

Moore has also had a lifelong fascination with Lovecraft, one that appears even in *The Watchmen* with its peculiar use of a familiar-looking tentacled monstrosity. Over the last decade, he has produced a number of metafictions about Lovecraft's monstrosities and even the phenomenon of Lovecraft. He's widely read enough in Lovecraftiana to skillfully, and sometimes savagely, bring the subtext in Lovecraft's stories and biography to the forefront.

Moore's series *Neonomicon* made use of a drug that allows one to understand the dark speech of the Old Ones and explored the sexual themes that often formed the "unspeakable" element of Lovecraft tales. The series borrows most directly from "The Shadow Over Innsmouth" and takes the idea of the Order of Dagon, a cult built around the notion of humans mating with the amphibious Deep Ones, to its logical conclusion. A vicious rape sequence forms the core of the tale, maybe the most harrowing set of comics panels that many readers have ever endured.

In 2015, Moore launched into a much deeper and wide-ranging and definitively odd exploration of Lovecraft, his art, and the meaning of horror as an aesthetic that intertwines how human beings suffer the terrors of history with the meaning of horror in popular culture.

Somewhat mysteriously entitled *Providence*, since the series doesn't take us to Lovecraft's hometown or even mention his name in the first few issues, we follow the exploits of a gay Jewish newspaperman and hopeful novelist named Robert Black, suggestive of the name of the unlucky main character in "The Haunter of the Dark."

Moore not only creates a fictionalized Lovecraftian world, he subverts the comics form in exciting ways. Each fat issue of *Providence* ended with pages and pages of text, often pages of Black's daybook and sometimes containing research materials that he has picked up along the way. At the time of writing, the series remains incomplete so it's an open question whether we will ever meet the Lovecraft who lives in this world and whose fictions have come to often horrifying life. Whether we do or not, Moore has succeeded in making the conservative young man's world, and the stories he wrote in them, crackle with new and fantastic possibilities, playing skillfully and thoughtfully with Lovecraft's own psychic wounds related to sexuality and race. Although in no sense an adaptation of Lovecraft's stories, it's the most dizzying achievement I've ever seen in the ongoing efforts to make sense of the dark and troubled prince of Providence.

Moore has provided some of the more compelling engagements with Lovecraft, especially if you are interested in the clash of values over sex, race, and art that appear in his work. But, just as interesting in its own way, have been the number of comic books and graphic novels making Lovecraft himself into a character. These stories often have little to do with what we might call "the historical Lovecraft" but are revelatory with regard to the perennial obsession with the man who made the stories as much as with the stories themselves. I noted that Arthur Conan Doyle also deserves some credit for having created a story cycle that lived beyond him. I don't know how popular Sherlock Holmes tattoos are these days since Benedict Cumberbatch has lent his peculiar and oddly alluring features to the character. But I doubt Holmesians are getting Doyle tattoos or wearing T-shirts with his face plastered across them.

This tendency to make Lovecraft himself into a character began with a story published by Frank Belknap Long and his 1928 tale "The Space Eaters" in which an easily recognizable avatar of his mentor becomes the protagonist. Another young protégé, Robert Bloch, used him in a contribution to *Weird Tales* entitled "The Shambler from the Stars." Derleth also used Lovecraft as a character in his Mythos tales, listing him with other scholars who had mysteriously died while investigating ancient tomes and the doings of the Great Old Ones. Subsequently, numerous authors have been unable to stay away from Lovecraft as a scintillating character whose peculiar biography holds all sort of fictional possibilities.

Traditional novels rather than the comics initiated this trend.

Arkham House actually traded on some of the darker elements of Lovecraft's biography by publishing, in 1985, *Lovecraft's Book*, a novel by Richard A. Lupoff that tells an alternative history of Lovecraft's racism and the fascist sputterings that made their way into his correspondence. Lupoff spins an entertaining yarn in which an organization of fascists bent on creating an American Brownshirt revolution contacts Lovecraft with the promise that they will arrange for the publication of a book of his tales if he will agree to write a kind of American *Mein Kampf* that will trigger their longed-for counterrevolution.

Luckily for this fictional Lovecraft, his friends Clark Ashton Smith, Lovecraft's estranged wife Sonia Greene, and even "Hardeen the Great," brother to the deceased Houdini, help him to see the error of his ways in throwing in with these right-wing extremists, a regular rogues' gallery of the 1920s that includes Nazi operatives, agents of Il Duce, the Grand Wizard of the KKK, and a Czarist revanchist married to the princess of one of America's robber baron clans. Lovecraft first becomes a kind of double agent in a tale that manages to work in an aviation adventure starring Hardeen and Lovecraft observing an undersea base being built by Germany off the coast of Marblehead, Massachusetts (that's, inexplicably, part of a Nazi plot in a Germany where Hitler will not come to power for another five years).

The most peculiar thing about this novel, other than the obvious re-creation of Lovecraft's world into one much more exciting than he ever wanted or experienced, is the obvious effort to fictionally redeem him from the racist far-right sentiments that Arkham House's publication of selected letters had made known to the world. Published almost fifteen years after the death of Derleth, who had hoped to mitigate Lovecraft's unsavory opinions, the novel suggests that Arkham House still hoped for at least a fictional revision of its dark patron saint's crudely racist conception of the world.

Comic book artists fascinated by Lovecraft's quirks have taken some extraordinary leaps of the imagination into an alternative history of his life. Perhaps the strangest and most creative series along these lines appeared from Action Lab comics from independent creators John Reilly (writer) with Tom Rogers and Dexter Weeks (art). *Herald: Lovecraft & Tesla* features a Nikola Tesla who's decided to use his inventions, including various ahistorical energy weapons, to search for Amelia Earhart. He ends up forming a partnership with the magic-wielding Lovecraft through the latter's association with Harry Houdini, made to appear in the comics as a much closer friendship than it ever became in Lovecraft's real life.

Fascination with Lovecraft abroad, particularly in Latin America and Spain, proved important for some of the most experimental efforts to make sense of both Lovecraft's work and his personality. In the 1970s, Argentinian Alberto Breccia used a Surrealistic style to portray the Great Old Ones. His collage-like effects have become somewhat common in comics over the last decade. Forty years ago, however, they deeply affected readers who confronted Lovecraft's terrors crawling out of the inky swirls of Breccia's creative use of comic panels . . . creatures that emerge within the hallucinogenic contrasts and horrific vagaries of Breccia's art.

His interpretation reveals the links between Lovecraft and the modern styles that the persona of the grumpy old Tory he attempted to create in his correspondence claimed to despise. Breccia gives us Lovecraft as Max Ernst or Dali might have drawn his monsters: an illuminated swirl of darkness, sometimes subtle and sometimes an effulgence of chaotic chiaroscuro.

Breccia chose this style wisely. The ambiguity of what Lovecraft's grotesqueries from beyond and beneath even looked like makes a literal reproduction of his horrors often underwhelming. Even great Cthulhu, perhaps the Elder terror for which Lovecraft provided the closest physical description, has been so often reproduced that it's lost some of the power that first comes to the reader of the original tale.

Breccia, however, captured his inspiration's ability to create that moment of suspension between seeing and not-seeing cosmic horror. In a special 1979 "Lovecraft" edition of the adult fantasy magazine *Heavy Metal*, Breccia penned an adaptation of "The Dunwich Horror" that managed to capture the physical horror of Yog-Sothoth and Lavinia

Whateley's nightmarish, multi-tailed, and serpentine-headed monstrosity of a child. Yet the art also forces on the eye the dizzying lack of solidity that Lovecraft implied about the creature, a terror that curls up in our minds as at once slimy and insubstantial, a perversion of natural law that Breccia sends crawling across your brainscape like unseen slugs.

Alberto's son Enrique continued and expanded on his father's obsession with Lovecraft. Enrique Breccia's *Lovecraft*, written by Hans Rodionoff and published by Vertigo comics in 2003, hearkens back to the elder Breccia's fever dream of Lovecraft's monsters. Perhaps more interesting, however, the junior Breccia presented his work as an alternative biography of the Providence writer that—unlike the other entries into sub-genre—sticks remarkably close to the actual life story of Lovecraft. However, it explains some of the more tragic aspects of his life by claiming that, at an early age, he came in contact with the Elder Things and their minions that shaped his later fiction. In this telling of the tale, for example, Lovecraft's father went insane when, in his Chicago hotel room, the beautiful woman he had bedded transformed into a slithering mass of tentacles. Guillermo del Toro and Clive Barker hailed the junior Breccia's *Lovecraft*, and John Carpenter wrote the introduction.

El Joven Lovecraft, a series of hilariously on-point graphic novels that began as an online comic strip by José Oliver and Bartolo Torres, imagines the childhood of a Lovecraft who learns the dark arts to help him with his homework, conjures ancient Egyptian deities who annoy him and, not unlike the real Lovecraft, has an obsession with *One Thousand and One Nights* that leads him to dress up like Abdul Alhazred. He has a ghoul for a pet but manages to convince everyone that it's an odd-looking dog who just happens to ink occult symbols with his eldritch pee on the streets of Providence.

Young "Howie," although much oppressed by bullies and his own anxieties, has managed to find something of a female soulmate, a cool punk girl named Siouxsie. Oliver admits in the introduction that he's aware of what he calls Lovecraft's "asexuality" and "general misanthropy" but wanted to give him some friends to "balance his temper" and make him more lovable to the reader. Some of the actual Lovecraft creeps through, including a strip in which Siouxsie first comes to his class and a nervous Howie's thought bubble as he looks at the empty seat beside him reads "Please God don't make her sit here!" Of course, she does and he thinks to himself "this is why I've been an atheist since seven."

Siouxsie and Howie's friendship has some pathos. Siouxsie's love of Poe and the macabre would have made her exactly the sort of friend he might have had in another era, another era in which he could have been a different person.

Lovecraft's enormous influence over artists drawn to horror across several generations partially explains the numerous imaginative leaps made in telling Lovecraft's story. Surely, someone who completely reimagined the world of fantasy has to be more than an emotionally stunted eccentric who lived with his aunts and played at being an eighteenth-century gentleman.

The Strange Adventures of H.P. Lovecraft, a comic series that appeared in 2009, imagined Lovecraft as meeting "outside shapes and entities on the known universe's outside rim" in his dreams, all in all not a poor description of how the actual Lovecraft nurtured his dark visions. Much less grounded in Lovecraft's biography than Breccia's work, series creators Mac Carter and Tony Salmons add a murder mystery and a beautiful high society love interest with the pulp heroine named Sylvia St. Claire.

The desire to create a cult of personality surrounding the author really has no precedent with any other writer of weird fiction with the possible exception of Poe. Even with Poe, however, it's much easier to find adaptations of his work than to find him transformed into a character in his own alternative world. What's most notable about the growing stack of comics and graphic novels dedicated to Lovecraft certainly is the recurring idea that Lovecraft did more than write fiction. The majority of the graphic novels that reimagine Lovecraft's biography, or even just his childhood, imagine him as a kind of mage who, not unlike some of his characters, knowingly or unknowingly opened portals to dread dimensions.

A 2015 novel entitled *Carter & Lovecraft* represents the most recent use of this formula. Dan Carter, a former police detective turned private eye after a traumatic encounter with a bizarre serial killer named for the villain of "The Horror at Red Hook," teams up with a female descendant of Lovecraft to battle a set of evil forces that the pair's ancestors had hoped they sealed off from the world in the 1930s. Allusions to Lovecraft's tales abound, and it's yet another sign of Lovecraft's notoriety that enjoying the novel depends largely on a very basic awareness of the author's work. The novel also makes Emily Lovecraft an African American woman, a fact that's never clearly explained but also a fairly transparent effort to use irony to close off the question of Lovecraft's racism.

These writers and artists are using more than their fertile imaginations in shaping this alternative history of Lovecraft and his world. The belief that Howard Phillips Lovecraft had reached out into the dark and felt something ancient, scabrous, and malignant reaching back began during his own lifetime.

～～

"Regarding the dread Necronomicon of the Mad Arab Abdul Alhazred—I must confess that both the evil volume & the accursed author are both fictitious creatures of my own."

Lovecraft explained this in response to a series of questions from William Frederick Anger in a 1934 exchange. Interestingly, he tells Anger that not only should he not bother trying to check out the *Necronomicon* from his local library, but that his "malign entities" such as Azathoth and Yog-Sothoth are merely "inventions." He further assures him that other dread volumes that appear in his work such as the *Book of Eibon* are only the creations of Clark Ashton Smith while yet another book of horror, the *Unaussprechlichen Kulten,* came from the imagination of Robert E. Howard.

Anger, to be fair, was a fourteen-year-old fan of *Weird Tales* at the time he made his inquiry. Moreover, Lovecraft's explanation of the terrifying grimoire that he, Smith, and Howard created and borrowed from each other doesn't suggest that Anger's letter signaled an actual belief in the supernatural. Lovecraft tells the young fan that he and his fellow writers created a "synthetic folklore" and traded "pet daemons" in order to give their world a "pseudo-authoritativeness." He doesn't feel it necessary to explain to Anger, as he was wont to do, all the reasons that matters spiritual and supernatural have an unlikely probability.[54]

Lovecraft unintentionally added to several generations of fans' confusion when he wrote a fictionalized history of his fictional book in 1927. The scholarly tone of the short note certainly sounds authoritative enough for those seeking to be fooled. Lovecraft places the origin of the book in "circa 700 AD" penned by Abdul Alhazred about whose loathsome fate "many conflicting and terrible things are told." During the Middle Ages, both the Byzantine and Roman churches seek to destroy all copies of the dangerous tome but Lovecraft traces, convincingly, its history of suppression and translation into Greek, Latin, and finally into English. He claims that even modern authorities attempt to suppress the book though copies reside in the British Museum, the Bibliothèque Nationale, the library of the University of Buenos Aires, the Widener Library at Harvard, and, as his tales frequently note, under lock and key at the fictional Miskatonic University. He notes darkly that "numerous other copies probably exist in secret."

Lovecraft never planned to publish *History of the Necronomicon (An Outline)* and sought only to use it as a reference guide for his own writing. Abdul Alhazred, a name that began to appear in Lovecraft's fiction in 1921, is a nonsense sobriquet that sounds convincing in English but makes no sense in Arabic. This is altogether fitting, since Lovecraft made it up as the name of a character he played during his boyhood fascination with *One Thousand and One Nights*. Lovecraft also alludes to his own stories in this *History*, mentioning that a Greek edition of the forbidden book belonged to the Pickman family of Salem though Upton Pickman himself went missing in 1926, the year Lovecraft wrote "Pickman's Model."

But even early fans believed Lovecraft had not shown his full hand, indeed that he might even be hiding some terrible truths under the guise of fiction. At least one member of that first, small group of Lovecraft aficionados refused to be convinced that their favorite *Weird Tales* author had not channeled dark realities with his work and that perhaps Lovecraft was fully aware of this and refusing to admit it.

Stuart M. Boland, a west coast admirer of Lovecraft and of weird fiction more generally, worked as a librarian for the Ocean View Branch of the San Francisco Public Library. He explored a variety of scholarly interests and, in the 1950s, wrote at least one article for a journal of Islamic studies. He also apparently had a delusional side to his learned intellect, insisting to Lovecraft that he had actually seen a copy of the dread *Necronomicon* during his extensive travels.

Boland wrote his letters close to the time of Lovecraft's death so their correspondence never flourished. Boland did apparently travel widely and mailed Lovecraft a series of photographs of Aztec ruins near Mexico City. Lovecraft told Morton about him in one of his final letters, describing him somewhat disparagingly as "a librarian of some sort" who "seems to possess occult leanings."

Boland became the first of many to either believe, or want others to believe, that Lovecraft had discovered very real dimensions of horror. The growing popularity of Lovecraft's work in the 1960s prompted an odd combination of fanboy enthusiasm and hoaxing. Devoted Lovecraft readers planted false entries in the card catalog of several university libraries. Reports I've not been able to confirm are that both Yale and UC Berkeley once had faux listings for the *Necronomicon* and its mad author in their holdings, a relatively easy prank in the days before digitization.

By the 1970s, the line between fandom, hokum, and quasi-religious devotion became intertwined in a fashion that Lovecraft would have viewed with ruthless cynicism and possibly some horror. Or perhaps he would have simply used it as exhibition of humanity's insistence on deceiving itself by any means necessary.

L. Sprague de Camp began the bizarre practice of creating fake

Necronomicons. Three years before the publication of his biography of Lovecraft, de Camp worked with Owlswick Press and an artist named Robert Dill to create the *Al Azif*, a phrase that Lovecraft had used in his own fake history of the *Necronomicon* as the work's original title.

The book, produced in a limited edition of 348 copies, featured calligraphy stylized so as to appear as an ancient Arabic text. De Camp and the press didn't have to worry about anyone translating it since it's not written in an actual language. In good Lovecraftian tradition, befitting a fake version of a book that never existed, its written in "Duriac," a fairly common surname in France but not an actual dialect spoken in an isolated Iraqi village as de Camp's "Preface" claims.

Lovecraft, and later de Camp, used the term *Al Azif* to evoke a somewhat chilling idiomatic phrase in Arabic. A colleague of mine in Middle Eastern history tells me that the phrase "*azif al-jinn*" refers to the sound made by the Jinn in the desert at night. The Jinn are powerful creatures made of smokeless flame in Middle Eastern folklore, creatures that fit rather nicely into the Lovecraftian conception of the Old Ones and their numerous servants.

De Camp, and perhaps in some cynical way Lovecraft himself, would be pleased that as late as 2014 the forty-year-old-hoax continues to cause consternation. Several Amazon.com reviews from recent customers complain that the text they ordered was all in "Arabic." However, at least one claimed, in all caps, that "IT'S NOT FAKE" while also insisting on the authenticity not only of the *Al Azif*, but of at least one of the numerous other fictional *Necronomicons* that have appeared since the 1970s. The reviewer based this assertion on the claim that "IT ACTUALLY WORKS IN MAGIC" and urged skeptics to "Light a single black candle in a safe spot in your bedroom, meditate on the candle a while, then place the *Al Azif* under your pillow and go to sleep." The reviewer jeered that unbelievers would know de Camp's hoax was no fake once they had "a wild night of incredible dreams."

Following de Camp's remarkably successful prank, various fictionalized *Necronomicons* appeared with some regularity. A group of Lovecraft aficionados in Great Britain organized to release *The Book of Dead Names* in 1978. "Translated" into English from an alleged compilation of Ancient Near Eastern texts from the British library, it's a tissue of fabrications although, as with de Camp, the lies are all out of affection for Lovecraft and the desire to give substance to his fictional world.

The Book of Dead Names reads more like Lovecraft fan-fic than most of the fake Necronomicons . . . although it's entertaining fan-fic. Part of the first chapter borrows, with few changes, an entire section of "The Dunwich Horror." The book takes images and ideas both from *The Case of Charles Dexter Ward* and the writings of early–twentieth-century mage/showman Aleister Crowley to make a convincing ritual for the invocation of Yog-Sothoth.

Probably the most popular, and for many the most convincing, of these Lovecraftian grimoires came from the pen of the anonymous "Simon" whose work, still available as a mass-market paperback, first appeared in 1977. Simon claimed that he received the manuscript from a priest "ordained through uncanonical methods" who then mysteriously disappeared.

Simon insisted that this manuscript, the true *Necronomicon*, revealed a relationship between the stories of Lovecraft, the writings of Aleister Crowley, and the deities and religious structures of the Ancient Near East. Lengthy introductory materials, meant to suggest the ominous nature of the work, contain an unintentionally humorous warning that *"there are no effective banishings for the forces invoked in the NECRONOMICON itself.* [emphasis in original]." The section urges that "People with unstable mental conditions . . . should not be allowed, under any circumstances, to see these rituals in progress."

A large part of Simon's *Necronomicon* paraphrases a very real ancient epic, possibly a hymn, called the *Enuma Elish*, a Bronze Age poem that locates the origins of the world, and the human race in a great theomachy, or battle between the gods. Much of the rest of the text conflates the ideas of Crowley, a smattering of knowledge of the Ancient Near East, and numerous allusions to Lovecraft.

The real story behind Simon's *Necronomicon* has been fully pieced

252 * W. SCOTT POOLE

together by those who have, if perhaps without too much effort given its absurdity, worked out the hoax. Authors Dan Clore, Jason Colavito, and Alan Cabal have reported that the text represented largely the work of Peter Levenda, a conspiracy theorist active in the occult scene in Chelsea during the 1970s. Although Levenda (somewhat laughingly) denied his involvement in the project in a 2009 radio interview, the U.S. Copyright Office does in fact list him as the author, under the pseudonym of "Simon."

Levenda only created the most successful of the fake Lovecraft grimoires. Creating a fake *Necronomicon*, among both Lovecraft devotees and occultists, has become a cottage industry. I counted forty-five books, films, and even musical interpretations that bear the title since 1978. A few of these are important pop culture artifacts, such as the classic collection of artwork by *Alien* (1979) concept artist H.R. Giger whose terrifying visions are, by his own account, heavily influenced by Lovecraft. A few are references to either the *Evil Dead* series or the work of zombie maestro George Romero. Most claim to be the forbidden text of the mad Arab Abdul Alhazred, now available in Kindle editions from self-published hoaxers, fans, and true believers.

The Age of Aquarius brought us more than the first fake *Necronomicons*. Lovecraft's horrors found surprising new homes in this age of religious experimentation, including San Francisco's much ballyhooed Church of Satan. Founded in 1966 by former carnival barker Anton Szandor LaVey (real name: Howard Stanton Levey) the organization did not teach belief in a literal Satan, but propagated a philosophy that seems equal parts half-digested Nietzsche and warmed-over Ayn Rand. LaVey did, however, claim to believe that rituals unleashed psychological energies that enabled the devotees to break with their reliance on Christian forms and myths.

LaVey's best-selling *Satanic Bible* represents a truly modern form; a forbidden grimoire that makes no claims to magical power. In a follow-up manual for aspiring Satanists called *The Satanic Rituals*, LaVey and Michael Aquino made use of their long acquaintance with the works of H.P. Lovecraft to create a series of rituals meant, not to invoke actual occult forces, but to unite "the constructive and destructive facets of the human personality . . . the keystone of Satanism."

In an introduction to two sections in the *The Satanic Rituals* that employ Lovecraftian themes, "The Metaphysics of Lovecraft" and "The Call to Cthulhu," LaVey and Aquino show significant awareness of Lovecraft's actual body of work and how far it departed from various revised versions of it. They are even aware of Derleth's effort to create a "Cthulhu Mythos" that told a tale of good and evil and occultist claims of the "reality" behind his stories.

LaVey came to understand Lovecraft from Fritz Leiber, perhaps one of the most acute observers of what his mentor had been attempting in his fiction. Leiber, largely out of curiosity it seems, attended some of LaVey's seminars at "The Black House" in San Francisco during the 1960s, a discussion group from which emerged the Church of Satan.

A few groups have taken the supernatural aspects of Lovecraft's mythos much more seriously. Kenneth Grant, a disciple of Aleister Crowley, created the most elaborate system of fakelore with a Love-craftian flavor. Grant's New Isis Lodge began in London in 1955, later taking the name of the Typhonian Order. Grant taught a confusingly elaborate mixture of western magic tradition as interpreted by Crowley, intertwined with some of the symbolism of the Kabbalistic tradition.

Lovecraft's work influenced Grant heavily, and indeed Grant's "Secret Chiefs" are something like Lovecraft's Great Old Ones. Grant has even claimed that Lovecraft came into contact with these Beings in his dream life. Writing under their influence, Lovecraft's limited knowledge of "true" magical systems led to misunderstandings in which the Great Old Ones, mostly benevolent according to Grant, appeared to him as monsters.

Such ideas have not been limited to individual cranks. A small group, now more than three decades old, exists in Eugene, Oregon (and claims lodges in "Australia . . . and Europe") that calls itself the "Esoteric Order of Dagon" and is led by "Grand Master Frater Obed Marsh." Their website claims they are influenced by Aleister Crowley, the work of Kenneth Grant, and "the great occult significance of the writings of H.P. Lovecraft." An even tinier sect in London, calling themselves simply "Krla," uses a mixture of tantric sexual ritual and Lovecraftian lore to find communion with the Great Old Ones.

The beginning of the appearance of fake *Necronomicons*, and tiny neo-religions attached to them, came at a peculiar moment in American cultural history. During the 1970s and 1980s, a wave of irrationalism that would have startled and depressed Lovecraft swept over the country. After more than three decades of "Flying Saucer" sightings, the term coming from an alleged sighting at Mt. Rainier in 1947, belief in the visits of extraterrestrials to earth became surprisingly common. During these decades, hundreds, perhaps thousands, of Americans claim to have experienced some kind of alien contact. Whitley Strieber's best-selling *Communion: A True Story* (1987), with its detailed descriptions of alien close encounters and a cover painting that has become the iconic representation of the bulbous-headed grey alien with enormous eyes, became the standard template for a multitude of ludicrous claims.

During the same era, "cattle mutilations" in the western United States and rumor legends about satanic rituals (both perfectly explicable by basic zoology or human psychology) became a cultural obsession. By the 1980s, the pseudo-psychology of repressed memory and free-floating cultural anxiety helped create what historians and folklorists now call "the satanic panic."

This widespread belief that "satanic cults" kidnapped children and ritually sacrificed them to Satan became remarkably common among evangelical Christians in the United States and among social groups that members of these churches and organizations influenced. Ironically, two fictionalized accounts that represented themselves as memoir served a similar role among evangelicals as did the fake grimoire among occult devotees. Michelle Smith's *Michelle Remembers* (1980) presented a falsified account of her abuse at the hands of a satanic cult that included her parents and neighbors, while Mike Warnke's *The Satan Seller* (1972) told a now exploded fiction of the author's time as a "high priest" of Satan in just such a cult. Both included sensationalistic and detailed descriptions of satanic rituals that led to a panicked public and prosecutions for "satanic ritual abuse" with no basis in physical evidence.

The myths of America's satanic panic had an oddly Lovecraftian flavor. Satan and his multitude of demons took the place of the Old Ones trying to find a way back into the human world. Cultists chanted in order to open portals using unnamable rites. Evangelical Christian leaders warned of the danger of Satanism and LaVey's *Satanic Bible* gave them a forbidden book to fear.

And yet, evangelicals like Warnke, Smith, and many imitators had produced tomes of truly horrific knowledge without the help of actual Satanists. Stories of human sacrifice and sexual deviancy appeared on the shelves of Christian bookstores alongside bibles. Youth pastors, parents, and evangelists passed along books they would never have allowed their young charges to read if they did not believe them cautionary tales. By the mid-1980s, as superpowers seemingly blundered toward nuclear winter, many Americans worried about the cultist on the corner, the Satanist waiting on the lane.

A fifteen-year-old Ramsey Campbell submitted his first short story collection to August Derleth and Arkham House in 1961. Born almost a decade after Lovecraft's death, Campbell quickly fell under his sway, as had many a young, hopeful writer before him. Many of his early stories take place in Lovecraft's world. The action in one of his best, "The Tower of Yuggoth," occurs in Arkham. Urged by Derleth to write about his native Britain instead of the New England he'd never visited, Campbell recreated the Miskatonic River Valley across the pond, with his imaginary towns of Severnford, Brichester, Temphill, and Cloton standing in for Arkham, Dunwich, Kingston, and Innsmouth.

Campbell, as he grew older and came out from under Derleth's shadow, found new ways to evoke *frisson* that makes the sturdiest reader of weird fiction sleep with the lights on. Maintaining a Lovecraftian timbre to his authorial voice, Campbell abstracted Lovecraft's aesthetic and made it his own in a contemporary world. His characters meet their fate in a terrifying present rather than the now-distant 1920s and '30s.

"Cold Print," a story written when Campbell was only in his early twenties, marked out his dark path. Sam Strutt, who lives a life of unquiet desperation amid the squalor of postindustrial England, attempts to escape his utter dread of life through violent, pornographic fantasies. He goes to Brichester, portrayed as a decayed, violent slum and a contemporary version of rotting Innsmouth, to find a bookstore said to contain volumes that cater to his very specific tastes in sadomasochistic erotica.

Strutt, like many a Lovecraft character, feels "abandoned in a tacitly conspiring, hostile world." Campbell compels us to feel this bleak dread not simply by describing Strutt's inner state but by evoking a world of terror in which neon signs blink "relentless as a toothache" and even Christmas trees seen by the lonely Strutt through grimy windows have "luridly sputtering lights." He already lives in a world of horror before the bookseller—who wants to show him a volume more terrible than anything he's read before—transforms into a Thing of sex and death, a compendium of the decayed world that Strutt already lives in.

Campbell has returned to Lovecraft's themes throughout his long career. For more than four decades, he's labored to produce both his own singular vision and become one of several of Lovecraft's truest heirs in weird fiction, a much-coveted title. Always experimenting with ways to communicate existential dread, making use of brutal sexual themes and employing film as a new sort of dreaded grimoire, Campbell keeps returning to his Lovecraftian roots. His 2003 novel *The Darkest Part of the Woods* employs the trope of mental illness to reimagine portals to horrific dimensions and the return of evil mages who make use of forbidden knowledge. The novel replicates, and in some ways surpasses, *The Case of Charles Dexter Ward* with its return of a sixteenth-century necromancer into the present.

Campbell once wrote that his ambition was "to write a single successful Lovecraftian story." His oft-noted modesty aside, he's written numerous such successes. Sadly, critics have noticed this more than readers. It's unlikely that you'll hear Campbell's name mentioned alongside Stephen King, Peter Straub, and other "masters of horror" in the popular press. But, as we know from the case of the Providence recluse who wrote the perplexingly frightening stories for the pulps, history has a way of rendering unexpected verdicts on the influence and importance of authors.

Stephen King offers a peculiar counterpoint to Campbell. He's also an illuminating example of the inescapable nature of Lovecraft's influence. Before the self-conscious effort to write a Lovecraft-inspired tale with *Revival* (2014), King made numerous allusions to his fellow New Englander's work. The short story "Jerusalem's Lot" (1978) has several references to Yog-Sothoth and at least one forbidden tome. His 1991 novel *Needful Things* has an inspired use of graffiti, "Yog Sothoth Rules," on a brick wall in the unlucky town of Castle Rock. At least one solid essay of literary criticism I came across, penned by John Langan, convinced me that King's famous short story "Graveyard Shift," with its unforgettably gruesome image of an underground world swarming with creatures that have embodied disease and death for centuries, represented King's attempt to place Lovecraft's 1923 story "The Rats in the Walls" in a contemporary setting.

These are, of course, rather simple shout-outs. King's as different a writer as can be from Lovecraft. King's deep interest in his characters, indeed in stories that make us care about what becomes of them, reveals a commitment to a literary project utterly foreign to Lovecraft. Normally, critics don't see a concern for character development as a failing in fictional constructions. However, if we are looking for a simon-pure Lovecraftian worldview, then King's certainly not our guy. In fact, as much as I find his prolix novels entertaining, I can't bring myself to place him in any meaningful way in the tradition of the weird tale that Lovecraft created, though it seems to me that King very much wants to see himself as an extension of this tradition.

There's a sense, however, in which King's success is unimaginable without H.P. Lovecraft. In fact, his fascination with horror and science fiction emerged out of the world of comics, pulps, and films that admirers of

Lovecraft created in the years after World War II. King himself has noted this, describing how he first learned of the weird tale tradition through a copy of Arkham House's 1947 *The Lurking Fear and Other Stories* that he discovered among his absent father's abandoned books.

King found his way to Lovecraft secondhand, through the pastiche of Derleth. The Arkham House volumes did, whatever their failings, cause him to think of the horror tale as something more serious than what you'd find, as he's written, "in B-movies." The popularity of the "new horror" in film, shaped by a generation of directors steeped in Lovecraft, made the 1970s much more receptive to King's work. *Carrie*, his first best-seller, reached that status after it provided the basis for a successful and much discussed film adaptation in 1976.

There may be one very direct influence from Lovecraft found in the tens of thousands of pages King has published. King's interest in placing us on the side of his characters, often in the head of his characters, deceives some critics. More than a few have accused him of sentimentality with regard to his subjects, surely an unforgivable sin for a writer of horror.

King may have learned a good deal more from Lovecraft than his desire to flesh out his characters would lead us to expect. King's Lovecraftian influence does appear in the various ways he destroys those characters he's made us care about. The mainstream success of King's novels and anthologies represents a remarkable achievement given his tendency to maim, kill, desolate, and drive insane personalities he's aroused our sympathy for over literally hundreds of pages.

This does not mean that King creates a sense of cosmic horror with his tales. Lovecraft, who always found reading about human experiences fatally boring, would not have cared about what kind of car King's characters drive or what brand of cereal they prefer. I expect, however, that the pair would have held a fascinating and pugnacious correspondence.

A number of best-selling writers, though never achieving King's mega–best-selling status, have used Lovecraft in more interesting ways. You can't read far into contemporary speculative fiction, for example, without finding yourself stumbling through the dark technocracies and Victorian steampunk dystopias of China Miéville. Miéville has received a good deal of attention as the leading practitioner of what's been called the New Weird, efforts to take the traditional weird tale and transform it with the admixture of related genres and the alchemy of contemporary concerns, politics, sexualities, and anxiety about modernity . . . and what comes next.

Miéville has been open both about his debts to Lovecraft and his desire to subvert certain Lovecraftian premises. Given his academic background in Marxist theory, it's not surprising that he's attempted a transubstantiation of the intent and direction of Lovecraft's horrors.

Calling some of his work an effort to "write behind Lovecraft's back," Miéville has most successfully reimagined the dread "Nameless City," draining Lovecraft's vision of its racist panic and obtuse attitude toward social and economic conditions. The cityscapes of Miéville are what would have happened had Dickens found a time portal that allowed him to shoot heroin with William S. Burroughs. Dark, huge, and seemingly subterranean even in daylight, these urban landscapes are home to oppressed populations that eke out their daily existence under the baleful eye of powerful, insidious elites. Unlike Lovecraft's urban denizens, they suffer the city's horrors rather than embodying them.

Miéville's imagery of the "cyclopean" city of terrors dwarfs Lovecraft's in its conception if not in the power of the language he uses to describe it. He frequently manages to create a much more terrifying gothic city, simply because his pockmarked and conflict-riven topographies closely resemble the urban realities of many an ailing metropolis in the western world and the contemporary global phenomenon of the rise of the slum city.

The most recent of Lovecraft's heirs would have utterly shocked the author himself. Victor LaValle has found exciting new ways to speak of Lovecraftian horror and monstrosity in his 2016 *The Ballad of Black Tom*, a novella he sets to a haunting blues soundtrack by making his main character an erstwhile street musician and hustler from Harlem named

Tommy Tester. Since the late nineties, LaValle has been producing beautifully rendered explorations of topics ranging from the experience of growing up young and black in Queens to descriptions of the beautiful and terrifying inner worlds of schizophrenia. LaValle, in a February 2016 interview on NPR's "Fresh Air," explained that he felt compelled to write his most recent novel in order to come to grips with Lovecraft. The racist from the early twentieth century has always been one of LaValle's most important influences as a writer, a man whose stories he'd discovered as an African American teenager growing up in Queens. The dedication of *The Ballad of Black Tom* reads "For H.P. Lovecraft, with all my conflicted feelings."

Victor LaValle sees his latest work as having a conversation alongside, or in his words just talking near, Lovecraft rather than "writing behind his back." *The Ballad of Black Tom* speaks alongside one of Lovecraft's notoriously racist tales, "The Horror at Red Hook," turning some of Lovecraft's own pathological prejudice on its head by exploring what precisely Lovecraft's white protagonists, and the author himself, truly feared. LaValle's work reveals what a writer can do with Lovecraft when his racism has been exposed in all its ugliness.

Of course, not all the new work that engages Lovecraft has equal merit. The pervasive power of Lovecraft over the horrific imagination can cause the unsuspecting reader to, as I've sometimes done, founder amid a cascade of anthologies, collections, and homages that claim a basis in his small body of work or purport to tell new tales about the Old Ones. Ellen Datlow, long the major American curator of short horror fiction, put together a 2014 anthology called *Lovecraft's Monsters* with an impressive line-up of horror and fantasy authors. Just in the final months of my writing this book, two new anthologies of tentacled horrors emerged in response to readers' feverish desire for more Lovecraftiana—one using the device of asking a number of horror writers to each tell a tale based on one of Lovecraft's mad, indifferent gods.

S.T. Joshi has edited three volumes of Lovecraftian tales, anthologies with titles like *The Black Wings of Cthulhu*. Robert M. Price seems dedicated to helping Chaosium games publish volume after volume of Lovecraft-inspired fiction to feed the imagination of its players. Along the way, Price has rescued plenty of twentieth-century pop culture artifacts, including Bloch's early pastiches of his mentor's mythos, otherwise likely lost among the piles of Lovecraftiana threatening to bury us.

I asked Joshi how his efforts to gather the best fiction inspired by Lovecraft differed from Derleth's attempts at the same. In fact, doesn't the printed logorrhea inspired by Lovecraft raise the possibility that more and more fans will read less and less Lovecraft while consuming second-rate, and easier to read, imitations?

Joshi defended his own efforts to gather these tales. He tells me that a number of new "weird" writers began sending him their fiction over the last decade, much of which he found "fresh and distinctive." The stories he's incorporated, he insists, "address fundamental issues in Lovecraft's work in a vital way" even as his stories are used by the authors as "springboards for expressing their own vision."

Still, some readers will likely find themselves in a morass as the line between what Lovecraft wrote and writing he inspired promises to become exceedingly thin. Certainly reading Lovecraft offers the only way to know Lovecraft. You have to lose yourself in his lush language, often feeling lost and uncertain of what's he's trying to do with you, to discover what all the chatter's really about.

The exception to this rule may be reading the work of Thomas Ligotti. Ligotti, more than any writer other than perhaps Ramsey Campbell, has successfully absorbed, transmuted, and yet remained firmly attached to Lovecraft's oeuvre. Arguably, Ligotti has done more than inherit Lovecraft's mantle. He's doggedly pressed forward Lovecraft's experimentation across a long and critically acclaimed, if not always commercially successful, career.

Ligotti's first volume of short stories appeared in 1986, during an era singularly unsuited for an author of serious literary horror. King, Straub, and numerous imitators cornered a market in which "true crime" stories obsessed with serial killers shaded the line between fact and fiction. Ligotti's *Songs of a Dead Dreamer* appeared from a tiny press called Silver Scarab, the book beautifully illustrated by Harry O. Morris (who also owned the press) and introduced by none other than Ramsey Campbell. The print run of three hundred copies has made the book highly valued by collectors today, though only connoisseurs knew of Ligotti's work when a second collection, *Grimscribe: His Lives and Works*, appeared in 1991.

Ligotti's hallucinatory writing style, unwillingness to place his stories in a recognizable place and time, profound lack of interest in plot and traditional narrative, and unremittingly bleak outlook assured that his work received limited circulation. As iron curtains came down and the 1990s economic boom began, the darkness that Ligotti unveiled proved anathema to all but the sturdiest of horror aesthetes. The limited run of his work also made him almost impossible to find.

Over the last decade, Lovecraft fans like me found their way to him through Lovecraft, though, in my case at least, I also found my way to better understanding Lovecraft by reading him through Ligotti. In a small but painstakingly crafted body of work, he has unlocked the infinite dark that Lovecraft continued to stare unblinkingly into at the time of his death in 1937. Ligotti's successfully realized 2010 novel, *My Work is Not Yet Done*, represented an achievement that many critics and scholars of the weird tale consider impossible as, so they claim, weird fiction works best as short tales.

Ligotti has begun to come out of obscurity at last. A 2015 Penguin edition offered his first two short-story collections to a mass audience. In 2014, HBO's pop culture phenomenon *True Detective* introduced the worldview of Lovecraft, Robert W. Chambers, and, most especially, Thomas Ligotti into a tale of two deeply troubled detectives rummaging in the detritus of America's forgotten rural worlds for a serial killer, or killers, who employ occult rituals and symbols in their gruesome crimes.

A controversy erupted around Nic Pizzolatto, the writer and showrunner of *True Detective*, when a number of Lovecraft aficionados claimed that he had "plagiarized" Ligotti in his script. They focused especially on the philosophical musings of Rust Cohle, whose cosmic sense of pessimism gave particular depth to Matthew McConaughey's character and made the show itself much more sophisticated than any police procedural has a right to be. An online journal called *Lovecraftzine* made an extended case that certainly proved the influence of Ligotti on the script.

A small literary brushfire has also sparked around Ligotti, one that's rather pointless in its particulars but interesting in its meaning for Lovecraft's long shadow. In the introduction to the Penguin edition of Ligotti's tales, best-selling author and accomplished critic Jeff VanderMeer insists that Edgar Allan Poe and Franz Kafka are primary influences on Ligotti. Curiously, an asterisk points us to a short note in which VanderMeer calls Lovecraft "an early influence" on Ligotti. However, VanderMeer proclaims, in a rather strongly put metaphor, that Ligotti "subsumed Lovecraft and left his dry husk behind."

Meanwhile, at least a few Lovecraft scholars have been more than a little reserved in their praise of Ligotti. Steven J. Mariconda suggested that Lovecraft has much more breadth and depth than Ligotti. He writes that in the twentieth century "far too many" authors tried to follow the path laid out by Lovecraft, resulting in the Cthulhu Mythos. Ligotti left behind the Mythos and "also jettisoned much else, perhaps too much else." Joshi has also been critical of Ligotti, suggesting that he cannot be compared to Lovecraft as he lacks his literary model's intense focus on technique.

Reading such comments from critics, indeed, reading the scholarly interchange in most academic disciplines, feels like learning about a battle in a war you've never heard of over aims that are unclear between adversaries whose motivations are obscure. Still, the need to position Lovecraft in relation to Ligotti, either as a standard to measure his work against or, alternatively, as a figure who secured his independence from his original master, underscores how completely Lovecraft has become a lodestone in scholarly discourse as well as in pop culture. The question the critics seem to worry over is whether he's Lovecraftian or not.

My own high opinion of Ligotti may seem to suggest that I think he out-Lovecrafted Lovecraft. One reader to another, I think he has done just that. As a historian of American culture, however, I'm dumbfounded at how the phenomenon of Lovecraft continues to outpace the biography of the historical Lovecraft, how the author so often accused of using too many adjectives has himself become an adjective that conjures up swirling images of tropes, fandoms, imagined and re-imagined fantastic worlds, and a particular kind of chill administered with a supreme lack of interest in our peace of mind.

Will Hart published a fanzine beginning in 1976 called *Eldritch Leanings.* A typescript newsletter with what he called "macabre" clip art, the first issue described his own discovery of Lovecraft's stories, including the discovery of a copy of the paperback copy of Ballantine's *The Colour Out of Space and Others* on the bookshelf of a girlfriend. This first issue lists his acquisitions from Arkham House and concludes with the lyrics to "The White Ship" by the band H.P. Lovecraft.

Hart first read Lovecraft in 1971, finding on a book rack a copy of *The Tomb and Other Tales* (first released from Ballantine books in 1970) that awakened his "morbid curiosity." Soon he discovered the work of Ramsey Campbell after hearing about the "Cthulhu Mythos" from a store clerk. He began a lifelong project of collecting Arkham House volumes, the emerging scholarly works on Lovecraft, and even pictures taken at conventions of Arkham House writers and materials related to Lovecraft's circle of friends.

Between 1976 and 1981, Hart published the newsletter as part of the Esoteric Order of Dagon Amateur Press Association, an allusion to both "The Shadow Over Innsmouth" and Lovecraft's own involvement in the early–twentieth-century amateur movement. Hart collaborated with and reprinted material from other zines at his home base in Anaheim, California. Gems in Hart's five-year run include interviews with Lovecraft correspondent J. Vernon Shea; a letter from E. Hoffmann Price—who had both corresponded, and to a limited degree, collaborated with Lovecraft; and numerous photographs of important figures in

Lovecraft fandom, including a record of Robert Bloch's induction into the Science Fiction, Horror, and Fantasy Hall of Fame. For one issue, Hart produced nametags labeled "Miskatonic Faculty" for some of his favorite Lovecraft scholars, including S. T. Joshi.

Hart was far from alone in his obsessive interest in Lovecraft and soon found, and helped create, a network of fellow fans and friends. Hart represents a growing number of Lovecraft fans in the 1970s and his zine—though one of the most long-running and consistently strong in content—represented only one of many such DIY fan newsletters that emerged in the 1970s and '80s with names like *Idiot Chaos*, *Night Gaunts*, *Dunwich Dreams*, and *Queer Madness*. Altogether, members of the EOD Amateur Press Association produced thirty-one different projects in the 1970s and '80s.

Lovecraft fandom emerged at a peculiar point in the origins of the fan phenomenon. The 1930s, '40s, and '50s can seem like the golden age of fandom as small associations, mostly male, met in the first conventions or "Cons" as they became somewhat unfortunately referred to. However, certain elements of mass culture, including the fandom that grew up around *The Twilight Zone* and *Star Trek*, began to attract a much larger number of adherents, as did a craze among children and teens for the classic monster films of the 1930s, '40s, and '50s.

Lovecraft fandom had a peculiar strength during this transitional period. Out of the emerging subcultures of nerddom, it alone produced a particular kind of scholarly fan who, over the years, professionalized themselves and their field into a thoughtful body of scholarship about the object of their obsession. Joshi represents this trend perfectly, moving from writing Lovecraft-inspired fiction to, by the time he was a teenager, planning a lifelong career of Lovecraft scholarship.

In this new world of Lovecraft fandom, sometimes you have to struggle to find the bright line between fandom and scholarship. A zine started by Robert M. Price called *Crypt of Cthulhu* incorporated both worlds.

Price told me he actually began *Crypt* out of admiration for the scholarly material that Joshi's *Lovecraft Studies* of the same era produced. Price soon produced so much writing on Lovecraft that it was turning "into way too much for him [Joshi] to accommodate" in *Lovecraft Studies*. Moreover, while Joshi's publication maintained what Price calls "a straight face," he wanted *Crypt of Cthulhu* "to inject some Stan Lee style fun!" The journal contained both fiction and scholarly criticism, some of the latter still cited by Joshi in the Penguin editions of Lovecraft tales. Price also included, in his words, "satire, puzzles, cartoons, and what-not." *Crypt of Cthulhu* became especially popular with a younger generation warming to Lovecraft even more than had the counterculture.

The end of the 1970s saw some changes to fandom as, for a brief time, the idea of the geek became utterly anathema in a decade that elected a president who ran, in part, on the need to overcome what his speechwriters called "the Vietnam syndrome" with a muscular new Americanism. America wanted the hard-body sculptured warriors played by Arnold Schwarzenegger and Sylvester Stallone, the latter literally refighting, and this time winning, the lost war in Southeast Asia in *Rambo II*.

Star Wars (1977), however, had made the obsessions of science fiction and fantasy fandom more mainstream, and profitable, than they had ever been before. Large comic book conventions had begun in the 1970s.

Lovecraft fandom expanded as well. Sandy Petersen developed his Call of Cthulhu role-playing game in the late seventies, in the middle of what became the golden age of tabletop RPGs. Peterson had been introduced to Lovecraft as a young boy, reading "Pickman's Model" in what he describes as a "tattered" Armed Services edition of Lovecraft's work. Like most fans I've read about or talked with from that period, he says he became "entranced forever."

In 1981, Petersen's Chaosium games began to produce a tabletop game called Call of Cthulhu that, as of 2014, has run to seven editions of updated rules for play. The year before Chaosium made a Lovecraft-grounded fantasy world, the enormous behemoth of role-playing popularity, Dungeons & Dragons, issued a version of its rules that allowed for the use of Lovecraft's gods and monsters in their players' adventures.

The odd boy from Providence had created a mythology responsible for thousands of pizza and beer–fueled gatherings where players invoked and fought Yog-Sothoth, Shoggoths, and Cthulhu with the role of a twenty-sided die.

Chaosium today has expanded into licensing complex board games such as Arkham Horror and the somewhat simpler Eldritch Horror that allow players to encounter the horrors of Lovecraft (and Derleth, Smith, Bloch, and more recent "Mythos" writers) in drawn cards and rolled die. The boxed Arkham Horror set functions as a set of collectibles as well as a game, with the artwork so evocative of a slick, glamorized Lovecraftian 1920s that Chaosium has released an oversized volume containing artwork from the series. Currently, Petersen has had some success with the *Cthulhu Wars* series that imagines the earth overrun by the Old Ones who now battle it out between themselves for control of the terrestrial plane.

The growth of Lovecraft fandom around gaming has, over time, made it much less the preserve of males than ever before. Strong, central female characters have become an important part of Chaosium's RPGs. Female scientists, researchers, authors, and a 1920s flapper packing heat are playable characters in the enormously popular board games.

Players attracted to the more freeform Call of Cthulhu rules can choose either male or female characters and indeed the rules themselves offer a number of female "ready-to-play" investigators, characters that players can begin playing without going through the sometimes laborious process of dice-rolling to figure out a character's various attributes. Ready-to-play characters include the adventurous "Rachel Hemingway," a journalist with significant knowledge of the power of the Old Ones. The newer editions of Call of Cthulhu also add an African American surgeon and "a torch singer and actress" along with the various professors and independently wealthy scholars of old New England families that Lovecraft himself mostly favored as his protagonists.

Call of Cthulhu calls for hours of attention, in fact some fans build their lifestyles around it. Players with less time on their hands can enjoy the satirical universe of Steve Jackson Games's Munchkin Cthulhu, a card game that can take as little as half an hour to play. Purposefully refusing to take itself seriously ("munchkin" is an old slang term for RPG newbies), the Lovecraft expansion packs allow gamers to fight "The Grape Old Ones" and even the unquiet spirit of Derleth ("Aughost Derwraith" in the game) while playing professors, investigators, cultists, or "monster whackers." Steve Jackson Games has also produced a fast-moving Cthulhu Dice game and a card game for slightly (only slightly) more serious players called The Stars Are Right.

The highly entertaining Steve Jackson Games aside, the phenomenon of Lovecraft RPGs has been remarkably faithful to the atmosphere the author tried to create. Players of Call of Cthulhu and Arkham Horror face the possibility of being devoured by Lovecraft's monstrosities. Even coming in contact with them can cause the loss of "sanity points" that drive your character to madness.

The success of these games underscores the reasons for the influence of Lovecraft's fiction more generally. The games, like the stories, unite a sense of social realism with the possibility of transcendent horror. Lovecraft's worlds are more enticing, seductively so, than middle earths or galaxies far, far away precisely because they recreate a world we recognize and hint—often ambiguously—about Things skittering around the edges of our diurnal reality. In Lovecraft's fantasia, we find a cosmic bleakness that we suspect just might tell us more than we know, or want to know, about the fate of all life.

I've already described myself as a Lovecraft fan in this book. It's a claim that's come to mean too many things. Fandom obsesses us to such a degree that at least some scholars of popular culture claim that our devotion to the numerous and complex literary and cinematic symbolisms we're offered draw on elements of the religious impulse.

Large numbers of people list their religion as "Jedi," and the "Campus Crusade for Cthulhu" (started at MIT) had an enormous following on Facebook. Still, these are clearly parodies of the religious impulse. A relatively tiny number of people join Lovecraft-inspired religious sects or choose to delude themselves with faked *Necronomicon*s and exploded ideas about a connection between Lovecraft and Aleister Crowley. More often, fandom replaces religion rather than offering a new form of it.

Fans, whatever else they are, represent archetypal consumers. When they run out of somewhat practical things to buy that represent their love of a pop culture symbol system (T-shirts, key chains, dog collars), they begin to collect for the sake of collecting, hoping to, in some sense, own the thing that they love.

Capitalism, to paraphrase William Davies, depends on our enthusiasm, our willingness to become fans. This diversion of the religious impulse has a special relationship to the twentieth century, to the explosion of consumer goods that has attended ongoing industrial and technological revolutions. Consumption, in recent decades, has become a patriotic duty. In the aftermath of 9/11, George W. Bush, in a telling reversal of what earlier generations have been asked in times of national crisis, encouraged Americans to take vacations and go to the mall. Acting otherwise would "let the terrorists win."

Acquisitive and entrepreneurial impulses are not new to fandom. The desire by Robert Barlow to own a complete file of *Weird Tales* and collect author signatures (and to try and sell fellow fans complete runs of magazines less important to him than *Weird Tales*) reveal it present in the midst of the Great Depression. However, few would compare this essentially personal bartering among early devotees to the mass production of plastic action figures snatched up by adult collectors and left in the plastic. Or the ability to walk into a big box department store and buy into *Star Wars*, *Star Trek*, or MCU (Marvel Cinematic Universe) fandom with a T-shirt purchase. Lovecraft, though following a different trajectory, has finally been monetized.

You and I are implicated in this process. Later today I might play a game of Arkham Horror or interact with Lovecraft-inspired monsters on one of my gaming consoles. I'll go online and contemplate the purchase of a polystone, collectible Cthulhu statue or a small, intentionally humorous vinyl figure of the madness from the sea. I'll be wearing a Miskatonic University T-shirt. Perhaps before the day passes I'll even take time to actually read the stories of the Providence author who worried over whether or not our "mechanical" civilization would substitute commerce for art.

———

The popularity of Lovecraft continues to grow and his literary reputation seems secure since his 2005 admission to the Library of America. But crucial aspects of his memory, as he's grown in stature, have come under siege.

The World Fantasy Convention announced in 2015 that its prestigious award, long known as the "Howies," would no longer feature an abstract sculpture of the head of H.P. Lovecraft.

A campaign mounted by a significant number of authors within the fantasy community began in 2013 to make the change. A petition to redesign the statue circulated, garnering around 2,600 signatures— although it's not clear whether all these signatures came from authors— and it failed to reach its goal of 5,000 signatures on Change.org.[55]

Daniel José Older, a WFA nominee in the "best editor" category for his elegant, idiosyncratic collection *Long Hidden: Speculative Fiction from the Margins of History*, wrote the petition. The statement acknowledged the contributions of Lovecraft to the genre but insisted, correctly, that the author had been an "avowed racist" and, tendentiously, "a terrible word smith." The petition further urged that the award, in a symbolic move, replace Lovecraft's head with that of Octavia Butler, an African American writer that any objective observer would describe as one of the greatest fantasy and horror writers of the twentieth century, one whose work in many respects exceeds the boundaries of genre.

The controversy gained a public face as early as 2011. Nnedi Okorafor won a much-deserved Howie that year for her novel *Who Fears Death* that offers readers a heartbreakingly beautiful story set in an African future, an alternate Africa that still resonates with the varied history of the gigantic and diverse continent. After winning the award, a friend of Okorafor's showed her some of the racist poetry that Lovecraft wrote in his early twenties. She confessed in a December 2011 blog post that she had been aware of "Lovecraft's racial issues, anti-Semitism, etc." but had not known his beliefs had been so "focused and specific."

Interestingly, the thrust of the post concerns her tangle with the racist enthusiasm, not only of Lovecraft, but of many of her genre's past masters. She called herself "conflicted" and described how she, time and time again, found herself struggling with a variety of racist legacies in some of her favorite authors and filmmakers, being forced to confront the horror that "many of the Elders we learn and need to learn from hate or hated us." At the time of that post, December 2011, Okorafor did not call for a change in the award. Instead, she insisted that there must be thoughtful discourse about the image and meaning of Lovecraft, "the talented racist," within the community of fantasy writers.

Sofia Samatar won the 2014 Howie for her novel *A Stranger in Olondria*. Samatar raised the issue in her acceptance speech in 2014, calling it "the elephant in the room." She thanked the board for taking the controversy seriously as it was "awkward to accept the award as an author of colour." She made clear in later comments, as have many other writers who believed the award must be changed, that she in no way thinks that Lovecraft's work should be censored. In fact, she teaches Lovecraft to her students, a seminar many of us dream of auditing.

Confusion about "censorship" and the meaning of the award's change abounded. The Twitterverse remained very divided after the announcement and I noted not a few young fans of Lovecraft who felt a bit betrayed by the news. Joyce Carol Oates expressed support for the change only to have a young male fan, of both her work and Lovecraft's, tweet to her a reminder that she had edited a collection of his stories. Oates certainly needed no reminder of this and the fan's non sequitur of a critique underscored the inability of many enthusiasts to discern the difference between the critical reading of an author and rooting for an author like she's your favorite sports franchise. The latter attitude has the effect of transforming art into a "brand," ironically one of the aspects of modernity that Lovecraft despised.

S.T. Joshi came out, rhetorical guns blazing, in response to the news. He returned his own two World Fantasy Awards in protest. In a letter to the co-chair of the World Fantasy Convention Award, Joshi called the decision "a craven yielding to the worst sort of political correctness." Joshi mortally wounded his own case on his personal blog when he used a phrase associated more with the privileged grumpiness of Gamergaters than serious discussion. He called those who wanted the award changed "Social Justice Warriors," an inexplicable term of derision among males who see geekdom as their personal treehouse, the NO GIRLS ALLOWED sign still hanging outside. The insult "Social Justice Warrior" (or "SJW" in online flame wars and sexual harassment) rather appallingly overlooks what the ideals of social justice have meant in both American and global history. Most who know that history, the story of social justice warriors ranging from feminists like Victoria Woodhull to labor activists who fought for workers' rights like César Chavez, hope that they are "SJWs."[56]

Joshi, in his calmer moments and sometimes even when he's riled, has, however, made some telling points. Major awards in horror and science fiction are also given in the names of Bram Stoker and John W. Campbell, both poorer writers than Lovecraft with much less influence over the direction of the modern weird tale. Campbell, whose fame recall comes in part from his dumbed-down version of *At the Mountains of Madness*, made a career out of right-wing activism and actively opposed the Civil Rights Movement. Joshi's also noted, quite rightly, that the works of Edgar Allan Poe are thoroughly tainted with racism, especially "The Gold-Bug."

Finally, it is worth remembering that, as Joshi points out on his personal blog, he was for many years the only "person of colour" working in Lovecraft scholarship. He does not, as he could have, remind critics that he's been, for several decades, the most important scholar working on Lovecraft, period. Worse, attacks on him as a "right-wing" racist himself are utterly absurd as he's openly and systemically described himself as a man of the left. He's also never been shy about talking about Lovecraft's racist attitudes, even if he sometimes dismisses them with the unfortu-nate "he was a product of his times" argument.

Moreover, as much as the "he was a product of his times" argu-ment fails to fully map out the history of race, and the struggle for racial justice that was very much a part of his own times, those who have con-fessed themselves shocked by Lovecraft's attitudes have done little his-torical thinking on the subject. Many of those horrified by Lovecraft's virulent racism would likely find themselves equally horrified at the less exuberantly expressed racist attitudes of Lincoln and at Mark Twain's self-confessed love of the minstrel show.

When we begin calling historical figures racist without being will-ing to examine the historical structures of racism, where shall we stop? How many of the multifarious prejudices of individuals before the late twentieth century need to be catalogued before we convince ourselves that, in an odd reversal of the typical tale of the afterlife, we've revenged ourselves on their ghosts?

Still, an unwillingness to fully engage with the sources and meaning of Lovecraft's racism deserves the blame for the controversy. Had Love-craft scholars not long sought to close off discussions of his racist belief system and how it played a role in some of his more important tales, a critical discourse about the topic could have emerged. Instead, the some-times simplistic, juvenile assertion that "Lovecraft's a racist" ironically threatens to prevent thoughtful explorations of how racism structured his worldview, what we can learn about the forms white supremacy took in his era, and—as good history always does—show how the roots of new forms of racism are hatched by the old.

Tellingly, at least a few of those who have damned Lovecraft for his racial attitudes, especially those who have damned him without recog-nizing his inescapable influence, are using concepts they haven't exam-ined. They are telling us he is a racist without any willingness to critically engage the concept of race and what it's meant in the United States or to speak more fully about how race continues to structure economic and social life even as symbols of racism disappear.

Looking into the dark eidolon of the past helps us understand Love-craft and the roots of contemporary racist structures of power. In Love-craft's lifetime, white supremacy structured law, politics, public space, and even science and medicine. Tens of thousands of Ku Klux Klan members marched in the streets of Washington, D.C., some of the coun-try's most prominent citizens expressing their public distaste for black people, Jews, and anyone who did not confess the Protestant faith. Most of America, de jure in the South but de facto in much of the rest of the country, had been utterly segregated with a legal system that fully backed the practice with the Supreme Court's *Plessy v. Ferguson* decision in 1896.

Lovecraft's prejudices remain central to understanding him, while also something of a mystery. He married a Jewish woman, one of, if not the most, brilliant raconteur he ever met. His dear friend James Morton dedicated his life as a white ally to the beginnings of the freedom struggle in the 1910s and 1920s.

The most we can say is that racism so completely structured the worldview of the white ruling class—even its down-at-the-heels part like Lovecraft, who had lost in their struggle with industrial America—that an otherwise brilliant man succumbed to the blandishments of fascist rhetoric. He called for a "fascist socialism" and a country ruled by elites even after he became supporter of Roosevelt and the New Deal in his final years.

Changing the furniture in the master's house obviously isn't the same as burning it down. Lovecraft's literary reputation, and certainly his invincible place in popular culture, remains as secure as the many white racists who wrote before and after him.

———

In 1997, someone tried to dig up H.P. Lovecraft. The December 4 issue of *The Providence Journal* reported that the amateur resurrectionist dug three feet into the family plot before giving up. Obviously, exhuming a grave proved more difficult than "Herbert West—Reanimator" made it seem.

Devotion to Lovecraft manifests at Swan Point Cemetery in less macabre, if arguably more intensive, ways. Providence locals have complained to me that tourists ask about his grave's location more frequently than any other of the town's many points of interest. A Lovecraft fan, who asked not to be named but who lives near the cemetery, claims that Lovecraft's grave receives about ten visitors a day.

On the day I made my visit to his graveside, a couple clad in Cthulhu T-shirts had just finished paying their respects and the grave itself featured offerings not only of flowers but fan art, burnt-out candles, a now-soggy edition of Poe tales, and an equally weathered edition of Simon's *Necronomicon.* One informed fan had left Lovecraft's remains a picture of their cats, noting on the back that one of the midnight black felines bore the name Ulthar while the other had been christened Howie.

Such devotion and affection for this odd man comes from awareness that he has more to say than his stories, at first glance, suggest. He's become one of the most important figures in American culture because he's regarded as a dark sage that offers something that our entertainment and influencing machines cannot provide.

Neil Gaiman once said that the typical ending of a Lovecraft tale has the protagonist screaming out their last bit of sanity as an ellipsis brings their existence to a close. The conclusion of his tales acted as a warning to the reader of what awaits them. Doomed narrators beseech us to destroy the manuscript in our hand, not to share the knowledge we have learned with the world lest we unleash the idiot wisdom of discovering the truth.

Horror, true cosmic horror in Lovecraft's opinion, meant, in his words, "a profound sense of dread," a sort of "cosmic panic." Pure, screaming horror refuses the blandishments of the modern world. It ignores politics because politics either asserts a pragmatic art of the possible or dreams utopian dreams of right or left. Horror calls on chaos, evokes the primitive, demands that we recognize that most of what we believe about progress and the possibilities of human experience are lies.

Howard Phillips Lovecraft built this haunted house. It's one of the many ironies of the man and his influence that the Rhode Island gentleman who wanted to pose as a man of the Enlightenment created an art of the irrational that André Breton and his Surrealists never achieved.

He did something that even Poe failed to do. Poe could walk the fringes of human madness and suggested the possibility that our insanities corresponded to the cold, dead heart of the universe. He pronounced the utter terror of cosmic horror, the possibility that the human race merely treads water above the great maelstrom of atavism.

Lovecraft, meanwhile, dreamed monsters that embody our Id but much more besides. They are desire, death, immolation, misery, suffering, the problem of evil, the impossibility of noble thought, the end of rationality.

Lovecraft's obsession with the eighteenth century seems peculiar once we've spent much time at all with his fiction. Diderot and Voltaire, Pope and Dryden, dreamed for us a dream of reason untrammeled, the human race free from history, art as the expression of a levelheaded contemplation of a clockwork universe. Lovecraft, dead as the greatest catastrophes of the twentieth century began to reveal themselves, unraveled these dreams, knew that the twentieth century could only be a corpse-haunted city that waited for the rising of the final revelation, the last evil, great Cthulhu in whatever actual form our doom would take.

This image, the tentacled Thing rising out of the sea, can represent exactly what some of my interviews with Lovecraft fans have suggested . . . something fun to draw, a great tattoo, a good story that takes you to stranger places than other horror writers dare, a monster worth our time in an age of recycled horror films from the eighties.

But the more you immerse yourself in Lovecraft's world, the more you discover that something more sinister lies behind tentacle terror. Lovecraft brought to life the final dread, the thing that lies behind all our culture's many, many apocalyptic fictions.

Did H.P. Lovecraft make himself afraid? We know of his terrors of the night gaunts, that he at least sometimes wrote of the inhuman terrors that waited for him on the other side of the walls of sleep. Lovecraft once described a meaningful exercise in horror as "the work of one shudder-ing himself." What did he fear and what did he hope would frighten us in his stories?

In 1992, Francis Fukuyama declared the end of history in a much-debated book. Whatever the reservations of more careful scholars, Fuku-yama perfectly captured a zeitgeist that believed liberal democracy and free markets had ended the traditional conflicts of history. Historical experience had given way to an enlightened self- interest. The past disap-peared and the future, shiny with new commodities enjoyed democrati-cally, spread an open horizon ahead of us.

Perhaps, as historian Paul Buhle once suggested, this is the true American horror that waits in Lovecraft, a horror that we try to ignore by almost any means. Only an American neoconservative could declare the end of history with optimism. The terror in the work of Lovecraft, the terror that has stalked us for the last century, precisely concerns the possibility of losing history, of history falling helplessly into a hungry void and taking us screaming with it.

Robbing the grave of Lovecraft initiates us into the terror that he saw waiting behind every horror story. Our minds can travel to his witch-haunted towns and read forbidden volumes. We can imagine the kinds of monsters he usually loathed describing in detail, monsters so inhuman and unintelligible that they break our rationality.

So we try to control them. We fight for Lovecraft's place in the literary pantheon or read Lovecraft-inspired comic books. We play Arkham Horror or spend decades sifting through his literary influences. We even try to co-opt him for trendy philosophical systems that trick us into thinking we are in control of the crazed cosmos. We do our best to contain his malign and terrible vision.

These things, these new strange things he made, help explain the appeal of the Lovecraftian. But only seeing yourself in the final lines of his stories explains Lovecraft.

Lovecraft told the secret, the secret about ourselves and the universe we temporarily inhabit. The secret is death.

A BRIEF NOTE ABOUT SOURCES

My interpretation of Lovecraft builds on an enormous amount of material sifted through by a deeply dedicated group of Lovecraft scholars, led by the inimitable S.T. Joshi. However, I should note that in my email exchanges with Joshi, the redoubtable scholar made it perfectly clear to me that he would in no way endorse opinions derogatory to Lovecraft's legacy. Although I disagree with him on what counts as derogatory, I know these pages contain ideas he does not subscribe to and so I feel it my duty to make it clear that my use of his work and his conversations with me in no way implicate him in these interpretations. My own emphasis on certain aspects of Lovecraft's character is just that.

My work in part seeks to place Lovecraft, and Lovecraft fandom, firmly in historical context. Several books by twentieth-century historians proved useful and their insights on everything from the Victorian era to contemporary America are easily recognizable. I'd like to especially note Lynn Dumenil's *The Modern Temper: American Culture and Society in the 1920s* (New York: Hill and Wang, 1995); T.J. Jackson Lears's *No Place of Grace: Antimodernism and the Transformation of American Culture,*

1880–1920 (New York: Pantheon Books, 1981); Peter Gay's *Modernism: The Lure of Heresy* (New York: W.W. Norton & Company, 2008); Carroll Smith-Rosenberg's *Disorderly Conduct: Visions of Gender in Victorian America* (New York: Oxford University Press, 1985); Lizabeth Cohen's *A Consumer's Republic: The Politics of Mass Consumption in Postwar America* (New York: Vintage Books, 2003); and Tom Engelhardt's *The End of Victory Culture: Cold War America and the Disillusioning of a Generation* (Amherst: University of Massachusetts Press, 2007).

All quotes from Lovecraft's work come from the three-volume Penguin edition of his tales (1999–2004), edited and heavily footnoted by S.T. Joshi. I also employed Leslie Klinger's beautifully conceptualized and executed *The New Annotated H.P. Lovecraft* (New York: W.W. Norton & Company, 2014). I found the notes to each extremely informative and especially made use of them in recreating the chronology and context of the tales. However, the interpretations and any possible errors in the discussion are my own doing.

The only exception to my use of Joshi's or Klinger's editions comes from Lovecraft's critical essay "Supernatural Horror in Literature," where I quote from *Eldritch Tales: a Miscellany of the Macabre*, a U.K. edition of Lovecraft's materials put out in 2011 by Gollancz Press in London.

Readers will automatically recognize that I leaned on Joshi's *I Am Providence: The Life and Times of H.P. Lovecraft Vol. I and II* (New York: Hippocampus Press, 2010) for many biographical clues, details, and a number of revealing anecdotes. I trust they will find my own reading of the same material very different. I also found Paul Roland's recent *The Curious Case of H.P. Lovecraft* (London: Plexus Publishing, 2014) useful, especially in his willingness to engage some of the more controversial aspects of Lovecraft's character.

The Selected Letters: H.P. Lovecraft from Arkham House (edited by Donald Wandrei and August Derleth, 1965–1971) provided a number of little-known quotes. However, I depended—as will all future work on Lovecraft—on more carefully edited editions of the letters largely from Hippocampus Press and assembled primarily by S.T. Joshi and David E.

Schultz. Most of the quotes from correspondence that did not come from *Selected Letters* can be found in *Letters to Alfred Galpin* (2003), *Letters to James F. Morton* (2011), *A Means to Freedom: The Letters of H.P. Lovecraft and Robert E. Howard* (2 volumes, 2009), and *Essential Solitude: The Letters of H.P. Lovecraft and August Derleth* (2 volumes, 2013). S.T. Joshi and David E. Schultz also edited the letters of Lovecraft and Barlow in a volume entitled *O Fortunate Floridian: H.P. Lovecraft's Letters to R.H. Barlow* (Tampa, FL: University of Tampa Press, 2007). This volume also includes Barlow's memories of his time with Lovecraft as well as a revealing autobiographical note.

Lovecraft Remembered, edited by Peter Cannon (Sauk City, WI: Arkham House, 1998), offers a treasure trove of memories from those who knew Lovecraft well to those who barely knew him at all. Many of the memories of his classmates are drawn from this collection.

Interviews with individual fans and experiences and impressions I received from them were, by their nature, informal. I interviewed S.T. Joshi by email and Robert M. Price in the same way, thus having a kind of automatic transcript of our discussion. I interviewed Christopher Geissler in person about his experience as curator of the Lovecraft collections at the Hay Library and made a tape recording and a transcript of that interview. Interviews with Lauren Patton and Andrew Clarke were conducted in person and via email. Transcripts are available by request.

The John Hay Library itself, as one might expect from such a mysteriously Lovecraftian archive, yielded plentiful insights. I came across a few facts about Lovecraft that other writers have missed or bypassed and that shed new light on his relationships and attitudes. The Sonia and Nathaniel Davis collection, eight huge boxes, proved illuminating, as did some of the material on R.H. Barlow. The Rhode Island Historical Society allowed me to learn a bit about the Suffrage movement during Sarah Susan's lifetime. They also maintain a file of contemporary clippings on Lovecraft whose contents are reflected in my text.

I engaged selectively with the immense scholarship of literary criticism on Lovecraft. One of the most useful volumes, quoted frequently in the text, is *An Epicure in the Terrible: A Centennial Anthology of Essays in Honor of H.P. Lovecraft,* edited by David E. Schultz and S.T. Joshi (New York: Hippocampus Press, 2011). Two other anthologies proved useful in placing Lovecraft in popular culture and I drew from them freely. These are *New Critical Essays on H.P. Lovecraft,* edited by David Simmons (New York: Palgrave, 2013), and *Lovecraft and Influence: His Predecessors and Successors,* edited by Robert H. Waugh (Lanham, MD: The Scarecrow Press, 2013). I'd especially like to note the essays in these volumes by Kenneth W. Faig, Gina Wisker, Sara Williams, Chris Murray and Kevin Corstorphine, Joseph Norman, Michael Cisco, and John Langan.

My work on the fake *Necronomicons* came from looking at the texts themselves, although my interpretation is clearly influenced by Jason Colavito's excellent *The Cult of Alien Gods: H.P. Lovecraft and Extraterrestrial Pop Culture* (Amherst, NY: Prometheus Books, 2005) and John L. Steadman's *H.P. Lovecraft and the Black Magickal Tradition: The Master of Horror's Influence on Modern Occultism* (San Francisco: Weiser Books, 2015).

Two books proved compelling sparring partners. I am a devotee of Maurice Levy's *Lovecraft: A Study in the Fantastic* (Detroit: Wayne State University Press, 1988), a translation from the original French edition. Its valuable insights are only sometimes marred by an attachment to the "Cthulhu Mythos" idea. The controversial Michel Houellebecq sees in Lovecraft something of a fellow traveller in the war with modernity. This makes his work *H.P. Lovecraft: Against the World, Against Life* (London: Gollancz, 2008) required reading for its insightful, combative, infuriating claims.

John D. Haefele's *A Look Behind the Derleth Mythos: Origins of the Cthulhu Mythos* (no place of publication given; Cimmerian Press, 2014) offers a detailed history of Arkham House and an attempt at defending Derleth from the general consensus of Lovecraft scholars. He does make a good case that a "Cthulhu Mythos industry" exists though he certainly fails to show that Lovecraft would have had the least bit of interest in this beyond curious derision. The hefty volume should be read for some interesting counterarguments to points made in this book. Haefele's marred his book, unfortunately, by what almost has to be described as obsessional attacks on S.T. Joshi. Joshi has excoriated the book rather forcefully.

I chose to lightly footnote the text, giving preference either to items that I looked at in manuscript at the Hay Library or to citations that I used in making new claims about Lovecraft, especially those that might seem controversial or tendentious.

ENDNOTES

Guide to Endnote Abbreviations

ES: *Essential Solitude: The Letters of H.P. Lovecraft and August Derleth: 1926–1931 and 1932–1937* (New York: Hippocampus Press, 2013).

IAP: S.T. Joshi, *I Am Providence, Vol. I and II* (New York: Hippocampus Press, 2013).

LAB: L. Sprague de Camp, *Lovecraft: A Biography* (New York: Doubleday and Company, 1975).

LR: *Lovecraft Remembered*. Edited by Peter Cannon (Sauk City, WI: Arkham House, 1998).

SL: *Selected Letters: H.P. Lovecraft Vol. I-V*. Edited by Donald Wandrei and August Derleth (Sauk City, WI: Arkham House, 1965–1971).

1. SL, 1:46.
2. A quote from Lovecraft's 1927 tale "The Colour Out of Space."
3. See www.cthulhuforamerica.com; accessed January 1, 2016.
4. Some of the more horrific examples of Lovecraft praising fascism appear in letters about Mussolini to James Morton regarding how he [Lovecraft] and Galpin regarded democracy. See *H.P. Lovecraft Letters to James F. Morton*. Edited by David E. Schultz and S.T. Joshi (New York: Hippocampus Press, 2011, 22–24). He took issue with elements

of the Nazi agenda in 1933 and yet also defended Hitler's general program to Morton. See 322–26.

5. An unusual report from the front lines of the much ignored (even at the time) conflict appeared in *Stars and Stripes*: "Yanks in Russia Still Fighting in Bitter Cold," *Stars and Stripes* (Paris, France), March 28, 1919, vol. 2, No. 8, Library of Congress.

6. IAP, Vol. II, 1034.

7. Ibid, 1036.

8. Called "Cats and Dogs," Lovecraft wrote the piece in 1926 as a lark and for private circulation among his New York set. It's delightful, even for a confirmed dog person like myself. Lovecraft, at least half in jest, points out that the dog appeals to "superficial, sentimental, emotional and democratic people." Oh, well.

9. IAP, Vol. I, 24.

10. SL, 1:33.

11. "Letter to J. Vernon Shea," July, 1931, manuscript, Hay Library.

12. SL, 4:172.

13. LR, 175.

14. LAB, 93.

15. Joshi quotes the poem in full; IAP, Vol. I, 16.

16. Quoted in LAB, 54.

17. Kenneth W. Faig in *An Epicure in the Terrible: A Centennial Anthology of Essays in Honor of H.P. Lovecraft*, edited by David E. Schultz and S.T. Joshi (New York: Hippocampus Press, 2011), 65, 69; IAP, Vol. I, 341; Derleth in LR, 36.

18. LAB, 61, 66.

19. Ibid, 54; LR, 175; LAB, 318.

20. See Robert E. Howard, L. Sprague de Camp, and Lin Carter, *Conan the Wanderer* (New York: Ace Books, 1968), 100.

21. LR, 23.

22. LR, 29.

23. Carroll Smith-Rosenberg, *Disorderly Conduct: Visions of Gender in Victorian America* (New York: Oxford University Press, 1985), 197–216.

24. LR, 50.

25. Folder 1, "A Brief History of Women's Suffrage in Rhode Island," Rhode Island Historical Society.

26. IAP, Vol. I, 301.

27. ES, Vol. I, 75.

28. Maurice Levy, *Lovecraft: A Study in the Fantastic* (Detroit, MI: Wayne State University Press, 1988), 64.

29. Wilson's now infamous critique appeared as "Tales of the Marvellous and Ridiculous" in *The New Yorker* (November 1945); reprinted in full in *H.P. Lovecraft: Four Decades of Criticism*, edited by S.T. Joshi (Athens: Ohio University Press, 1980), 46–49.

30. LAB, 194.

31. A complete discussion appears in George Chauncey, *Gay New York: Gender, Urban Culture and the Making of the Gay Male World, 1890–1940* (New York: Basic Books, 1994), see especially 12–23 for a discussion of nomenclature.

32. IAP, Vol. I, 66.

33. "RE HPL" Box 1:31a, Sonia and Nathaniel Davis Collection, manuscript, John Hay Library.

34. SL, 2:116.

35. SL, I:351–2.

36. Reinhardt Kleiner, "Bards and Bibliophiles" in *Lovecraft's New York Circle: The Kalem Club, 1924–1927*, edited by Mara Kirk Hart and S.T. Joshi (New York: Hippocampus Press, 2006), 226.

37. SL, 1:348.

38. SL, 2:28.

39. Wilfred B. Talman, *The Normal Lovecraft: 1890–1937* (published in a limited run in Saddle River, New Jersey; author's collection; 1973).

40. ES, 28, 140–1.

41. ES, 51.

42. Letters to James F. Morton, 252.

43. Letter from Bloch, June 12, 1935, manuscript in John Hay Library.

44. Brobst correspondence, manuscript in John Hay Library.

45. IAP, Vol. II, 1041.

46. Correspondence between R.H. Barlow and Harris Collection and "Brown University Correspondence Files," Lovecraft collection, John Hay Library.

47. Barlow letter, 30 June 1946, John Hay Library.

48. Greene and Davis Papers, Box 1:27 and Box Six, John Hay Library.

49. LAB, 308.

50. T.J. Jackson Lears, *No Place of Grace: Antimodernism and the Transformation of American Culture, 1880–1920* (New York: Pantheon Books, 1981), 17.

51. Lloyd Briggs letter to Winfield Scott, John Hay Library.

52. Carpenter quoted in "Introduction" to *Lovecraft* by Hans Rodionoff, Enrique Breccia with Keith Griffen (New York: DC Comics, 2003).

53. "H.P. Lovecraft and the Horror of Comics"; www.comicbook resources.com/?page=article&id=28632; accessed May 10, 2016.

54. SL, 5:16.

55. Text of petition at www.change.org/p/the-world-fantasy-award-make-octavia-butler-the-wfa-statue-instead-of-lovecraft; accessed May 10, 2016.

56. Alison Flood, "H.P. Lovecraft Biographer Rages Against the Ditching of the Author as Fantasy Prize Emblem," *Guardian,* November 11, 2015; see Joshi's blog post for November 10, 2015 at www.stjoshi .org/news2015.html; accessed November 11, 2015.

THE TALES

The following provides the reader with a chronological, lightly annotated listing of H.P. Lovecraft's tales in the order he wrote them. I have also included information on several of the stories he revised. Some seem to have been so thoroughly rewritten that they deserve at least secondary notice as Lovecraft conceptions. Dates of writing and publication are based largely on the voluminous research done by scholars such as S.T. Joshi and David E. Schultz.

The date Lovecraft wrote the story follows each title. The notation then lists the date it was published professionally in his lifetime, noting also if *Weird Tales* published it posthumously. Many of his stories appeared in the pulp for the first time in 1937–41 as readers demanded more Lovecraft after his death.

Three groupings of stories meant to provide guidance for new readers follows the chronological listing. I assembled these descriptions according to my own view of what readers, at different stages of encountering Lovecraft, are most likely to enjoy. I also noted tales with an eye toward what readers must absorb in order to truly encounter Lovecraft.

So, read Lovecraft. Then read Lovecraft some more. The wearing of Miskatonic U. tees while doing so is entirely optional.

"The Tomb." 1917. Published in *Weird Tales* in 1926. Swan Point Cemetery, his own final resting place, provided the inspiration.

"Dagon." 1917. HPL's first story accepted in *Weird Tales* in 1923.

"Polaris." 1918. Not published professionally in HPL's lifetime. Appeared in *Weird Tales* after his death in 1937. Sometimes viewed as a story influenced heavily by Lord Dunsany but in actuality written before Lovecraft read the Anglo-Irish author.

"Beyond the Wall of Sleep." 1919. Published in *Fantasy Fan* in 1934 and then in *Weird Tales* after his death in 1938. The title provided the inspiration for a song on Black Sabbath's first album.

"The Statement of Randolph Carter." 1919. Appeared in *Weird Tales* in 1925. The first of Carter's five adventures.

"Memory." 1919. Never published professionally in Lovecraft's lifetime. Notable as one of Lovecraft's first efforts at using fiction to explore the indifference of the universe to humanity.

"The Doom that Came to Sarnath." 1919. Appeared in 1935 in a Scottish journal called *Marvel Tales*. Published in *Weird Tales* in 1938.

"The Transition of Juan Romero." 1919. Never published in a professional journal or an amateur one in his lifetime. He apparently only showed it to Barlow in 1932.

"The White Ship." 1919. Appeared in *Weird Tales* in 1927. The mystical lighthouse keeper in this tale reappears in *The Dream-Quest of Unknown Kadath*.

"The Terrible Old Man." 1920. Appeared in *Weird Tales* in 1926.

The shortest word length of any of Lovecraft's completed weird tales, setting aside his prose-poem "Nyarlathotep."

"The Tree." 1920. Not published professionally in HPL's lifetime. Appeared in *Weird Tales* in 1938. The only of his tales set in the world of classical myth.

"The Cats of Ulthar." 1920. Appeared twice in *Weird Tales*, 1926 and 1933. Barlow made Lovecraft a gift of tale as a small booklet from his personal printing press in 1935, due to their mutual love of cats.

"From Beyond." 1920. Appeared in *Fantasy Fan* in 1934 and reprinted in *Weird Tales* in 1938. Stuart Gordon adapted it for his film of the same name in 1986.

"The Temple." 1920. Published twice in *Weird Tales*, 1925 and 1936. One of two HPL tales that make use of German U-boat warfare in WWI.

"Celephaïs." 1920. An odd publication history as it appeared in Sonia H. Greene's amateur journal in 1922 and then in *Marvel Tales* in 1934 and then became one of the *Weird Tales* posthumous reprints to meet the demand for more Lovecraft in 1939.

"Nyarlathotep." 1920. Never published in a professional journal. Ripe for rediscovery and shows Lovecraft's modernist temper.

"The Picture in the House." 1920. *Weird Tales* published it in 1924. Contains the first mention of the Miskatonic River Valley.

"The Outsider." 1921. Appeared in *Weird Tales* in 1926. Sometimes referred to as Lovecraft's "zombie tale." Has perhaps received more attention than it deserves due to August Derleth's love of the story.

"The Quest of Iranon." 1921. Published in *Weird Tales* posthumously in 1939.

"The Nameless City." 1921. Did not appear in a professional journal and *Weird Tales* twice rejected it. Something of a beta version of *At the Mountains of Madness.*

"Facts Concerning the Late Arthur Jermyn and His Family." 1920-1. Published in *Weird Tales* in 1924 under the pulpy title "The White Ape," which HPL despised. Reprinted in *Weird Tales* in 1935 as simply "Arthur Jermyn."

"The Moon-Bog." 1921. Published in *Weird Tales* in 1926. Prepared originally for a Saint Patrick's Day celebration for an amateur gathering. Sometimes seen as Lovecraft's ghost story but the protagonist encounters something more ancient and dreadful than mere ghosts.

"The Other Gods." 1921. Only appeared in *Weird Tales* (1938) after HPL's death. Contains the first mention of "Kadath," an important locale in the geography of HPL's dreamlands.

"The Music of Erich Zann." 1921. Appeared in *Weird Tales* in 1925 and 1934. A famed quote of Lovecraft's emerged in relation to the story. He supposedly said he described the Parisian setting so well because he had visited there "In a dream, with Poe." The quote is fake and the description of Paris in the story is not especially vivid.

"Hypnos." 1922. Not published professionally in Lovecraft's lifetime or reprinted in *Weird Tales*. Contains allusions to Sigmund Freud, Albert Einstein, and Poe.

"Herbert West—Reanimator." 1921 through 1922 for serial publication in *Home Brew*, a humor magazine. Famous as the basis of the

1980s cult horror film of the same name. Lovecraft received five dollars for each installment.

"The Lurking Fear." 1922. Published serially in *Home Brew* between January and April 1923, the second such series written by HPL.

"The Horror at Martin's Beach." 1922. Published by *Weird Tales* in 1923 as "The Invisible Monster" under Sonia Greene's name. The story appears to be a collaboration between Greene and HPL.

"The Hound." 1922. Published twice in *Weird Tales*, 1924 and 1929. Contains the first mention of the *Necronomicon* and Lovecraft's first use of the cannibalistic ghouls (who are a bit canine in his conception).

"The Rats in the Walls." 1923. Appeared in *Weird Tales* in 1924. Lovecraft claimed that he came up with the tale after hearing the wallpaper crack in the middle of the night.

"The Unnamable." 1923. Appeared in *Weird Tales* in 1925. The second installment in the adventures of Randolph Carter, and a horror tale that features an aesthetic argument between the characters, based on an ongoing dispute between Lovecraft and his friend Maurice W. Moe (the latter loses in this tale, though Lovecraft lets him live).

"The Festival." 1923. Published by *Weird Tales* in 1925. First tale based on his acceptance of Margaret Murray's thesis in *The Witch-Cult in Western Europe.*

"The Loved Dead." 1919–1923. Published in *Weird Tales* by C.M. Eddy in 1924 but heavily revised to the point of rewriting by Lovecraft in the previous year. The story, which hinted at necrophilia, resulted in this issue of *Weird Tales* being pulled from shelves in some locales, especially the Midwest.

"Under the Pyramids." 1924. Ghostwritten for Houdini and appeared under the title "Imprisoned with the Pharaohs" in *Weird Tales*, both in 1924 and 1939.

"The Shunned House." 1924. Appeared in *Weird Tales* after Lovecraft's death in 1937. R.H. Barlow printed a few booklets of the tale. Lovecraft based the house on one he saw in Elizabeth, New Jersey, but also conflates it with one at 135 Benefit Street, Providence, where he sets the story.

"The Horror at Red Hook." 1925. Appeared in *Weird Tales* in 1927. Sonia Greene believed the story's racial elements came from the experience of HPL encountering some "rough, rowdyish men" while dining with the Kalems.

"In the Vault." 1925. Rejected by *Weird Tales* at first, later accepted in 1932 when August Derleth took it upon himself to resubmit the story.

"He." 1925. Published in *Weird Tales* in 1926. Apparently written in one night, August 10–11.

"The Strange High House in the Mist." 1926. Rejected at first by *Weird Tales*; later accepted and published in 1931.

"Cool Air." 1926. Rejected by *Weird Tales*, later published in *Tales of Mystery and Magic* in 1928. One of Lovecraft's tales most frequently filmed for either shorts or for television (a version of it appeared in Rod Serling's *Night Gallery* series in 1971).

"The Call of Cthulhu." 1926. Rejected by *Weird Tales* but later accepted (without changes) and published in 1928. Certainly Lovecraft's most famous tale and monster.

NECRONOMICON: A FAKELORE

Pulp writers of the 1920s and '30s, many of them friends and disciples of Lovecraft, created ancient forbidden books of evil. They loved the notion, suggested in a Hawthorne fragment but fully explored in Robert W. Chambers's *The King in Yellow*, of a book that not only granted forbidden knowledge but actually offered a portal to forbidden worlds.

Lovecraft's *Necronomicon*, first mentioned in his 1922 tale "The Hound," became the model for these fictional grimoires and the inspiration behind the peculiar hobby of creating forged versions of the dread volume.

The following offers the reader an annotated list of the best known and most influential hoaxes, texts of ceremonial magic, fakelore and pop culture renditions of Lovecraft's book of unnamable horror.

History of the Necronomicon: An Outline by H.P. Lovecraft. Written in 1927, this short piece provided a fictional history of the *Necronomicon* from its origin in 700 AD from the pen of "Abdul Alhazred, a mad poet of Sanaa" through various Latin, Greek, and English translations. He alludes both to his novel *The Case of Charles Dexter Ward* and the story "Pickman's

Model." Several fans, including Robert E. Howard, later urged him to write a complete *Necronomicon*. He demurred.

The Wollheim Hoax. In 1936, Donald A. Wollheim, later the founder of science fiction and fantasy publishing giant DAW Books, wrote a falsified "review" of a translation of the *Necronomicon* for a small Connecticut newspaper.

Publishers Weekly has the *Necronomicon* for sale: the 7 July 1945 issue featured a joking advertisement from the Grove Street Bookstore searching for copies of the *Necronomicon*, along with several other forbidden tomes created by Lovecraft's circle.

1960s: Various hoaxers placed card catalog citations for the *Necronomicon* in several major university libraries (unconfirmed).

The Dunwich Horror. Film, 1970. In this Roger Corman production, a handsome, counterculture Wilbur Whateley played by Dean Stockwell tries to get his hands on the *Necronomicon* and instead ends up seducing a Miskatonic University student played by Sandra Dee. The Old Ones that are summoned are a bit like aging hippies in a psychedelic sequence that involves ancient monoliths, LSD, and an attempt at occult erotica with the *Necronomicon* as a prop.

De Camp's *Al Azif*. Printed in a limited run by Owlswick Press in 1973, the first of a forest of faux *Necronomicons*. The publisher had to write to at least one academic, warning them that one of their grad students had been taken in by the hoax.

Colin Wilson's *The Book of Dead Names*. 1978. Notable for the claim that Lovecraft had inherited his knowledge of the *Necronomicon* from his father who, Wilson alleged, had been a Freemason who learned the mysteries of the eighteenth-century sorcerer Cagliostro. It's not clear whether Wilson was serious.

Simon's *Necronomicon*. 1977. The most popular of the hoaxes and still a perennial mass-market paperback. An odd compendium of Lovecraft's stories and ideas current on the occult scene in New York of the

1970s conflated with bits and pieces of Ancient Near Eastern myth. The text includes love spells that would seemingly hold little interest for Lovecraft's cold and indifferent Old Ones: "To Win the love of a Woman chant the following three times over an apple or a pomegranate; give the fruit to the woman to drink of the juices and she shall surely come to you." Usefully, the next incantation allows the user "To Recover Potency."

A section called "the Magan text" offers a rough paraphrase of an actual Babylonian epic poem, the *Enuma Elish*—a copy of which dates to the seventh century BCE. It's worth noting that Lovecraft never mentioned the myths of the Ancient Near East in his work and seems to have had little knowledge of them.

The Al-Raschid Necronomicon. 1983. Allegedly unearthed by an English occultist named Elizabeth Ann Saint George (likely a pseudonym). Along with claims that she chased KGB agents with the help of psychic powers and her dog, the author insisted that she had found the *Necronomicon* in a private collection in Peru during the 1960s. It's unclear why she changes the name of the author from Lovecraft's "Abdul Alhazred" to "Al-Raschid" but there are many peculiar things about this pamphlet, which includes advice for pregnant women and a description of how irrigation came to the Ancient Near East.

The Evil Dead trilogy. Films, 1983–1993. Directed by Sam Raimi. Features both a "Book of the Dead" and a *Necronomicon* that opens time portals. Interestingly picks up on bits of the "Sumerian" connection in the Simon *Necronomicon*. In *Evil Dead II*, cult film hero Ash (Bruce Campbell) explains the book as "a passageway to evil worlds." The recent *Ash vs. Evil Dead* television series (premiered October 31, 2015) has already introduced us to a Dark One who claims she authored the *Necronomicon*.

Cast a Deadly Spell. Film, 1991. Imagines an alternative 1940s L.A. where magic and its use have become very common. A detective named H. Phillip Lovecraft, a Sam Spade–style character dropped into an occult noir, must chase down the *Necronomicon*, Maltese Falcon–style. We hear part of the text read that borrows from quotes in "The Dunwich Horror" and "The Whisperer in Darkness."

The Necronomicon: A Compendium of Ceremonial Magick. 1999 by "Merlyn Stone" (real name Joshua Free; not to be confused with the female author Merlin Stone, who propounded a controversial view of feminism centered on worship of "the Goddess" in the 1980s). Stone's book borrows from the Kabbalah and the Simon *Necronomicon.* He makes the claim that Aleister Crowley uncovered the original *Necronomicon* "carbon dated to 6,000 BC" but it's not clear whether he thinks, or wants the reader to think, his own publication represents a translation of that text.

Necronomicon. Edited by Joshua Free (the former Merlyn Stone). 2009, reprint 2014. Free, on his website, says he began his "planetary mission" at age twelve when he became initiated into a Druidic magical tradition. His latest *Necronomicon* makes extensive use of a mishmash of Ancient Near Eastern ideas that he calls "the Mardukite path." He alludes to Lovecraft in the introduction by simply saying that the *Necronomicon* is "more than a book imagined by a fantasy horror writer." The turgid read runs to 243 pages of tiny print and mixes ceremonial magical rituals with references to various Near Eastern gods and ideas from the Gnostic tradition.

A PDF has been floating about online for several years claiming to be "The Necronomicon—NOT FICTION!" and presents itself as a 1586 John Dee translation, hearkening back to Lovecraft's own fake history (though Lovecraft wrote that Dee's translation had never been printed . . . I suppose it had to wait for digitization). I found it mentioned on a gamer site as the inspiration for the popular 1990s video game *Quake,* which did in fact draw its inspiration from Lovecraft's work more generally.

In July of 2015, an author using the pseudonym of "Abdul Alhazred" began selling a Kindle edition of what Lovecraft described as "a book rigidly suppressed by the authorities of most countries, and by all branches of organized ecclesiasticism," since "Reading leads to terrible consequences."

ACKNOWLEDGMENTS

Studying an alleged recluse has pushed me out into the world more than I would have expected. The protagonists of Lovecraft's tales often pursued their dread secrets alone. Given his enormous popularity, it's impossible to piece together his story in solitude.

My students, with their questions and ideas, have always played an important role in my writing. Never has this been truer than with this project. I teach courses on the history of American horror, and many of my students want to talk about Lovecraft, tell me their favorite tales, or, simply curious, sit in my office asking about what stories they should read and why. One even used me as an NPC (non-player character) in his *Call of Cthulhu* RPG group, the tale of a professor who teaches about monsters but doubts the Great Old Ones and goes mysteriously missing. Apparently they valiantly tried to rescue me from my fate, but cultists fed unlucky Professor Poole to some of Lovecraftian horror or other. I was tremendously pleased. Cthulhu gets us all, someday. I also appreciated the students who, without class credit, took part in a Lovecraft reading group with me. Laura Rashley's insight and interest added much to the group and how I wrote about some of the tales.

Special thanks are due to Christopher Geissler at the John Hay Library and his important and groundbreaking work in maintaining that fascinating and enormous archive. He pointed me to a number of materials I would not have come across on my own, as well as took extra time to show me the amazing Robert Bloch drawings.

I'd very much like to thank Counterpoint Press and particularly Dan Smetanka. His skills as a reader and editor are matched only by the enthusiasm he has for his authors and their work. I also appreciate and will miss working with Sharon Wu, a very talented publicist who has left Counterpoint to pursue graduate study. Megan Fishmann and Bethany Onsgard, both extremely attentive and encouraging, responded quickly and thoughtfully to anxious author emails. I really love everything about my press and the people who work there.

Rounds of copyediting became much less of a chore through the talent and attention of Matthew Hoover. Irene Barnard did an outstanding job as an outside copyeditor and I much appreciate Diane Turso's work on the final proofs. They take credit for making this a sounder volume, and any and all mistakes herein are, trust me, mine and mine alone.

My agent, Deirdre Mullane, deserves special recognition for this project. She pushed me to see the significance of bringing together my own Lovecraft fandom with a critical historical reading of his importance. Her unfailing encouragement and direction has help shaped how I write and indeed how I think about the meaning of writing. Thank you, Deirdre.

I must mention that, although I have only recently begun to get to know them, Victor LaValle and Grady Hendrix have become sources of writerly wisdom and enormous inspiration. I have read their work for years and I'm pleased this project has given me the chance to get to talk with them.

My colleagues at the College of Charleston have provided me with their interest and very direct help in pursuing my writing. I'd like to thank the entire Department of History for allowing me time and funding to research this book. I especially thank my colleague Dr. Rana Mikati for taking time to answer my strange questions about the "Al-Azif" and confirming that "Duriac" is indeed a fake dialect. Dr. Richard Bodek helped me think about the nature of the pulps as an industry and commodity. I am excited to read his forthcoming work on that fascinating world of formulaic ideas and strange ideological crosscurrents. My department chair, Phyllis Jestice, cheerleads for all of us and she has my gratitude for this and for her friendship.

Family and friends have been willing to endure my macabre interests for many years. I want to thank my parents, Clarence and Joan Poole, for always asking about my work and Ruth Vandiver for being my grandmother and being willing to take me to see *Star Wars* in 1977, despite how much she inexplicably hated the movies.

Heather Richardson Hayton read the galley proofs even though, for the best of reasons, Lovecraft is not her style. Only she fully knows how much our talks and time together contribute to my writing and my life, and I hope for many more years, forty or so, of that ongoing conversation in the infinite library. Alan Richard and Honor Sachs encourage me from afar, always. I am lucky to have two of the most interesting people I've ever met be my compatriots, since we were three in Alan's case. Tammy Ingram is both one of my favorite writers and best friends and she drinks with me. This is, of course, essential for authors to do together. I owe her a great deal, much more than she realizes. Leah Worthington read large parts of the early manuscript and caught numerous errors, as well as set me straight on some important points. Moreover, her friendship was crucial for me at key moments in the project. Hannah Conway shares my Lovecraft enthusiasm and is responsible for many of my earliest conceptualizations of the problems I needed to deal with in this book.

Beth Phillips's support for me has always been unwavering and, though no HPL fan, she has endured all of this willingly. She listened to more Lovecraft anecdotes than she should have had to. Her strength and fundamental goodness inspire me, even if I cannot imitate her. I hope she knows how grateful I am for her concern and love, and for how frequently she puts aside her own needs to attend to mine. This means more to me than I can effectively put into words.

My brilliant friend Emily Owen Farrier Fahl's influence over this book may be less apparent to her than some of my previous work. However, our conversations about everything that lives and moves under the sun (feminism, horror movies, goats, *Star Wars* collectibles, the work of Margaret Atwood, gourmet jelly beans, gin v. bourbon, Asheville, Gustav Klimt, *Buffy the Vampire Slayer*, et al.) shapes much of my writing life in ways obscurely secret and gossamer clear to anyone who knows her and has read my work. Across the years and almost two thousand miles, E&S has flourished. This book is dedicated to her.